Triple Crown Winner: The Earl Sande Saga
Tragedy to Triumph

*Jennifer
Enjoy the ride
Rick*
*Remington Park
10-10-10*

Triple Crown Winner:
The Earl Sande Saga
Tragedy to Triumph

By Richard J. Maturi

Richard J. Maturi

Foreword by Sande Tomlinson

Good luck from Equine Artist, Joyce Conaday

Check out website *www.triplecrownwinnerearlsande.com.*
21st Century Publishers

Books by Richard J. Maturi and Mary Buckingham Maturi
Will Rogers, Performer (hardcover 1999, expanded paperback edition 2008)
Beverly Bayne: Queen of the Movies
Francis X. Bushman
Nevada: Off the Beaten Path
Wyoming: Off the Beaten Path
Cultural Gems: An Eclectic Look at Unique United States Libraries

Bios: Richard J. Maturi, author of more than 1,200 articles and 21 books, earned finalist status in the International Imitation Hemingway Contest and won the 2008 National Society of Newspaper Columnists' Will Rogers Writing Competition. He is a member of the Denver Press Club. Mary Buckingham Maturi's freelance credits include seven books plus articles in regional and national publications. The Maturis live in the Laramie Range of the Wyoming Rockies.

Original Cover Art: *Gallant Fox, Earl Sande Up; 1930 Triple Crown Winners* by Joyce Canaday, thoroughbred equine artist. Please see additional paintings on Website: www.JoyceEquineArts.com, Email: JoyceEquineArts@yahoo.com

Cover Design: Lee Lewis Walsh, Words Plus Design, www.wordsplusdesign.com

Frontispiece: Earl Sande on scales. Courtesy Keeneland-Cook, Lexington, Kentucky

Library of Congress Control Number: 2009910255 (paper)

Maturi, Richard J.

Triple Crown Winner: The Earl Sande Saga, Tragedy to Triumph
by Richard J. Maturi
p. cm
Includes biographical references and index.
ISBN 0-9607298-5-2, 978-0-9607298-9-0 (revised, paper edition)
1. Sande, Earl (1898-1968). 2. Jockey-United States-Biographical Historical Novel
3. Horse racing-United States-I. Maturi, Richard J. II. Title

1 2 3 4 5 6 7 8 9 0

21st Century Publishers, 1320 Curt Gowdy Drive, Cheyenne, Wyoming 82009, 307-399-0894.

First and foremost,
To Earl Sande,
thanks for the great ride.

To Doc Pardee
who inspired this book.

"No sports hero had more panache than a handy guy like Sande bootin' a long shot in, but this great adventure tale is no long shot. It's a sure-fire winner, a movie-in-the-making. Saddle up and sit tight for one rare ride." —Edward Hotaling, horse racing author

"I enjoyed *Triple Crown Winner: The Earl Sande Saga*. As a jockey, I knew of Sande and his accomplishments but not the whole story behind the man. This interesting book shows just how hard it is to win the Triple Crown and how Sande came from nowhere to become one of the greatest jockeys of all time." —Jean Cruguet, 1977 Triple Crown Winner aboard Seattle Slew

"A Handy Guy like Sande says it all. The book explains Sande and all of racing in the 1920s' Golden Era of Sports. I was fascinated by the description of the leaky-roof circuit. As good as I've read anywhere. " —Tom Gilcoyne, national turf historian

"Jockey's Triple Tale A Winner." —New York Daily News

"A sure shot winner. Riveting. I simply couldn't put it down." —Manny Marquez, Zia Park

"Weaves a fascinating tale of Sande's life." —Buffalo News

"Pacy, complex and addictive tome . . . deeply moving account of tragedy and triumph . . . gripping adventure . . . Maturi has a hit." —Pacemaker, U.K. turf magazine

"Remarkable . . . readers will be enthralled with engaging Sande story."
—Midwest Book Review

"Triple Crown Winner: The Earl Sande Saga leaves Seabiscuit in the dust." —Boise Weekly

"A Dandy Was Sandy." —San Diego Union Tribune

"The Greatest Jockey Who Ever Lived." —New England Horse Talk

"An incredibly intriguing book." —The Jockeys' Guild *Jockeys' News*

"Saluting All-Time Greatest Jockey." —USA Today Newsview

"While the book will be an immediate hit with racing fans, it is a good read for anyone who likes sports or horses." —White Mountain Independent

Interviews:
    Kentucky Public Radio live from Churchill Downs during Derby Week, Fox Sports' *The Drive,* HRTV's *Race Day America* with hosts Carolyn Conley and Scott Hazleton, Arizona Public Radio, *Daybreak USA, Down the Stretch, Good Day USA,* Oregon Public Radio, *Sirius at the Race and Beyond*, South Dakota Public Radio, Wyoming Public Radio, *Sports and Race with Felix Taverna, Thoroughbred Connection, Trackside* with Carol Holden, Fox 23 Albany, NY, WLEX Lexington, KY and many local radio and television stations.

Acknowledgments

Special thanks to the Earl Sande relatives. Their generosity in providing background materials and family photos adds insight into the life of one of horse-racing's greatest jockeys. Additional thanks to Earl Sande nephew, Sande Tomlinson, for race photos capturing Earl's most important races and famous mounts.

Great thanks to Keeneland Library for vintage Keeneland-Cook photos, Ken Grayson for invaluable photos from his L. S. Sutcliffe collection, and Josephine Scott Werner for providing information and photos.

Gratitude also to Allan Carter of the National Museum of Racing; Steve Cauthen, 1978 Triple Crown winner on Affirmed; Dr. James Claypool, author of *The Tradition Continues: The Story of Old Latonia, Latonia, and Turfway Racecourses*; Brett Crompton, editor of the "Power County Press;" Jean Cruget, 1977 Triple Crown winner on Seattle Slew; Tom Gilcoyne, the retired but still official horse-racing research historian; Chris Goodlett of the Kentucky Derby Museum and Bowles Collection; Dr. William Rex Hinshaw for his insight into Doc Pardee and photos from the Doc Pardee Library; Ed Hotaling, author of *The Great Black Jockeys* and other racing books; Valerie Hoybjerg, American Falls Historical Society; Bob Magee, Susquehanna Lockhouse Museum; Phyllis Rogers, associate librarian at the Keeneland Library; Heather Schader, marketing coordinator for the Arizona Biltmore Resort & Spa; Cathy Schenck, librarian at the Keeneland Library; Stacy Swenson, owner of "The Groton Independent," and Michael Wirtz, archivist for the Sharlot Hall Museum.

I also wish to extend my appreciation to the helpful research staffs at the Aberdeen Room Archives and Museum, Inc., the Arizona Historical Foundation, the Arizona State Library, the Arizona State University Library, the

Boise Public Library, the Boston Public Library, the Canadian Horse Racing Hall of Fame, the Cincinnati Historical Society, the Denver Public Library, the Enoch Pratt Free Library, the Fair Grounds Race Track, the Harford County Public Library, the Idaho Historical Library, the Kenton Public Library, the Maryland Horsebreeders Association, the Oregon State Library, the Palo Alto Library, the Phoenix Public Library Arizona Room, the Prince George's County Library Bowie Branch Selima Room, the City of Bowie Museums, the Salt Lake City Public Library, the Salem Public Library, the Saratoga Springs Public Library, South Dakota Cultural Heritage Center, South Dakota State Library, *The Times Picayune*, the Toronto Public Library Special Collections Center, the University of Arizona Library, the University of Nevada Las Vegas Library Special Collections, and the University of Wyoming Coe Library.

New Edition Acknowledgments

We wish to thank Arlington Park, Calder Race Course, City of Bowie Museums, Coady Photography, Four Footed Fotos, Jim Lisa Photos, Jose Naveja, Steve and Stacy Swenson and Yavapai Downs for use of photos. We are also indebted to the following race venues which aided our telling the Sande story with program announcements, track interviews and/or other means: Alameda County Fair, Arlington Park, Arapahoe Park, Brown County Fair, Calder Race Course, Canterbury Park, Churchill Downs, Delaware Park, Emerald Downs, Fonner Park, Gulfstream Park, Hollywood Park, Hoosier Downs, Los Alamitos, National Racing Hall of Fame, Nebraska State Fair Park, Pimlico, Portland Meadows, Remington Park, Saratoga Springs Race Course, Suffolk Downs, Thistledown Racetrack, Tillamook County Fair, Western Montana Fair, Will Rogers Downs, Woodlands Race Course, Wyoming Downs, Yavapai Downs and Zia Park.

Contents

New Section

Introduction

The Earl of Sande: Saratoga 1924
by Richard J. Maturi
As it appeared in the August 1, 1988 Saratoga Springs
Raceway issue of "Horse World USA"

On August 6, 1924, at Saratoga Raceway, the racing career of one of the greatest jockeys ever to leave the starting gate almost came to an abrupt halt. Earl Sande, noted jockey of the 1920s, up on Spurt, rounded the far turn in second position. Sande's hands sent a message to his mount's brain while his knees pressed the horse's sides urging speed from the horse. Senor, with Benny Marinelli up, was on the outside ready to make his move toward the rail. In doing so, he nudged Gnome Girl causing her to crash into Sande's fast charging Spurt. Shocked cries from the stands pierced the air as the tangled mass of man and beast hit the turf. When the dust cleared, Sande lay with his leg crushed and mangled. Medical authorities pronounced the end of Sande's racing days.

"If a guy can't ride, he's not living," was the Earl's response. Never a quitter, Sande worked hard at rehabilitating himself, and the following spring he guided Flying Ebony to win the Kentucky Derby. Once again he was the top man, the "Earl of Sande,"

The following verse reflects Sande's answer to Fate:

Fate called a Quitter from the crowd
And barred his pathway to success;

1

At each new blow he wailed aloud,
Or faltered in the crushing stress;
And Step by Step Fate Dragged him low,
And yet he struck no counter blow,
Or upward tried to fight his way.
And at the end he cursed the fate,
That Swept him to such wretched state.
Fate called a Fighter from the throng,
And barred his pathway to the goal;
At each new blow, with purpose strong,
He fought back with a stouter soul;
And step by step he drove Fate back,
And soon before the last attack,
Fate fled in terror from his way.
And at the end he blessed Fate's whim,
That helped to make a man of him.

Sande was the idol of the public. Immortalized by sportswriter Damon Runyon's 1920s verse, Sande represented horse racing's contribution to the "Golden Age of Sports." His name rests amidst such fabled figures as Babe Ruth, Lou Gehrig, Jack Dempsey, and Red Grange.

Sande was an all around jockey whether he was setting the pace or trailing the leader waiting for the right moment. His judgment of pace reflected pure horsemanship at its finest. Sande hand rode to perfection, but if necessary, in a close finish, he used a whip effectively.

Sande perfected hand riding. His hands transmitted to the horse a loving, gentle, soothing mother's touch; feelings of strength and protection of a friend; and the iron grip of Hercules taming a rogue.

Damon Runyon's famous words ring true. Runyon immortalized Sande in 1923 with the following verse.

Maybe We'll have another,
Maybe in 90 years!
Maybe we'll find his brother,
With his brains above his ears,
Maybe—I'll lay agin it,
A million bucks to a fin.
Never a handy guy like Sande,
Bootin' them babies in!

Even today, Sande's statistics remain impressive. He started professional thoroughbred riding in 1918. He rode 3,673 mounts over his career, winning with 968, placing with 717 and showing with 552. His percentage of winners reached 26.4% and 61% of his mounts finished win, place or show. He was the leading money winning rider in 1921 with $263,043, in 1923 with $569,394, and in 1927 with $277,877. His total career earnings were $2,998,110.

Many of his most impressive wins and a majority of his purses were for the Rancocas Stables of Harry F. Sinclair, a frequent racing representative at Saratoga Raceway. Among his racing achievements are three Kentucky Derbys, five Jockey Club Gold Cups, four Withers Stakes, five Belmonts, three Dwyer Stakes and one long sought after Preakness. Earl Sande claims the distinction of being one of only ten riders to have won the coveted Triple Crown.

Sande was elected to the Jockey's Hall of Fame, receiving more votes than any other member. He has also been inducted into the Arizona Racing Hall of Fame and the Racing Hall of Fame located in Saratoga Springs, New York.

Throughout his career, Sande was noted for winning the big races. In 1923, he brought Zev home at 19-1 odds to win the Kentucky Derby. Flying Ebony, on whom Earl won the 1925 Kentucky Derby, never won another stakes. To his credit he seldom failed to win with a good horse and many times won with a mediocre one.

Years later Sande would say, "Man o' War was the greatest horse I ever rode. Gallant Fox, too, was a great horse, but entirely different from Man o' War. You couldn't let him get too far out in front or he would try to loaf. But he was mighty tough to beat once another horse looked him in the eye."

Other noted horses with whom the Earl of Sande won significant races include Saxon, Mad Hatter, Mad Play, Haste, Chance Shot, Sarazen, Silver Fox, Diavolo, Sir Barton, Grey Lag, and Little Chief.

On January 21, 1918, a freckle-faced kid won his first race on a recognized track, Sande brought home Prince S., a second rate thoroughbred. During the following 12 months, Sande rode a winning streak that led to one of the greatest racing days of his career during the fall of 1919 at Havre de Grace.

Sande lost the first race. He then guided El Mahdi to victory in the second and Wodan in the third. Murmurs buzzed through the racetrack crowd. "This kid Sande has got a double." African Arrow carried Sande into the winner's circle in the fourth, Milkmaid in the fifth! The crowd surged to the betting windows. "Sande in the sixth, Sande in the sixth," they clamored.

Frenzied cheering greeted Sande at the finish line as he won on Sunny Hill in the sixth race and on Bathilde in the seventh and last race of the day. Six straight winners. Fate smiled on Sande that day at Havre de Grace.

Sande's best year proved to be 1923 when he occupied the position of star rider for Harry F. Sinclair's Rancocas Stables and won 39 stakes races and a half million dollars in purses. This included his first Kentucky Derby victory on Zev and his outstanding victory with Zev in the international match race against Papyrus, winner of England's Epsom Derby.

After his young wife's death in 1927, Sande left racing and purchased a stable of horses, becoming a trainer. Financial difficulties forced him to sell his stable in 1930, and at age 32, overweight and broke, Sande attempted a comeback.

Gallant Fox's owner told trainer Sunny Jim Fitzsimmons, a regular on the Saratoga circuit, he wanted the best jockey to ride the colt. "That's Sande," was Sunny Jim's reply. Offered a flat $10,000 fee to ride Gallant Fox, Sande held out for a percentage of the winnings. "Gallant Fox is a winner and I want a part of him," he said. He got it and rode Gallant Fox to victory in Sande's only Preakness win, leading to the Triple Crown in 1930.

Damon Runyon's pen stroked another verse to the Sande legend:

> *Say, have they turned back the pages,*
> *Back to the past once more?*
> *Back to the racin' ages,*
> *An' a Derby out of yore?*
> *Say, don't tell me I'm Daffy,*
> *Ain't that the same ol' grin?*
> *Why it's that handy guy named Sande,*
> *Bootin a winner in!*

The following years found Sande working as a trainer, stable owner and even as a professional singer during a brief stint at New York's famed Stork Club. In 1953, at age 55, Sande rode the circuit for the last time, after a 21-year hiatus. He placed third on Honest Bread, a 7-1 shot. Asked why he returned to racing after such a long absence, "You might say I'm racing for the creditors," answered the Earl of Sande. He gained the winner's circle on his tenth month, Miss Weesie, then hung up his tack for good.

An unmistakable note of pride filled his voice, "I had a good ride," he said.

The young boy who bought his first pony for $15 and four live ducks made his mark on the world of horse racing. Earl Sande died on August 21, 1968.

Upon hearing of Sande's death, fellow 1930s jockey Sammy Renick recalled a race he rode against Sande at Saratoga. "Sande and I were coming down to the wire, side by side. Suddenly I felt as if I were on a merry-go-round. Sande had grabbed my knee and was holding me back. Then he let go and went on to win.

"I didn't say anything to Sande then, but the next time we rode together I did the same to Sande and I won. When we got back to the dressing room Sande said to me, 'Young man, do you realize you grabbed me and held me back?'

"I said, 'Yes, Mr. Sande, but you did the same to me last week.'

"And Sande replied, 'Ah, yes, but I did it with finesse.'"

6   Triple Crown Winner

Foreword by Sande Tomlinson

Uncle Earl

I first met my Uncle Earl when I was 10 years old. My mother, Frances Audrey Sande Tomlinson (aka FAST), had two sisters and two brothers, however, it was Uncle Earl whom I found most intriguing. Mother told me about her youth in American Falls and she described Earl as a wonderful athlete and horseman. Most people use the term horseman to describe one who rides a horse. In Earl's case, my mother called him a horseman because she thought he was "part man and part horse." Mother knew how much Earl loved horses and riding. She believed he could not only communicate with horses but that they could understand him. To say the least, I had my doubts. This skepticism, however, totally disappeared following our first meeting in 1952.

Uncle Earl came to Salem, Oregon, to visit my grandmother and grandfather, John and Matilda (Mimi or Tillie) Sande, and his sister, my mother, Frances. It was during the summer and the Oregon State Fair was in full swing, including the horse races at the fairgrounds. Uncle Earl and I went to the horse races.

I will never forget the events that took place that day in Salem. We stood alongside the fence next to the paddock, where they walked the horses and prepared them for the upcoming race. One of the horses in the paddock started to act up. The young man walking the horse took a whip to him. When he whipped the horse, it became even more agitated. The horse stood up on its rear legs and kicked at the young man with its front feet. The noise from the commotion drew the attention of many fans.

The next thing I knew, Uncle Earl jumped over the fence into the paddock, walked up to the young man, and yanked the whip from his hand. The boy stared at him in amazement. The horse still reared on its hind legs, kicking and thrashing with its front hooves. Uncle Earl stepped directly in front of the horse, just beyond its flailing hooves. He then slowly raised his arm and put his hand out towards the horse's face. The horse looked at Uncle Earl and kicked in his direction once and possibly twice. To everyone's astonishment, the horse stopped kicking, walked up to, and nuzzled its nose into, Uncle Earl's hand. The crowd became absolutely quiet. Uncle Earl slowly stroked the horse's head, walked alongside it, and rubbed its neck. A few minutes later, Uncle Earl reached out, took the horse's reins, and walked over to the young man with horse in tow. He handed the reins to the young man, together with the whip, and admonished him never to whip a horse again.

Now I knew exactly what my mother meant when she said my Uncle Earl was a horseman. I personally witnessed his ability to communicate with a horse and the obvious ability of the horse to understand that with my Uncle Earl he was in the best of hands.

When Uncle Earl won his first Kentucky Derby on Zev in 1923, he gave his mother, my grandmother, and each of his sisters a half-carat diamond ring. My mother had her diamond reset into a man's ring, which she gave to me when I graduated from college. My sister, Kaye, has Grandmother Sande's diamond. My ring will always remain in my family and I presently wear it every day knowing that it was a gift to my mother from her brother and my uncle, Earl Harold Sande, the horseman.

Part 1

In Search of Earl Sande

Chapter 1

A Rude Awakening by Doc Pardee

A persistent irritating noise breaks the silence. Amber numbers glow through the darkness. Five a.m., an ungodly hour. Realizing the incessant ringing won't stop, I seize the phone.

Before the receiver reaches my ear, a gruff voice fires a question. From the labored breathing on the other end, an image of an old codger forms.

"You this fella R. J.?"

Before I answer, he asks again, "Well, are you?" The questions come in staccato fashion, like cracks of a whip.

"Yeah, what about it?"

The gravelly voice spits out another question. "You the fella who wrote that there Will Rogers book?"

"You bet. Mighty proud of it."

"Fine man Will was. Didja get to talk to his boy, Jim?"

"Yes, a real down-to-earth horse person. Same sense of humor as Will. Real pleasure to meet him."

"Earl Sande! Didja write about him?"

"Yup, twenty years ago. Found information on Sande in Idaho and wrote an article on him. First one I ever sold."

"Then you wrote about Sande to make big money?"

"Not unless you call $25 big money."

The direct questions and deliberate pauses signal close scrutiny. The voice measures my worth with shrewd precision. I feel like a bronc under the hard gaze of a seasoned horse trader. After another long pause, the voice demands, "Then why didja write it?"

"Found his life interesting. A story filled with tragedy that needed to be told and—"

"But, didja know that thousands upon thousands of jockeys raced the American turf, and only ten captured the Triple Crown?" the grizzled voice demands. Without waiting for a response, he continues on, "Sande started as a young farm kid with nothin' but his hands and horse sense. He struggled through disaster and rose to the peak in horse racin', the Triple Crown. Not many can claim that. He's a legend."

"Yeah, you're right. Mind telling me who you are and what the heck all of this is about?"

"Well, been stewin' over the hoopla surroundin' Seabiscuit. A great horse without question. Now Sande, there's the real story. The ultimate jockey. Not just for one year or two but throughout the 'Golden Age of Sports.' George Woolf had a lot of flair and the newspaper boys ate that up. Sande took to the track and won with class. He avoided all the fanfare and won race after race on major tracks. His winnin' percentages still rank among the top in all of horse racin'. As for Seabiscuit, he came into the racin' game after Sande's ridin' days ended. Betcha didn't know Sande trained Stagehand, the horse that beat Seabiscuit with George Woolf up in the Santa Anita Handicap. Sande ranked as the leadin' money-makin' trainer that year."

"While this is all very interesting, it's been twenty years. Right now, it's a bit vague, especially at 5 in the morning."

"Sorry 'bout the time. Reckon I didn't figure you for a late riser. As for myself, up all night with a mare foalin'. She had a fine colt! Back to this Sande thing, been eatin' at me for some time. Don't seem quite right, all this fuss made over Seabiscuit, Pollard, and Woolf. Why, they couldn't hold a candle to Sande. Early on, Sande stayed with me for a year, best hand rider in the business. Say, why don't you come on down to Prescott so we can talk about it?"

"Who did you say you are?"

"Didn't say yet. Figure you're the fella to talk to. Name's Pardee, Doc Pardee. Betcha didn't know that Man o' War owner Sam Riddle let me ride Big Red. Got the picture right here on my wall. Only man in the world, other than exercisers and jockeys, to ride that champion. Man o' War pranced around like on springs. What a horse."

I try to get a word in, but Doc Pardee continues rambling. "Sande won that Triple Crown in 1930 on Gallant Fox. They didn't call it the Triple Crown till he won the three toughest American races; the Preakness, Kentucky Derby, and Belmont. Came out of retirement to do it, too!"

"Everyone always knew the difficulty of winning those three races. Now, the jockeys and horses get their deserved recognition with Triple Crown honors."

"William Woodward, the fella who owned Gallant Fox, named a colt in my honor. Called it Pardee, he did. That horse won a few stakes races. Woodward wrote me, 'Pardee is a damn nice horse. Can't beat the good ones, but the bad ones can't beat him. He's honest and game. So that suits his namesake. He's won about $22,000 in two years and he is still sound and good.' But 'nough of that, I'll be expectin' you in Prescott next week. Don't matter which day. Easy to find, ask anybody in Prescott for directions to Doc Pardee's Pony Restaurant Feed and Livery. Look for a stone buildin' made from river rock. Built it with my own hands. You can't miss it. Just down the street from the Brinkmeyer Hotel on Montezuma. 'Whiskey Row,' the local bronco busters call it. Proud to say, I never touch the stuff."

In the next instant, the phone clicks and the voice disappears before giving me a chance to tell him I do not intend to drive to Prescott. Doc's pronouncement, "Never touch the stuff," explains why he calls someone so early in the morning. I disconnect the telephone line from the wall jack lest Doc Pardee thinks up more urgent thoughts. Consciousness fades as my head hits the pillow again.

Brilliant sunshine sneaks through the edge of the window coverings. A cold floor signals the fire expired during the night. I mull over the early morning call. Doc's insistence points out the elusiveness of America's Triple Crown. Only ten jockeys and eleven horses ever achieved that distinction.

Sure, Earl Sande's life told an interesting story. However, why call before the crack of dawn years later to discuss it? Doc Pardee's life must entail more important things. That afternoon, I try to put Pardee out of mind. While packing and storing away research materials from my last book, he and Sande keep creeping back. Just before the oak file drawer closes, my fingers grab an aged Earl Sande folder and plop it down on my desk.

In the background, my favorite Sons of the San Joaquin tape, "Great American Cowboy," harmonizes western tunes. An adventure novel rests in my lap while my eyes drift time and again to the Sande file. Finally, I quit the pretense of reading, cross the room, and revisit Earl Sande once again.

Yes, Sande certainly started out in rural America, rose to the top of horse racing, and experienced tragedy and triumph. Even so, who wants to go traipsing down to Prescott to find bits and pieces on a forgotten jockey? Besides, Sande died years ago. The writing challenge lies in creating new and exciting works, not dwelling on past projects. After the late nights and grind of writing, rewriting and rewriting yet again; it's time to celebrate. The Sande folder lands back on the desk with a thud.

The drive into Laramie ends at the Cowboy Saloon & Dance Hall. Country music reverberates throughout as young couples entwine their arms and stomp cowboy boots to "Cotton-Eyed Joe." Heavy smoke hovers over the billiard and pool tables while cowboys shift their talents and attention from a hard week on the range to a weekend of relaxation and recreation. The cue ball skitters across the green felt and the six ball falls in the side pocket. A pretty young girl wearing a white cowboy hat, leather vest, short skirt, and fringed cowboy boots siddles up to the pool player. With a cigarette dangling out of her mouth she says, "Nice shot, cowboy."

"Haven't seen you in here for awhile, R. J. Where you been hiding?" Cody asks from behind the counter as burly hands push the bar rag back and forth. His faded denim shirt stretches to cover broad shoulders. Behind him, a bullet hole in the mirror echoes of rowdier nights.

It hasn't been so long that he forgot my drink preference. Cody pours a gin and tonic, adds a twist of lime, sets the glass on the bar, and gives it a calculated shove. It stops directly in front of me.

"Spent the last few months holed-up completing a book. Sure nice to put all that work behind me."

"Don't know how you do it. Can't imagine writing a book. Takes me darned near a month just to read one. Some folks finish reading a book in a single sitting. Not me, seems like it takes forever. How do you find the discipline?"

"Well, Cody, what about the peculiar habit of eating three times a day? No writing, no eating. Simple as that."

"That mean you're working on a new book now?"

"Nope. Just going to take it easy for a while. Let the batteries recharge before diving into a new project."

"Any ideas for a new book? Say, how about writing on famous Country and Western groups that used to travel the bar circuit? You know, bands like Bob Wills and His Texas Playboys. That would make a great book. They're selling more CDs and tapes of their music now than in their heyday. Their song, 'San Antonio Rose,' a real classic."

"Thanks for the idea. That's not exactly my field of expertise. Besides, it's probably already been done."

"Yeah, maybe. Bet a smart writer could dig up new material, add a new twist here and there, and make it interesting again."

"You might have something there, Cody. I'll give that some thought. First, though, let me run this by you. Did you ever hear of Earl Sande?"

"Sande? Sure. All of us cowpokes know about Sande. Top jockey in my book. One of the few to win the Triple Crown. Smarty Jones and Stewart Elliott made a run at it and lost in the final race, the Belmont. Just goes to show you how hard it is to win the Triple Crown. Few people know the names of those who won the first two races and failed to win the third. Everybody in the racing game remembers Sande's name. Many regular folks do, too."

"You're right. He's one of only ten jockeys to win the Triple Crown and one of seventy-seven jockeys in the National Museum Racing Hall of Fame. Taking away the steeplechase members leaves an even smaller number of racetrack jockeys among the anointed few. Sande's lifetime winning percentage stills ranks near the top of the list at 26.4 percent. Compare that with other top Hall of Fame jockeys since Sande's time: Avelino Gomez at 24.0 percent, Willie Shoemaker at 21.9 percent, and both Eddie Arcaro and William Hartack at 19.8 percent. The renowned George Woolf only won 19.1 percent of the time. Seabiscuit's jockey, Red Pollard, not even in the Hall of Fame ranks."

"Hold on, there, R. J. I'm convinced. You're trying to convince yourself to tackle this Sande project. Go for it. It's a great story."

The door of the saloon closes and I head back home. The transmission downshifts as my 4 x 4 pickup rises from the plains and mounts Sherman Hill fourteen miles east of Laramie. Honest Abe sits atop the highest point on I-80 which straddles Wyoming's Laramie Range. Lincoln's large sculpture commemorates the 1913 route of the first transcontinental highway: The Lincoln Highway. An impressive monument to a great American admired by folks across the country.

I exit to the right, cross the overpass, and round the bend of Happy Jack Road, named after an area pioneer who always whistled while he worked. Cheyenne's lights glimmer forty-five miles away on the eastern horizon.

Drifting clouds break to reveal a glowing full moon hovering high in the sky. Spirit Rocks of Vedauwoo tower and cast their shadows in the moonlight. An Arapahoe legend speaks of animal and human "earthborn spirits" captured in the odd-shaped rocks. Despite all of the crazies drawn out tonight by the lunar pull, an eerie feeling that I am the only one left on earth sends chills up my spine. No cars pass in either direction during the final fifteen minutes of my drive home.

Wyoming winds whip up snow ghosts and scatter light powder across the road, causing brief whiteouts. The tires turn off Happy Jack and crunch through the frozen gravel leading up to my log home. A small brown, pink-eared bunny startles at the sound of the truck door slamming and scampers away, disappearing into a light fog bank hovering close to the ground. One hundred yards beyond the house in a pile of large rocks stands a lone coyote. He arches his neck upward and lets out an ancient, chilling, high-pitched yelp.

After a night of honky-tonking in Laramie, Garth Brooks's song, "I'm Too Young to Feel This Damn Old," runs through my head. I lean against the truck, gaze up at the star-studded sky showing through fleeting clouds, and take deep breaths. The crisp air of a Wyoming night at 7,700 feet clears my head of barroom smoke. Within moments, the frigid cold drives me inside. A cowboy mix of the coffee grounds and eggshells brews while hot water tumbles into a long clawfoot tub. Coffee slides down my throat as my body sinks into the steaming water.

What a relief to know I can sleep till noon and gather much-needed rest. I dive under the down comforter and, as usual, slip into the twilight zone before my head hits the pillow.

Saturday morning dawns. Once again the Sande folder beckons. Faded headlines read, "Millions of Americans Admire Horse Racing's Greatest Jockey." With the car packed, I rationalize that a trip to Prescott serves as a good break before starting another writing project. After all, it doesn't make sense to drive 1,000 miles to Arizona to meet some fanatic ranting and raving about thoroughbreds, horse races, and jockeys buried more than seventy years ago in the vaults of history.

High plains and herds of bison on the outskirts of Cheyenne transform into industrial parks, strip malls, and suburbs around Denver. North of Colorado Springs, the weather turns wintery and vehicles slow to navigate icy Monument Hill. Raton Pass, just south of the Colorado border in New Mexico, offers more driving challenges. Several cars without snow tires or

4-wheel drive spin out and create a heap at the bottom of the gully, like bison driven off a cliff by Indians. Traffic inches up the mountain. The slow traveling delays arrival into Albuquerque until after sundown. Supper in Old Town precedes bunking down in a clean 1930s bungalow hotel.

Day breaks with cold, clear skies. Heading west of Albuquerque, it's hard to believe an early morning phone call from a grizzled old cowpoke set this trip to Prescott in motion.

A stop at the famous El Rancho Hotel & Motel in Gallup, New Mexico, conjures up cowboy and western images. During its glory years, numerous movie crews and stars made the hotel their home base. A parade of movie star photos adorn the walls. Kirk Douglas, Alan Ladd, Humphrey Bogart, and Ronald Reagan help date the historic hotel's heyday. The hotel opened in '37 as a business venture of R. F. Griffith, the brother of movie tycoon D. W. Griffith. The area surrounding Gallup provides a panorama of buttes, painted desert, mesas, and cacti, which gave a dramatic backdrop for many famous westerns of that era. Although Doc Pardee exists only in voice, for some reason, I picture him riding into Gallup on his horse.

Returning to the road, bright sunshine turns into a beautiful magenta sunset and dusk. An evening stop at Flagstaff avoids night driving on the winding mountain road to Prescott. The next morning dull brown rangeland gives way to gorgeous red rock formations around Sedona. A switchback road rises steadily upward until it snakes through Jerome, which clings to the mountainside like a goat. The highway weaves through Yavapai Indian Reservation before thrusting my pickup out onto Prescott's E. Gurley Street. I turn the corner on Montezuma and edge over to the curb.

The sun is deceiving and the cold, high-altitude air of Prescott takes my breath away. Stone letters on top of the corner building designate it as the Brinkmeyer Hotel. A glance down the street fails to identify either a rock building or a livery stable. "Just down the street" in Doc's mind could mean one block or one mile. I opt to eat before searching out Doc Pardee and enter Zuma's Mexican restaurant.

After paying my meal ticket, I ask, "Do you know the location of Doc Pardee's Livery?"

"Don't know of any livery by that name. Maybe Doc Hinshaw can help. He's a veterinarian and knows every place to do with animals in Prescott. Been here forever it seems. You're in luck. That's him sitting back there."

The corner table offers a good view of the street. A man in his late seventies or early eighties watches pedestrian traffic. His hands perch on an

Doc Pardee in Prescott wearing his trademark unshaped cowboy hat, circa 1915. Courtesy Sharlot Hall Museum & Archives, Prescott, Arizona.

empty coffee cup. He wears a white cowboy hat, worn blue jeans, and western shirt. He turns and slowly scans my six-foot frame, salt-and-pepper hair, weathered face, Indian beaded belt, and scuffed cowboy boots. Finally Doc Hinshaw says, with a glint in his eye, "Can I help you, young man?"

"Trying to locate Doc Pardee's livery or stable. Supposed to meet someone there. How far down Montezuma is it?"

Hinshaw's face clouds and his forehead wrinkles before he answers, "You half crazy or pulling my leg?"

"Neither. Just seeking directions to Doc Pardee's place. Can you help or not?"

Hinshaw continues to stare without speaking.

I turn to leave Zuma's but a hand pulls at my coat.

"I think you better sit down." He pauses. "Well, son, I don't know how to say this. You're in it. I mean, this sure is the spot where it stood. The original livery building is long gone, of course. You're not from these parts, are you? Maybe your friend meant to tell you to meet him at a bar called The Stable. That's what they called this place before it turned into a Mexican restaurant. Guess it was called The Stable 'cause of Doc Pardee's Livery from long time ago."

"I'm sure he told me to meet him at the livery, however, that could be wrong. His call came awfully early in the morning. Woke me up out of a

Doc Pardee on Man o' War. Courtesy Ken Grayson Collection.

dead sleep. That could have caused the message to get mixed up a bit. If this isn't the livery any longer, can you tell me where I can find Doc Pardee?"

Hinshaw's eyes lock on mine.

"Well, that's easy enough but won't help you much."

"Why not?"

"Doc Pardee's been in boot hill for over twenty-five years. Died at age ninety."

Doc Pardee's dead? Who in the heck called the other morning -- or was there a call?

Hinshaw leads me back to his place, where he digs out and dusts off his files on Doc Pardee. I explain the early morning phone call and demand to come to Prescott.

"Well, Doc Pardee sure was mighty persistent when he got a bug in him about something or other." Hinshaw pauses, "Never knew him to cross over before, though. You sure he said he was Doc Pardee?"

"Sure as the sun sets in the West."

"OK, son, if you say so. Let me tell you all I know about my hero, Doc Pardee. Doc was known as Mr. Arizona back when folks still knew who he was. These young kids today don't recognize the impact he had on Arizona and our state's horse racing. Doc never drank nor smoked nor put a shape to his hat. Just plunked it on his head right off the hat block."

Almost with reverence, Hinshaw hands over two photos. The first shows Doc Pardee astride a horse on a dirt Prescott street, around 1915. Doc's trademark cowboy hat and a fine pair of fringed chaps add character to his bulky frame. Underneath the saddle, an Indian design saddle blanket protects the horse. Doc Pardee was no drugstore cowboy. The second photo shows Doc Pardee up on Man o' War.

"He told me, in that early morning phone call, he was the only one to ride Man o' War other than stable handlers and jockeys. Is that true?"

"That's the way I heard it. A very exclusive club. Pardee led an interesting life. Champion bronc buster, Wild West Show producer, bit player in Tom Mix western movies filmed hereabouts, arena director for the Northern Arizona Fair and Prescott Frontier Days, livery stable owner in Prescott, and stable manager at the Arizona Biltmore in his later years."

"He lived a full life. Why did they call him Doc?"

Hinshaw laughs. "Doc was a lot of things but never a licensed veterinarian. They called him Doc because he briefly attended a veterinary school. He used to say that his training and horse sense qualified him to be a vet until better-schooled veterinarians came along. Despite his modesty, Doc authored the Veterinary Department column in the county paper, dispensing mighty sound advice for years. Many's the time I asked Doc Pardee about a particularly perplexing ailment bothering one of my animal patients. And wouldn't you know, he'd be right on the money with his prognosis."

Hinshaw takes the photos from my hand and studies them for a minute. As he returns them to the protective envelope, he says to himself, "Wonder when all the years slipped away."

He turns back from the file cabinet. "Pardee towered six feet tall when men were a lot shorter. As you saw from the photo, he carried a bulk of 200 pounds. Had a tuft of red hair and blue eyes. His wide smile appeared wherever there were horses. Doc loved rodeos and horse racing with a passion. Used to tell me, 'I couldn't shut out the siren call that was rodeo.' Made friends wherever he went. Doc knew horse people all over the country. You could say that the rodeo brought him here to Prescott."

"What do you mean?"

"When Doc won the 1912 world's championship bronc busting in Dewey, Oklahoma, Tom Mix stepped out of the audience and congratulated him. They struck an immediate friendship. To earn extra money, Pardee provided livestock and played a bit part in a Mix film being shot near Paw-

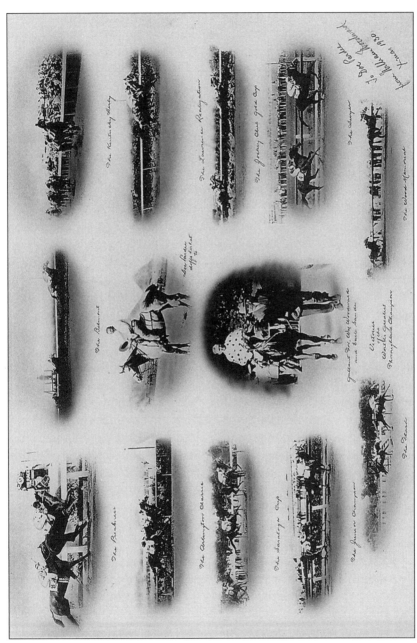

Doc Pardee and collage of 1930 races of Earl Sande on Gallant Fox. Courtesy Doc Pardee Library, Phoenix, Arizona.

nee, Oklahoma. In 1913 a flat-busted Doc -- he would say he was never really broke but often badly bent -- took up Mix's trail to Prescott and played more bit parts for $25 per week in the Mix films produced by Selig Polyscope around Prescott."

"Seems like he moved around a bit in his early years. What made him stay?"

"Doc just found his home here. Horse racing always played a big part in Prescott's history, starting with match races in the days of early miners. Since 1913, the Yavapai County Fairgrounds hosted Fourth of July and Pioneer Days celebrations with horse racing and rodeo events as major attractions. Pardee won bareback bronc riding here in 1914 and 1916, saddle bronc in 1916 and 1923, relay race in 1922, and the wild horse race in 1927. He could do it all, and what better place than Prescott to do it."

"That explains how Doc Pardee got here, but what is his connection with Earl Sande?"

"As Pardee told it many times, that Sande kid arrived in Prescott around 1916. Just showed up one day. Tagged along after horse trader Burr Scott, chasing the county fair horse racing circuit. By this time Doc ran a couple of quarter horses, Vanity Fair and Tick Tack, at county fairs and other races across Arizona. Doc saw right away the kid had a knack with horses and offered him a job. Sande worked his way up from stable boy to chief rider. He won twenty-three races in one day for Doc at Springerville. Sande stayed a year or so then headed east for the big tracks and fame. He never forgot his friendship with Doc Pardee and visited Doc on and off over the years. Met him myself once with Doc Pardee at Turf Paradise in Phoenix."

Offering proof of Doc and Earl's closeness, Hinshaw hands over a framed photo collage. Many photos of Earl surround one of Doc Pardee. The Sande photos show him winning stakes races aboard Gallant Fox in 1930, the year he won the Triple Crown. The matting is autographed to Doc Pardee by Gallant Fox owner William Woodward.

"This hung in Doc Pardee's office for many years. Made him mighty proud of his influence on Earl Sande, one of the best jockeys ever to wear the silks. Come to think of it, Doc played a big part in Sande's getting to ride Gallant Fox the year he won the Triple Crown. He was instrumental in convincing Woodward to hire Sande to ride Gallant Fox that year. Guess I talked your ear off, son. Any idea what you are going to do now?"

"One way or another Doc Pardee wanted to spark an interest in Sande again. He's certainly accomplished that. Nothing to do but head for Groton,

South Dakota, and then on to American Falls, Idaho, to see where Sande grew up and what made him tick."

"Looks like Doc roped you into this one, son."

Chapter 2

Growing Up in Horse Country: Groton, South Dakota

Thanks to Doc Pardee, there's no rest between book projects. Doc Hinshaw and I spend time in Prescott at the Sharlot Hall Museum and Archives, researching more background on Doc Pardee and the area's early horse racing. Seeds for Sande's story take root. Adrenalin pumps on the way back to Wyoming. Mental notes shape *Triple Crown Winner: The Earl Sande Saga*. I stay home only long enough to get a change of clothes, pack the laptop computer, and grab assorted writing supplies. Before departing, I place two phone calls to Groton, Earl Sande's birthplace.

As expected, the small town library yields little information. The next call reaches the Groton newspaper.

A female voice answers. "'The Groton Independent,' may I help you?"

"Yes. Is the editor available?"

"You're speaking with the publisher, editor, and owner. I'm Stacy Swenson."

My heart starts to race, anticipating a wealth of information. "Name's R. J. and I'm working on a book about the famous jockey, Earl Sande. He was born in Groton and lived there with his family. Do you have any clipping files on him?"

"We're too small to have clipping files. Don't know anything about an Earl Sande. Haven't been here that long. Just bought the paper a few months ago. However, you're welcome to go through the newspaper file morgue. We maintain bound volumes of all 'The Groton Independent' issues, way back to the 1890s. If you don't mind dust, they are at your disposal."

Reality dashes wishful thinking. Instead of a few hours photocopying an organized clipping file, the research will entail eye-straining hours poring over page after brittle page of musty, yellowed newspapers. I accept my fate and respond, "Will be there in a couple of days if that works for you."

"No problem." With that she hangs up the phone.

Before I leave, the phone rings and Stacy Swenson speaks. "I have to apologize. When we talked I thought maybe you were some flake. I reasoned, sure, I'm going to waste hours of my time researching my old newspapers for some guy who may or may not ever write about Earl Sande. Not likely. Then I checked out your credits on the Internet. You really are a writer and Sande, a super jockey."

"Sande's life tells a great story. I hope to do it justice."

"This is great news for our town. I'll try to scan through the back issues before you get here and organize them somewhat. Can't promise anything with deadlines pressing in on us. I'll also put a blurb in the paper asking anyone with information on Sande or his family to call the office."

"Super. Appreciate all the help. See you soon. Can you recommend a bed and breakfast or good hotel in Groton?"

"Forget it. Not many authors visit Groton. You must stay with me and my husband, Steve. We wouldn't have it any other way."

"Will that be a bother?"

"Not at all. It's settled. You're staying with us."

"OK, thanks. See you Friday."

A snow-packed Happy Jack Road drops 1,700 feet to the southeastern Wyoming plains. Antelope forage through the snow for shafts of yellow prairie grass. North of Cheyenne, the road heads toward the Black Hills of South Dakota.

In Deadwood, I book a room at the restored Bullock Hotel, built in 1895, just three years before Earl Sande's birth. From a large wall photo, Seth Bullock and his cowboys at Teddy Roosevelt's 1905 Inauguration stare across more than 100 years of history. Close inspection of the rough looking cowhands and bronc busters fails to discover a young Doc Pardee. Stranger things have already happened.

A short walk up the street brings me to The Midnight Star Casino. Upstairs, Kevin Costner's Jake's Restaurant serves the best food in Deadwood. The setting offers a warm fireplace and good stiff drinks to fight off cold night mountain air. Afterward, back at the Bullock, a video poker machine relieves me of $25. With any luck, tracking down Earl Sande should prove more rewarding.

Fueled by a cup of coffee, the drive across South Dakota's Badlands goes well. By mid-morning, the Greek and Roman architecture of the South Dakota Capitol in Pierre rises from the prairie. Governors Drive leads to the South Dakota State Library. There, a reference librarian helps locate Earl Sande biographical source material. Unfortunately, the State Library contains no Sande clipping files or photos.

"Try the South Dakota Cultural Heritage Center just up the road."

The brown-tone structure blends into a hill. Dedicated to pioneer women, the sculpture "Citadel" guards the walkway. A quote from John Steinbeck's Grapes of Wrath captures the spirit of the art.

> She seemed to know, to accept, to welcome her position. The citadel of the family, the strong place that could not be taken.... She had dignity and a clean calm beauty...as a healer, her hands had grown sure and cool and quiet;...as arbiter she had become as remote and faultless in judgement as a goddess.

The Heritage Center librarian heads to the catalogues while reciting, "The South Dakota State Legislature created the State Historical Society in 1901. State Archives contain more than 10,000 cubic feet of records dating back to the 1850s, recording the history of South Dakota and prominent residents. You should be able to find material on Mr. Sande without any trouble."

Despite her assurances, no bio, photo, or clipping files exist on Earl Sande. By scouring various records, bits and pieces of Sande family history emerge. The 1905 South Dakota State Census documents Earl's father, John, at age 34, living in Groton and working as a railroad section foreman; mother, Tillie, at age 30, registered as a housewife with three children; Earl, a student at age 6; Lester, age 5; and Eva, age 3. On March 11, 1908, John Sande filed his Declaration of Intention for Citizenship with the Brown County Clerk of Circuit Court. He declared himself a resident of Groton, born in Aalesund, Norway, who entered the United States after arriving at the port of Quebec, Canada, on the vessel Caro in May 1891.

The librarian provides directions to the South Dakota Department of Vital Records, where an official copy of Earl Harold Sande's November 13, 1898, birth certificate can be requested. The clerk enters Earl's birth date into a computer terminal behind her. As she takes my $10 bill, she hands over a Notification of Record Search indicating no record found.

She explains, "This is not unusual for someone born in 1898 in South Dakota. We were barely a state at that time, and only twenty percent of people from that period have official birth certificates."

"You mean it cost $10 to find out you have no record?"

"Well, we did perform the search, and it's state law that we charge for that work."

Determined to get my money's worth, I return to the Cultural Heritage Center and pore through historic materials on Groton. The town's Centennial History provides a vivid picture of life in the town during Sande's young years.

Groton dates back to 1881 and owes its existence to railroads that crossed the prairies supplying new settlers and hauling crops to eastern markets. Aberdeen, twenty miles west of Groton, forged itself into a major railroad hub. By 1880, The Chicago, Milwaukee, and St. Paul Railroad graded its route across the Groton site and the first train reached the town on June 18, 1881, with mail service beginning in August. Passenger service, excursion, and circus trains followed.

The Milwaukee Road built stations on its main South Dakota line, one of which it located at Groton. The Chicago & Northwest Railroad also served Groton beginning in 1887. Adding to the town's railroad infrastructure, C&NW constructed two new stockyards along its track on the outskirts of town. Groton citizens used the Milwaukee depot for various functions including voting and Sunday services. The town supported three lumber yards, nine grain elevators, and three farm implement dealers, all using the railroad for shipment of goods. Groton took on the role as center of the area's large grain trade. Farmers transported their wheat and other crops as far as forty miles and often had to wait a day or two to unload.

The influence of the railroads and influx of people westward contributed greatly to the town's growth. Businesses sprouted up, adding hotel, mercantile, banking, and other commercial enterprises. By 1889, the Groton Opera House provided an elegant venue for many public activities, from stage productions to political rallies. Groton's population grew to 410 by 1883, and 1,300 in 1911.

Another facet of early Groton history revolves around horse racing. The 1892 Fourth of July program listed no less than five races with purses of $40, split $20 to the winner, $12 to second place, and $8 to third place. A 1906 editorial commented on a new racetrack and the existence of three previous tracks: Bowler's Racetrack and Ball Field, south of the Milwaukee Road railroad tracks; Krueger's Park, one mile west on August Krueger's pasture land; and a horse racing track west of the present athletic field.

That background sets the stage for a visit as I leave Pierre. The route travels through flat farmland bearing cornstalk stubble. White fences and horse stables dot the landscape. The sky meets land without interruption as far as you can see in every direction, except for sporadic clusters of protective elms and cottonwoods around farmhouses and outbuildings. At the rail hub of Aberdeen, the road passes by the South Dakota Wheat Growers silos, the skyscrapers of the prairie, and a myriad of railroad tracks before heading out of town.

John Sande joined the rush of immigrants to pioneer South Dakota. He made his living farming near Bristol. Earl's mother, Tillie, was born in the small agricultural community of Lake Elizabeth, Minnesota. She moved with her family around 1891, at age seventeen, to a farm near Lily, South Dakota, fifteen miles southeast of Bristol. She met John Sande at market in Groton. They attended rural barn raisings and dances together while their relationship blossomed. John and Tillie married in a double ceremony with her sister, Julia, and John Sundin of Groton on January 31, 1898. With a wife to support, John Sande gave up full-time farming, moved from Bristol to the bustling Groton community, and took a job as a Milwaukee Road section foreman.

A sign on the edge of Groton reads, "Welcome Earl Sande author, R. J." Nice touch. Downtown, a blue, wooden building at 16 Main Street houses the newspaper offices. Gold lettering on the window proclaims, "The Groton Independent."

Inside, to the right, shelves and shelves hold bound, yellowed newspapers; the morgue I will be spending hours with later. Against the adjoining wall, an uninviting, well-worn sofa faces the street. To the left, rows of books and maps feature Groton, Brown County, and South Dakota history. A copy machine, coffee maker, boxes of supplies, and file cabinets line walls on either side of the long narrow building. Used coffee cups and filled ashtrays cover every available flat surface.

A tall redhead emerges from her office beyond the morgue, a trail of

Double wedding of John Sande and Tillie Peterson and John Sundin and Julia Peterson. Courtesy Earl Sande Family Collection by Marion Jensen

smoke following her. A ponytail controls her long curls.

"I recognize you from the picture I found on the Internet and, of course, your black cowboy hat. You're R.J. Must have been a long ride from Wyoming. How about some coffee to clear the dust?"

"Sounds good. Take it you're Stacy."

She nods and extends her arm. The firm handshake shows she's a take-charge woman. In an instant she grabs the pot and pours a round. Then she plunks down copies of issues containing articles on Earl Sande that she ran in her paper's most recent issue. One is a reprint of the article on Sande I wrote twenty years ago. Another highlights Sande's connection to Groton.

"The folks here take a strong interest in their native son. It sure is a – no, let me correct that. It is 'the' source of conversation in coffee shops all over town. In fact, the interest is so great that we're holding an open house sort of town meeting here tonight. Anyone with information on Sande and horse racing around Groton will be dropping in to meet you and tell what they know."

"I appreciate all your help in arranging this warm welcome."

"Glad to do it. I found a little time after deadline to do some research. Called our school system but they have no record of Earl or his siblings attending school. Their yearbooks only go back to 1930, so they're of no help either. Did find a photo of an eighth-grade class identifying one of the youngsters as Earl Sande. But the picture is driving me crazy because its 1917 date does not tie in to your research that Earl and his family moved to American Falls by that time. Perhaps your digging in our old issues will help solve this puzzle."

With that, the no-nonsense Stacy gets up and walks over to a table stacked with papers, books, ad layouts, and other newspaper office items. She clears the deck in a hurry and steps back with a look of satisfaction.

"There's your office, as long as you want it. Not much. It will have to do. I'm sure you'll need to get to work before the townfolks start descending. Feel free to go through anything on the morgue shelves. If you need a photocopy, don't wait around for anyone to help you. The machine's right over there. Make yourself at home."

Stacy disappears into her office and smoke curls out of the doorway once more. She needs to do her work, and it's time to start mine. I open the 1898 bound volume and start researching. Turning each page with care, I work my way up through 1904 with no mention of Earl or his family in the school news, personal notes, sports, features, or any of the other sections of the paper. The phone rings numerous times and people come in and out of the newspaper office on a regular basis. A number of old-timers stop by to share their Groton remembrances and horse racing knowledge.

Stacy sticks her head out and asks, "Any luck?"

"Nope. Beginning to think that despite newspaper accounts claiming this town as Sande's birthplace and childhood home, the Sande family never lived in Groton."

"Well, maybe you'll find something soon."

Stacy's husband, Steve, slips in carrying sandwiches from Laura's Latte. With a welcoming grin he says, "This will provide nourishment for getting through the rest of the newspapers. Laura's makes delicious food. Dig in."

I reach for my money clip to pay. Steve, sensing my intention, says, "Forget it. Our treat."

He places the lunch down on the worktable and pulls up a chair. Steve serves as the paper's reporter, feature editor, advertising director, and chief gopher.

"Is Stacy going to join us?"

Steve leans back in his chair, points to Stacy's closed door and laughs, "I learned a long time ago to steer clear when that happens. Computer probably went down again. Not a pretty sight. She'll come out when she's hungry."

"In my short time at 'The Groton Independent,' I notice a big difference between the pace of researching and writing a book or magazine article and the grind of putting out a weekly newspaper. One week does not give you enough time to track down story leads, interview sources, take photos, write and rewrite copy, drum up ad business, and get the paper laid out and sent to the printers. You work at a demanding pace."

Steve nods, "There's not much time for recuperation following putting the paper to bed. After a night of relaxation, morning brings another week's deadline. This scenario goes on in town after town across America, as family owned and operated papers deliver the news to citizens of their communities. We take great pride in providing this service."

A call summons Steve to his office and directs my attention back to the looming stack of newspapers. Persistence pays off in the form of an item in the January 20, 1905, personal column.

"Hooray! I finally found proof of the Sandes in Groton."

Stacy and Steve both emerge from their offices to see the treasure. The single line reads, "Mrs. John Sande spent Sunday at Bristol."

Steve exclaims, "Well, that's a scoop if I ever saw one!"

Stacy laughs. "Makes your trip worthwhile, doesn't it?"

"You bet. At least it's a start. A small, but important start."

Further research uncovers other items on the Sandes. A February issue reports, "John Sande moved his shoemaker shop and stock to Waubay, and will open up there. His family will remain here for the present. Mr. Sande went to Waubay the first of the week."

A few weeks later, another edition confirms John Sande's return to Groton. "John Sande is again a permanent citizen of Groton—back in his old place as an employee of the Milwaukee Road. Mr. Moxness, who took his place here, has returned to Bristol, and his family will move back there in a short time." In July, the paper notes, "Mrs. John Sande returned last Friday evening from her visit to Minnesota."

The newspaper office door opens and a man enters in a Schwan's Ice Cream uniform with the name Duane embroidered on it. He looks around and asks, "Well, what kind of convention do we have going on here?"

Stacy answers, "R. J's a writer from Wyoming working on a book on our famous Groton native jockey Earl Sande. Do you know any stories about Sande?"

"Well, let's see. The name's familiar enough to me because of my friend. Of course, I haven't thought about this in years. It's not about Sande directly. I grew up around here on a nearby farm. My best friend from school was a chap named Vern. He just idolized Earl Sande and always told me that he was going to be a top jockey like his hero. Ever since he was ten or eleven he had a dream that someday he would follow Sande's lead and ride a Kentucky Derby winner. We all have dreams, and most of us grow out of them. But not Vern."

Sensing another story, Stacy asks, "What happened?"

"His family raised quarter horses and thoroughbreds. That sparked his interest in horses. He was kind to horses and spent hours currying them. He made their coats so sleek and glossy that they shone like some sort of metal. Guess he was born with the passion to race. He and his brother Bernie, rode every chance they got. They were favorites at the Brown County racetracks and moved up to the bigger tracks and did all right. They both made it to the big time. On Vern's way to achieving his dream of riding in his very first Kentucky Derby he died in a plane crash." Duane's voice trails off.

Steve deftly shifts the conversation to an order for the next week and we all silently go back to work. The Schwan man leaves without revisiting his friend's story. While he exits, in strolls a man whom Stacy introduces as Gene Cassels. I remember running across "The Groton Independent" articles about Herb Cassels as a prominent businessman and that Mr. Cassels owned a local farm implement dealership. He also bought and sold horses. Mrs. Cassels took pride in her fine stepping horses.

Gene explains his family's connections to Earl Sande. "My grandfather had a farm just outside of town and my father, Leon, was born here in 1899, a year after Earl. Dad and Earl became close friends from day one. I remember him telling how he and Earl Sande used to ride Grandad's horses in the fields. Here's an article from the 1920s saying Earl learned to ride horses on H. W. Cassels's farm. I can take you out there if you want." His quiet voice masks the importance of the offer.

Stacy grabs her camera and I stuff a notepad in my vest pocket. We follow Gene out Fifth Avenue and then cross a double-laned highway.

Stacy says, "You can be sure those lanes weren't around when Earl came out here to ride. This was just a rural trail, and the farm was way out in the country then."

The dirt road hooks left, Gene pulls over to the shoulder, and stops in front of a farm. The farmhouse stands on a narrow plateau that drops off into low-lying fields of crop stubble. To the right, a dilapidated old barn with a caved-in roof leans toward the earth.

"That's the only building left from Grandad's original farm. I don't know the year for sure, but I can guarantee you that right out there is where Earl Sande learned to ride horses!" Gene exclaims with determined confidence.

As if on cue, a horse rounds the corner of his stable and stops next to the old barn. Stacy raises her camera and captures the Sande "spirit" horse for her paper. I hear a distant voice yell, "Come on Earl, let's go ridin'." The winds whip the powdery snow into an image of two young, barefooted kids racing across the field riding bareback. All of us look at each other and head back to our vehicles without saying a word as the light of day begins to fade.

Stacy suggests, "Let's stop and see Ben Anderson on the way back to the office. He's an old-timer and may know something about Sande."

Sande "spirit" horse. Courtesy "The Groton Independent."

"Good idea."

Anderson lives across the street from the Groton High School athletic field. The man who greets us could pass for Lionel Barrymore: heavy set, bushy white eyebrows, and husky voice. His hands rest on his cane like Mr. Potter's in *It's A Wonderful Life*.

"I'm old, nearly ninety, but not old enough to have known Earl Sande as a boy. My father had a drugstore, and Dad told me that Earl used to come in and order a soda once in awhile. Dad talked about Earl's racing career and his ties to Groton a lot."

Stacy nudges Ben. "Tell R.J. about the racetracks rumored to be near here."

With surprising speed, Ben's hand sweeps through the air. "Rumors nothing. Well, it's right over there in that pastureland. You can still see ruts in the soil and how they banked the track."

Before we return to the newspaper office, Stacy and I do indeed check out the pasture in dusky twilight for signs in the soil and notice the banking of the land and ruts described by Ben.

"Sande's house is just beyond the school." Stacy says. "Wthout a doubt, he could easily see the racetrack and hear the roar of the crowd as jockeys and their horses raced to the wire. I can just hear his mother admonishing, 'Earl Sande, you get back in this house and finish your schoolwork and chores before you sneak off again to that racetrack.'"

I join in the fantasy and voice Sande's reply. "Aw, Ma. I'll do my chores when I get home, and I'm no good at book learning."

"Earl Sande, you speak properly. Ma is not my name. You know you should call me Mother."

We look down the street where the echo of his running lingers as Earl heads around the corner and sneaks under the racetrack bleachers.

Back at my worktable, newspaper research continues for additional Sande family mentions. Nothing appears in the remaining issues of 1905; nothing in 1906; nothing in 1907.

A group of men and women enter the office. All are dressed up, distinguishing them from the working townfolk, who conduct business at the newspaper office. Stacy goes over to talk to them. After a bit, she turns to me and says, "I have a surprise for you. These are Earl Sande relatives from around the area, and they are here to see how they can help with your research. They drove from Aberdeen, Conde, Brookings, and Mitchell."

"Saving the best for last? Aren't you and Steve the sneaky ones!"

After handshakes, Betty Jensen, Douglas Jensen, Eunice Jensen, Marion Jensen, Carmen Wika, Delmar Maeschen, and Louise Maeschen gather at the worktable. A genealogy chart shows how they are descendants or spouses of descendants of Karl O. Peterson, Earl Sande's maternal grandfather.

I explain my research for a book on Earl's racing career, and they assess whether to trust information about him to a writer. The presentation of autographed copies of *Will Rogers, Performer* and copies of my article on Earl help convince them I am capable of doing a credible job on his life as America's top jockey.

"Have been trying to pin down when the Sandes left Groton and moved to Idaho. The family lived in American Falls by 1915, but there's conflicting evidence about when the family left here."

With a wide grin, Marion says, "I think I can clear that up." He hands a colorful, fringed, leather postcard across the table.

I inspect it carefully. It carries a May 4, 1908, Groton postmark and a receiving postmark at Lily, South Dakota, the next day. Writing on the reverse side reads, "Will start for Idaho about 2 weeks. Try and come see us before we move, I can't get away. Baby isn't very well yet. Oh, how hard it will be to leave you all so far behind. Tillie."

Marion says with satisfaction, "I guess that postcard puts to rest when John, Tillie, and the kids left Groton."

"Thanks for clearing up that mystery."

Over the next several hours, Sande relatives share stories about Earl and his family as well as precious family photos. I thank them for the great amount of help and for traveling to Groton in the dead of a South Dakota winter. All enjoy the savory food Stacy and Steve provided. Family memories spring to life as old photographs and yellowed newspaper clippings pass back and forth.

After they leave, the postcard date serves as a starting point to further confirm when the Sandes left Groton. The proof comes in the May 21, 1908, personal notes section of the newspaper. "John Sande loaded a car with his household effects for shipment to American Falls, Idaho, on Tuesday of this week, and will establish his home in that irrigation region, where so many former Grotonites have cast their lot."

John Sande corresponded with friends who left Groton earlier to move westward to American Falls. They encouraged him to join them out West. Holding an envelope in his hand he pleads his case. "Listen Tillie, I know it's hard to leave friends and family, but there are great opportunities in Idaho. Our old neighbors, the Farnhams, moved there and are already homesteading. It's not a pipe dream. I don't want to be a railroad section foreman forever. I showed I know how to farm back in Norway and here in Bristol, too. I'm not afraid of hard work."

"I know you're a hard worker, John. That's not the point."

"Under this homesteading, we can prove up the land and it will be ours free and clear in a matter of years. I already filed my first citizenship papers, and all we need to do is work the land. Here, take a look at this American Falls Commerical Club brochure sent us by the Farnhams. It says right in here that new settlers are coming to American Falls from almost every state in the Union. It's the biggest movement West since Oklahoma homesteading. Earl and Lester are big enough to lend a hand with clearing the acreage and farm chores while little Eva can help you out."

"Do we just up and leave our family and friends, John?"

"With the Farnhams and other Groton families already there, we would have ready made friends. The soil is fertile lava ash, and there's 275 days of

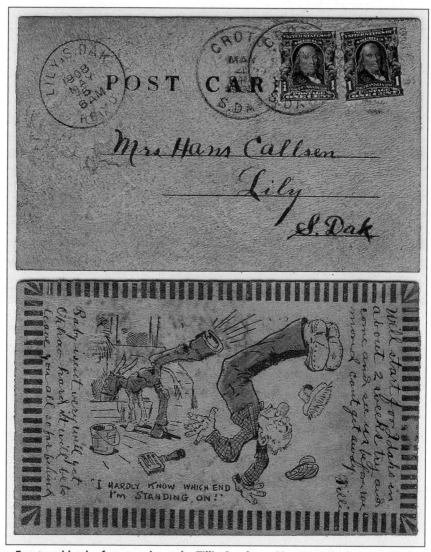

Front and back of postcard sent by Tillie Sande on May 4, 1908. Courtesy Earl Sande Family Collection by Marion Jensen.

sunshine yearly. There's ample below-surface water for wells and irrigation. Look at the size of these irrigated crops. And there's plenty of dry farming of wheat, alfalfa, barley, rye, oats, and potatoes. The main route of the Oregon Short Line Railway serves American Falls, so we aren't locked into

John Sande and son Earl shortly before the family moves to American Falls, Idaho. Courtesy Earl Sande Family Collection by Marion Jensen.

local prices for our crops. I know I could earn a decent living for our family in Idaho," John states with firm conviction.

"But John, I'm due to have a baby in August. How can we make this move now?"

"I know it will be hard with another new baby coming, but we can't afford to wait. In the first part of this year new settlers took 50,000 acres and built several hundred farmhouses. Unless we act now, all of the choice lands will be taken. Of course, I could go on ahead with you and the kids following later, after the birth of our baby."

"We will have no separation. I can see you're of no other mind, John Sande. We will move together and make new friends and a new life in Idaho. Now go, I've planning and preparing to do for the move West."

Morning comes early in the western horse country. Steve has already taken off to conduct an interview for a front page story. I help Stacy feed her horses, hauling out feed amidst a scurry of barn cats. Despite wanting their feed, the young horses keep a cautious distance. The older horse moseys over to the hay and munches without paying any attention to a stranger. Stacy treats her to a good rubdown.

"My long history with horses is one of the reasons your phone call to the newspaper office about Earl Sande intrigued me. I always owned Arabian horses. In fact, Arabians are the foundation horses credited with the origin of thoroughbreds. This is my Arabian soulmate horse, Zakamora. She was shown before I got her and qualified for Nationals. I hear she was a real pistol when she was young, and that's one of the reasons she did so well. She's nineteen years old and I've owned her for most of the past twelve years."

"What do you mean, most of?"

"Well, a few years back, my life was a mess. An addiction to prescription drugs left me unable to care for myself, let alone my kids and horses. I lost my job, and my savings barely supported our family. I hated to part with Mora, but I had to sell her in order to make ends meet. My friend, Sandy, bought her. We knew each other for years, but Sandy hadn't ridden in a long time. She is such a great horse that Sandy felt comfortable with her and started riding again. While happy for her, I lost my best friend."

"How did you reunite?"

"Well, R. J., another friend and I often went down to Sandy's place to visit my horse. After treatment, Lisa saw how hard I worked to put my life back together again. She knew that I missed Mora beyond description. Secretly, Lisa talked with Sandy about selling Mora back to me. One day Lisa came over to tell me that Sandy decided that my horse and I were a team and we should be back together. Being very close with her previous horse, Ibn, Sandy understood the bond. Lisa put up half the money, and I arranged a bank loan for the other half needed to buy back Mora. The next day we arrived at Sandy's for the move. We all cried as we loaded the trailer."

"Wow, powerful. You have some great friends. That says a lot about you."

"There's another chapter to this story. Last year I was reading 'Arabian Horse World Magazine' and noticed a contest for free breeding to a six-time national champion stallion. The owners of Alada Baskin 1 asked people to write a short letter explaining why winning a breeding to their stud would be a dream come true. I thought about it for a long time before submitting an entry explaining how losing Mora and getting her back was such an emotional time for me. I attached a photo of us to the entry, sent it out, and forgot about it. What a thrill when the notification arrived. I still can't believe I won. She will be bred this spring via artificial insemination to Lad."

"Congratulations. I must say, you earned getting Mora back and winning that contest."

"So that explains my horse passion and why I was so quiet when that horse came around the corner of the old barn where Earl learned to ride. When I said it was the Sande "spirit" horse, I really felt it. Horses connect to a part of me that goes very deep. I don't think that horse stood and looked at us the way he did all by himself."

"This research on Earl has taken on a life of its own. The call from a dead Doc Pardee, your love of horses that got you interested in this project on Earl, the Sande "spirit" horse, and Duane's touching story are just the beginning."

"I'm sure you will keep us posted on how things progress. Right now, I need your help. Could you grab that bucket over there and fill it up from the faucet in the far end of the barn? Thanks."

I follow directions and haul enough water to satisfy the horses for the day. Hunger has overcome the younger horses' caution, and they now feed heartily without bothering to look up as water from a stranger pores into their trough.

"When did you first have horses?"

"I developed a love for horses at an early age. Lucky for me, my parents supported my passion. Owned horses most of my life and feel nothing can take the place of looking out my window to see 'the girls' running along the pasture as the trains go by. They fill a need in me for beauty and compassion."

"Earl must have experienced similar feelings."

"In my opinion, no other breed in the world compares to the Arabian. Living here in quarter horse country helps me develop a thick skin about horse breeds. I take a lot of ribbing for my Arabs, but on the other hand, many around here know my Arabs and recognize the close connection they have with people."

Our chores done, Stacy turns and says, "I guess we won't be seeing you for a while, cowboy. Good luck on your search for Earl Sande." She gives me a firm handshake and adds, "Thanks for bringing a lot of excitement to Groton."

Her ponytail swirls as she jumps into her truck. The tires spit out gravel and she heads down the driveway. Her hand waves out the window.

With my Groton work finished, the trip to American Falls takes shape after several calls to Idaho. As in Groton, the local library does not have clippings files on Earl Sande, nor does the State Historical Society in Boise. The Boise Public Library holds more promise since the file on Sande discovered years ago originated there.

The librarian delivers bad news. "Sorry, there's not much here. We checked for files on Earl Sande, Idaho jockeys, Idaho athletes, horse racing, and every other conceivable connection, but only came up with a single folder with two 1960s articles on Sande.

That material could have been misfiled or lost over the years. That's why we moved the rare and irreplaceable items into the Idaho Room with limited access. Sorry I could not help you more."

The librarian promises to photocopy the two articles and mail them to Wyoming. How ironic. The file that triggered my interest and article years ago, and initiated this renewed quest for Sande no longer exists — or at least — cannot be found.

I obtain better results with the next call. Brett Crompton, owner and editor of the "Power County Press" in American Falls, promises to dig out the former "American Falls Press" issues prior to my arrival.

Brett says, "I wrote an article on Earl Sande myself for our Centennial Edition a few years back. Ran across some old news items on him that piqued my interest and thought the town should be reminded of his roots here in American Falls."

The folks in Groton have been wonderful and it appears from the phone call that the welcome at American Falls will be equally hospitable. I think about Tillie's strength and courage to leave Groton pregnant and travel across the country to homestead in Idaho. Her determination reminds me of the "Citadel" statue in Pierre.

After one last tour around Groton, Sande's stomping grounds as a young kid, I wonder how he felt as he left behind his friend Leon Cassels, and the days of riding horses on the Cassels's farm. I've only been in Groton a few days and have already taken a liking to the town, its horse racing heritage, and its people.

Chapter 3

Bitten by the Racing Bug: American Falls, Idaho

"John Sande, if American Falls is as desolate as eastern Montana, we have a piece of talking to do. Are you taking us to the far ends of the earth?"

Even today, traveling the more than 1,000 miles across South Dakota, clipping the southwest corner of North Dakota, through Montana and dropping down into Idaho, takes nearly three days to traverse. In 1908, good roads were few and far between. The Sandes traveled in May and heavy spring downpours turned the roads into muddy quagmires. Tire blowouts and radiators boiling over on mountain grades extended the trip to three weeks.

Near the end of the third day of travel, a backroad takes me through Aberdeen. It's ironic that the Sande family moves one-third across the country and settles sixteen miles from another town named Aberdeen. I stop along the northern shoreline of American Falls Reservoir and watch wind gusts create ripples on the surface. Dusk creeps across the semi-arid landscape, while the sun casts a purple haze on distant sand hills. Clouds dot the sky with fleeting forms. Wild horses, urged on by ghost riders, race the cloud shadows to the horizon. The camera's shutter clicks, securing the image.

At the edge of American Falls, the American Motel provides the only available room in town. A pipeline contractor's crewcab pickups fill the parking lot except for one narrow space. The sparse but clean room comes with a colorful pamphlet on the town's unique history.

Most of the present town did not exist when the Sande family moved to Idaho. In 1923, the federal government undertook to move residents and businesses from the old townsite, on the east bank of the Snake River along the old Oregon Trail, to the present location. Contractors uprooted buildings and moved them via steam engines. The Oregon Short Line Railroad relocated its tracks at a cost of more than $500,000. Government contractors started construction on a dam in 1925 for the creation of the American Falls Reservoir.

By early 1927, the streets that Earl Sande walked as a youth lay underwater most of the year. Today, however, during the dry months, the water level recedes. At that time, you can walk among the foundations of the downtown structures, which teemed with activity as the Sande family arrived in 1908. One of the few remaining structures of the old town site, the Oneida Milling & Elevator Company concrete grain elevator, looms over the water's edge like a phoenix. Beneath the highway bridge, an original powerhouse stands empty on the rock island splitting the Snake River's flow.

Only minutes from the motel, an early morning light burns in the "The Power County Press" office at 174 Idaho Street. Brett Crompton and wife, Debbie, continue running the family newspaper, operated for years by his father and mother. To the right, a dark-haired man in his forties sits at a desk, poring over newspaper copy. He gets up as I enter and walks around his desk to greet me.

"You're up kind of early, R.J."

"I've been called a late riser. Saw the light on so thought I'd get an early start on the Earl Sande research. How did you know I was R.J.?"

"Not many folks hereabouts I don't know, so it was a process of elimination. Besides, your Wyoming license plate gave you away."

We shake hands and he motions me to a large desk covered with crumbling, bound newspapers.

"You can work over here. I brought up the early years of 'American Falls Press' from basement storage. Couldn't find some issues. They might be lost completely, or they may be over at our house. Because of a fire down the street, we took precaution and moved a lot of old newspapers out in case the fire reached our building. If they aren't at home, we may be able to locate a microfilm copy if you really need it."

"Thanks. I'll start my work and let you get back to your business."

"Yeah, deadlines are a constant at a weekly paper."

Brett walks over to his desk, hesitates before sitting down, and returns holding several newspapers.

"Here's a copy of our Centennial Issue. It provides background on American Falls and a copy of the article I wrote on Earl Sande. It references a 1920s article with some early information on Sande. Hope that helps. If you find any photos in the newspapers that you would like to have copied, don't hesitate to ask. We have fairly complete photo archives."

"Great. Vintage photos always help to illustrate a book."

"I also put a little article in the paper that you were coming to American Falls to research Earl Sande and requested anyone with information on Earl or his family to contact you or the newspaper office. No calls as of yet but the paper has not been out that long."

"Will probably run into the same thing here as in Groton. Anyone around when Earl lived here is dead and buried by now. However, people may remember their parents talking about Earl or have some photos or other remembrances of the Sande family. Thanks for your effort."

Knowing that the Sande family left South Dakota in May and arrived in Idaho sometime in June, the search begins in fragile issues of "American Falls Press." Much of the paper's news originates from eastern newswires and covers national events, sports, and politics, so the research moves along at a fast pace. In September 1908, the newspaper runs a Homestead Gossip column. That section, along with the personals and local news sections, gets line-by-line scrutiny.

I find the first American Falls Sande family reference in the December 5, 1908, issue. "Mrs. John Sande attended first religious service at Homestead Schoolhouse. Meetings are held every other afternoon at 3 o'clock with Methodist preacher." In the same issue, there's a line that notes, "John Sande brought a load of hay from town." A few days later, the paper reports, "John Sande expects to leave for Blackfoot today to attend business interests."

"Brett, do you know the location of the old Homestead Schoolhouse?"

"That's just northwest of American Falls, toward Aberdeen. Do you think the Sandes homesteaded there?"

"It's a possibility. But more concrete evidence is needed."

A mention of the Sandes in the Fairview Facts section of the newspaper narrows the focus and takes the research effort to the County Courthouse.

A knowledgeable clerk points out Fairview on the area map. A search through the giant plot record books documents J. C. Sande homesteaded and proved up Section 32, TW 65, R 31E on July 25, 1911.

The clerk explains, "It took three years to prove up and earn ownership of a homestead. Since the Sandes arrived here in mid-1908, they probably picked out a site shortly thereafter and settled in Fairview by July 1908. That section was all sagebrush and infested with jack rabbits back then. You can be sure they earned their land."

Armed with copies of the plot map and section description, I start to leave when the clerk calls me come back. Her voice reflects excitement. "I just remembered, there's local a man you should talk to. His family bought the old Fairview School where the Sande children would have attended. The Clingers lived in it for many years."

She dials and hands the phone over the counter.

Dallas Clinger picks me up at the newspaper office. We drive west out of town and then north on the way to Fairview School.

"The school was built in two stages," Dallas explains. "The first part in 1906 and then expanded in the 1920s. Typical two-room schoolhouse. You're lucky. Most of the country schools around here were built of wood and disappeared over the years. This one is built of concrete so remains. My dad bought the school in 1958 and sold it to the present owners in 1972. There's still a merry-go-round pole in the yard. By the way, just past the school is the old Sande place. When I was a kid it was abandoned and we called it 'the haunted house.' We'll stop there, too."

On Fairview Lane he pulls up to the former schoolhouse. Although now a country inn with new windows, the schoolhouse shape remains. A large tree in the backyard was probably a sapling when Earl Sande attended school here. Nobody answers the door, we continue on to the Sande homestead, taking a left on Fairview Road and traveling a few miles north.

I pull out the 1920s interview of Earl Sande which Gene Cassels had provided. Earl reminisced, "When I was nine years old, my family moved from Groton, South Dakota, my birthplace, to American Falls, Idaho. My sisters, my brother and I attended a school built by the farmers about three miles distant from our home. To reach it we had to walk on cow paths through the sagebrush, using a swinging bridge suspended from wires to cross the canal, which connected the irrigation laterals. Often I would run the full three miles at a dogtrot, for I had it in mind then that the way to keep in good physical trim was through exercise. And back in my mind

Sande family farm at Fairview outside of American Falls, Idaho, circa 1915. Courtesy Sande Tomlinson Collection.

was the thought that if I keep my muscles hard and my body lean I should be better suited for race riding when the chance came."

The tangled sagebrush and jack rabbit infestation remain only a memory. In their place, land plotted into neat fields and farmyards paint a different picture. The farmhouse, looks eerily similar to the Groton Sande home. The white frame structure is nestled behind a barrier of trees lining the road. The north side of the house sticks farther out than the rest and protects the front door from the wind with an alcove.

Dallas remarks, "It's easy to see why they called this section Fairview. To the southeast lies the river, and beyond rises Wild Horse Mountain of Idaho's Bannock Range. Stunning sunrises greeted the Sandes as they rose early to work the fields and care for their animals."

"You can see a lot of hard work went into making this farm a success. Thanks for taking the time to show the location of the school and farmhouse."

"Think nothing of it. The trip brought back a lot of good memories. Good luck with your project."

Further research back at the newspaper office shows that American Falls area residents used horses in both work and recreation. The Fourth of July and Pioneer Days coverage always carried news of horse races. The yellow and dusty issues unveil additional confirmation that the Sandes homesteaded outside of American Falls in Fairview.

— John Sande lost a valuable heifer this week. Too much frosted alfalfa.
— Lester Sande is first in cantaloupe at the County Fair.
— Miss Ruth Cronkhite (teacher at Fairview School) was a visitor at home of Mr. and Mrs. John Sande last Friday remaining until Sunday.
— Mrs. J. C. Sande and Mrs. Harry Anderson took a trip to Pocatello last Saturday.
— Miss Eva Sande is the proud possessor of a pet lamb a year old, which sheared 15 pounds of wool.
— J. C. Sande suffered a sore neck and shoulder for over two weeks as the result of being kicked by a cow.
— Earl Sande, Lester Sande, and Leonard Farnham took a trip to Neeley and enjoyed a swim in the Warm Springs last Sunday afternoon.

- Mrs. J. C. Sande gave a party last Saturday night in honor of Mr. Sande's birthday. About forty were present. They all enjoyed a pleasant time and went home at a late hour.
- A very pleasant meeting of the ladies club was held last Thursday at Mrs. Sande's. Delicious refreshments were served by the hostess.
- The all day get-together at the Fairview school last Saturday was a very satisfactory affair socially and financially. A very entertaining feature of the program was a recitation given by Frances Sande and five year old Karl Kampf.
- Miss Eva Sande and little sister, Helen, visited the Muller place last week and watched the combine at work there.
- A fairly good crowd attended the dance at John Sande's. It was a very severe night but everyone enjoyed themselves.
- Among those who attended the dedication of the Methodist Church at American Falls last Sunday were the Millers, Sandes, and Sweetwoods.
- Earl Sande spent Christmas at his home returning to the Falls in the evening to resume his duties in the Sheep Store.

Bits and pieces of Homestead Gossip, Facts from Fairview, and American Falls Personal Notes help build a picture of Sande family life in American Falls over the years. Hard work, fun times, and simple pleasures mark the Sandes' lives.

John Sande builds a successful farm, selling produce and stock throughout the area and to markets serviced by the Oregon Short Line Railroad. For relaxation, he joins friends Harry Anderson, Carl Johnson, Harry Wallis, and O. F. Crawley for periodic fishing trips, catching 900 mountain trout in a single outing near Arco. He takes his civic duty seriously, serving on the jury in American Falls, and running for Justice of the Peace; losing to E. E. Geesey by a vote of forty-four to forty-three. Tillie takes care of the home, participates in church and social club events, and entertains friends and relatives in their home.

The children share the farm workload and enjoy their own pleasures. Lester continues his interest in growing produce and wins several county fair competitions with his prize peck turnips and summer squash. All of the children participate in school activities, including singing in the Christmas program and acting in plays. Helen and Frances endure the typical childhood illnesses of measles and diseased tonsils. Older sister Eva travels to

Fall Creek Sheep Company Limited where Earl Sande worked in 1914 and 1915. Courtesy "Power County Press," American Falls, Idaho.

Interior of Fall Creek Sheep Company Limited where Earl Sande worked in 1914 and 1915. Courtesy Valerie Hoybjerg, Power County Historical Society, American Falls, Idaho.

Lava Hot Springs for paralysis treatments.

It is evident from the years of news clips that the Sande family forms a vital part of the Fairview and American Falls social scene. John Sande again proves his worth as a successful farmer and shrewd businessman.

"You were right, John. We have built a nice home and life here in Fairview. We and the children have many friends and much for which we should be thankful," Tille says as she and John sit on the porch of their farmhouse, and view the stunning Fall sunset.

"You gave up a lot to move to Idaho, Tillie. I appreciate the sacrifices you made and all the hard work you put in to make our house a wonderful home."

After Fairview School, Earl attends American Falls High School and starts working at the Sheep Store in 1914. The Sheep Store carries a wide variety of products for area residents, including cash-and-carry groceries, clothing, footwear, high fashion garments for the ladies, and tack and outfitting supplies for ranchers and farmers. In May 1914, the company reorganizes as the Fall Creek Mercantile Company, but local folks continue to refer to the business as the Sheep Store.

At age nine, Sande acquired his first horse, trading three 5 dollar gold pieces, four ducks, and a bicycle for the filly. The strawberry-colored horse could run like the wind. Sande named her Babe. The two engaged in impromptu races against dogs and horses of other area kids. At age fourteen, the lanky, freckle-faced Sande weighed only seventy pounds. On July 14, 1914, Earl rode in his first official horse race during the American Falls Fourth of July celebration activities. The notorious Burr Scott announced to the spectators that he needed a rider. Sande jumped at the opportunity and bounded out of the crowd. He rode the horse, Guise, to victory. Sande won a $10 purse. Scott rewarded the youngster with a silver dollar for his riding skill.

Sande later recollected,

> When Burr Scott, a burly Westerner, came striding along the fence at the race meet and called out for a volunteer to ride his horse, Guise, in the main event, a youngster wearing overalls and a blue shirt elbowed his way through the line of railbirds. That ambitious kid was myself, and since Scott knew that I understood something about racing a horse, he accepted my offer.

Power County Fair Grounds in American Falls, Idaho, where Earl Sande competed in horse races. Courtesy "Power County Press," American Falls, Idaho.

Horse Race at Power County Fair Grounds in American Falls, Idaho. Courtesy Valerie Hoybjerg, Power County Historical Society, American Falls, Idaho.

It was a roughly hewn half-mile track laid out in the sandy soil from which the sagebrush had been cleared. Back of the finish line was a little wooden structure we called the grandstand, large enough to give seating to several hundred people. Women and girls sat in the stands while the men and boys preferred to hang over the rail directly in front or to stroll around the grounds.

My saddle was made from a sweat pad to which the girth was riveted and from short leather loops swung for use as stirrups. Guise was a real thoroughbred, one of the few in that part of the country. He was an eight-year-old son of Peep O'Day. His front ankles were disfigured and although he had long since lost his best racing form, he could still step along at a lively clip over a short distance. This particular race was a quarter of a mile and I think that was as far as Guise, at his advanced age and crippled condition, wished to go. We started slow but after the first 100 yards Guise shot past the rest of the field and we were far out in front when we crossed the finish line.

I've had many a thrill on the big racetracks of America since then and I've ridden some wonderful horses, but I don't think I ever experienced the kick I got out of bringing Burr Scott's Guise home to victory.

After I had crossed the finish line, I brought Guise up to a fast stop and an angry Burr Scott came running quickly. He said, "What's the matter with you, kid? Are you plumb crazy stopping Guise like that? Do you want to ruin the best racehorse in this part of the country? Don't you know the difference between a racehorse and a plow horse?" Burr settled down after a bit but that began our relationship. He was a fine man.

The September 30, 1915, issue of "American Falls Press" reported the results of horse races at the Eighth Annual Power County Fair. Earl Sande came in first place in a mile race on Stranger Horse, winning $25; second place the next day, winning $15; and tied for first on the third day, splitting a purse of $40.

"Brett, have you ever heard of a Burr Scott? I see here that Sande won a few fair races for him in American Falls between 1914 and 1915. Sande supposedly left town with this Burr Scott fellow just before finishing high school in 1916. Some articles refer to Scott as an itinerant horse trader, and I spoke with a Doc Hinshaw in Prescott who told me that a man by that name brought Earl down to Doc Pardee's."

"No, don't have a recollection of any mention of a Burr Scott in my days in American Falls. I'll talk to some of the old-timers in town and see if any remember Burr Scott."

"With that deadend, it's time to call it a night, Brett. Been a long day. Thanks a lot for all your help. Collected great information on Earl and his family from your morgue. My work's done here so will be heading back to Wyoming in the morning."

"OK, keep us posted on your progress. We want to keep our readers informed on Earl. Good luck with the rest of your research. Make sure to come back for a book signing when it's finished."

"That's a date."

After a delicious evening meal at the Willow Bay Café near the American Falls reservoir, the waitress's advice that the pie is "to die for" is heeded. A thumbs up signals approval of her recommendation.. She's a non-traditional college student attending the university in Pocatello and working on a novel on the side. We trade writing war stories as the rest of the customers depart.

The phone's ringing disturbs my sleep. Outside it's still pitch black. A glance at the clock reveals 6 a.m. I pick up the phone, wondering who can be on the other end. Few know I'm in American Falls.

"Hello."

A woman's frail voice asks, "Is this R.J.?"

"Yes, who's calling?"

"My name is Josephine Werner. I live in Las Vegas but grew up in American Falls. Left with my husband in 1935, however, I still get the paper. Read the article about your research on Earl Sande and just had to call. You know, it's about time someone wrote a book about that boy. Oh, he so deserves it. You'll have to excuse my voice, Dearie, I'm just getting over this darned flu and was afraid I was a goner there for a while. Just had to hang on to talk with you about that boy, Earl Sande."

Almost as an afterthought she adds, "My uncle taught Earl how to ride race horses."

After hearing this claim for about the tenth time, I was a bit wary. Without a doubt, everyone has a relative who taught Earl Sande how to ride.

"Who was your uncle?"

"Otho B. Scott, known as Burr Scott by everyone. I'm sorry, I forgot to tell you my maiden name was Josephine Scott. Uncle Burr lived with us and that young Sande boy used to stay at our house the nights before he and Uncle Burr went out horse racing. Lots of relatives hung around our home and for a long time I thought that since Earl Sande came so much he was just another relative. I'm in my nineties now but was a young girl when Sande slept on our daybed in the living room.

"The night prior to their horse racing trips he would bicycle over to our house. Before he and Uncle Burr left, Earl would tell me and my brother, 'Now you snot-nosed kids leave my bike alone while I'm gone.' And, of course, as soon as he left, we laid that bike upside down and spun its wheels," Josephine laughs, relishing the memory.

"Let me get this straight. Your uncle was Burr Scott? Nobody in American Falls seems to remember him, and articles refer to him as an itinerant horse trader."

"Oh, no. Uncle Burr was a bachelor and lived with us. He and my father were in business together. Uncle Burr also had racehorses he would run in the off-season. Uncle Burr left American Falls in the 1920s so the folks there now would not remember him. I talked with that nice young man at the paper, Brett. I knew his parents long ago, but he would not remember Burr."

"Do you mind answering a question?"

"No, by all means, go ahead."

"By any chance do you know Doc Pardee?"

"No, never heard that name."

"Good. You'll have to excuse me about being a bit wary concerning early morning phone calls."

"I called Brett last night, but you had already left. I hesitated to disturb you so late. He gave me your hotel number in order to catch you before leaving town. Please accept my apologies for the early call. Yesterday, I sent out a package that may be of interest in your research on Earl Sande. It's being delivered to the newspaper office and should arrive overnight. Call me after you receive it but before you open the package. We'll go through each item over the phone to discuss its significance."

"Let me have your phone number to call you after the package arrives."

Mrs. Joseph Walter Scott and her children, Josephine and Conrad, circa 1916. Courtesy Josephine Scott Werner.

Still a bit gun-shy about early morning calls from strangers, moments after she hangs up I call Las Vegas information and confirm the number that Josephine gave me. I breathe a sign of relief. She does exist. My head spins with anticipation. What gems await in Josephine's mysterious package?

Brett grins as he lets me into the newspaper office. "Thought I'd find you here early this morning after that call from Josephine Werner last night. Looks like you found the elusive Burr Scott. I checked with my mother and she remembers Josephine well. Her parents lived here for years, but Burr moved early on to the west coast. Guess that's why nobody remembers him today."

He digs into his newspaper work while I jot down questions to ask Josephine about her uncle, Burr Scott, and Earl Sande. After two anxious hours, the overnight delivery package arrives. Brett, sensing a story, saunters over to see its contents when opened and listen in on one side of the conversation. I signal approval and dial Josephine's telephone number.

"Mrs. Werner, the package is here and still unopened, as you requested."

"Thank you, Dearie. You can call me Jo; everyone does. Now let's begin. I put the contents in the order that we will discuss them. I want to impart a sense of who the Scotts were, and then you can pick my brain on Earl Sande and Uncle Burr. Now, on top should be a photograph of a woman with two small children. That's my mother, Rose, my brother, Conrad Sailors Scott, and me. Conrad died at an early age. We were so close and I miss him still after all these years." Jo pauses before continuing.

"The Scotts were a big family, as you can see from the next photograph. There were fourteen children in total but only twelve were still alive when this picture was taken in 1902. Burr was thirty-four and is the man with the mustache, second from the right in the back row. My father, Nathaniel

Scott family children, circa 1902. Joseph Walter Scott in bottom row, Burr Scott second from right in back row. Courtesy Josephine Scott Werner.

Joseph Walter Scott and Burr Scott driving to a dance outing with horse team, circa 1907. Joseph Walter Scott is in middle back row wearing hat and Burr Scott sits second from left with arms folded. Courtesy Josephine Scott Werner.

Postcard photo of Burr Scott holding reins of horses pulling road grader, circa 1917. Handwritten text from Burr Scott on back of postcard reads, "Well ma here I am working on the state highway. Even the people have cold names here, in this (photo) the man's name is Snowball. Am getting $3.50 per day. Don't know when I can receive any mail as I don't know what PO (post office) we'll come to next. Love to all. O.B." Courtesy Josephine Scott Werner.

Postcard photo of Joseph Walter Scott, first on left holding horse rein, and Burr Scott, seated in wagon, with work team of horses, circa 1917. Back of postcard reads, "Dear Mother, I will write tonight, all well, hope this will find it the same. J. W. Scott." Courtesy Josephine Scott Werner.

Joseph Walter Scott, is the tall one in the middle of the bottom row, aged twenty-six at that time.

"OK, Jo. They're both located in your family picture. It sure clears up the Burr Scott mystery. Great to see a photo of him."

"Good, now on with my story. Grandfather Conrad Sailors Scott served in the Civil War from Indiana. Citizens elected my father sheriff of Grant County, Kansas, in 1904. He served until 1907 when he lost the next election. He moved to Dodge City, where they hired him as a deputy sheriff. That's where I was born. During this time, Uncle Burr and Father owned and operated livery stables, renting out carriages and horses. Horses were always part of our family as you can see from the next photo. It shows my father and Uncle Burr transporting their friends to a dance outing."

"A nice gathering. Sounds like lots of fun."

"Oh, we had great times back in those days. Father's older sister, May, married and moved to Portland, Oregon. Around 1913, she convinced the family to leave god-forsaken Dodge City and move to Oregon. On their way, my family got as far as American Falls and settled. Father and Uncle Burr first obtained work building the new high school in Pocatello and later in American Falls pouring cement sidewalks and hauling sand and gravel with their teams of horses. They worked for the county engineer, helping to build roads. I believe his name was Allred, and he lived up the street from us. The next two items show Father and Uncle Burr's team of horses and equipment. Excuse me for talking on so. I just want to get everything out before I forget."

"I appreciate all the items you sent and information you provided."

"So happy I can do it for that dear boy. Now back to my story. We lived in the old part of town. Our house stood four blocks from the Fall Creek Mercantile Sheep Company Store at Chestnut and Main Street. I think folks long ago just called it the Sheep Store. It was the largest and nicest store around. Our property went clear to the river; we only rented our home, never owned the place. We had a large barn in the yard and a house. You understand it's all under water now. The Power House was to our left as you faced the river. You can still see the deserted shell of that building. Kind of sad when you think about it."

"I'm sure there are lots of good memories even though the town as you knew it is gone."

"Oh, yes. Father and Uncle Burr each had a team of six work horses, and Uncle Burr had what he called racehorses. They burned the midnight

Earl Sande on Gallant Fox at Churchill Downs after winning the 1930 Kentucky Derby. Courtesy Josephine Scott Werner.

oil many nights shoeing the horses and repairing the gear for work. Father and Uncle Burr were always fixing the horse harnesses and often needed supplies from the Fall Creek Mercantile. You know, the Sheep Store. That's where Uncle Burr met Earl Sande. Sande worked there and admired Uncle Burr's horses when he helped him load his goods onto the wagon. They struck an immediate friendship and Uncle Burr always stopped to chat with Earl whenever he visited the store."

"What was it like living in American Falls back then?"

"I'm sure it was different for everybody. My folks and Uncle Burr worked hard, but we had a grand time at home. Uncle Burr played the violin and called dances. Father and the rest of us sat around the warm stove and sang. Earl would join in when he knew the words. Now about Earl and Uncle Burr. Earl sure had the right last name. He had a real sandy complexion, light sandy hair, and a face full of freckles. He used to call me Queen Josephine, just like Uncle Burr. Burr took a fatherly interest in Earl. He just saw something in that boy. Earl had a keen interest in horses, and Uncle Burr let him exercise them. Earl beamed as he walked the horses, like they were his very own. Uncle Burr helped to foster that spark in Earl. I remember Uncle Burr studying his race horses, watching their gait, how they led off, everything. He practically made himself into a horse trying to understand them. I'm sure Earl picked a lot of this up from Uncle Burr. I think we're ready now for you to open up that manila envelope."

The outside of the envelope has stamped on it: H. C. Ashby, Official Turf Photographer, Box 4, Latonia, Kentucky. Inside, I discover an autographed photo of Earl Sande on a horse. Earl's silks are the Woodward colors of white with red dots and he sits astride Gallant Fox with the twin spires of Churchill Downs in the background. He has just won the Kentucky Derby on the way to capturing the Triple Crown in 1930. On the back is written, "Dear Mrs. Werner, Just ran across your very nice letter that I had misplaced. Terribly sorry. Yes, I remember you folks quite vividly and Burr was a really wonderful friend. Hope you are well and happy. Also hope to see you sometime. Sincerely Earl Sande."

"Great photo, Jo. That's Sande on Gallant Fox. From the grandstand spires you can tell he's at Churchhill Downs. Looks like he just won the Kentucky Derby, the second jewel of the Triple Crown."

"Yes, but way before that happened, Earl had to get his training from Uncle Burr. Back then, Uncle Burr followed the county fair circuit in the summer, and in the winter he traveled what he called the outlaw circuit, going from Utah to Texas to New Orleans and Aqua Caliente in Mexico. He left by train and slept with the horses in the stock car. Earl went with him on many of these trips. Mother would be hopping mad when they returned because vermin infested their clothes. She burned the clothes and washed their hair in coal oil to kill the lice, muttering under her breath the whole time. Earl's missing school caused a big disturbance and troubled my mother. She would tell Father, 'The Sandes were here again looking for Earl.' As a mother, she knew the pain Mrs. Sande felt in her heart. But Earl liked to be around the racehorses and Burr, and the thought of earning money racing horses enticed him. That's all there was to it.

"Mother used to admonish Father, 'Why should I wash Burr's fancy white shirts when you don't have a silk shirt to wear? And he should not be taking that Sande boy down to racetracks where tobacco chewers, drinkers, and who knows what else hang around there.' Of course, Father knew better than to respond. After a while things blew over. At some point, Uncle Burr left our home and moved to Portland. I think Mother had something to say about Uncle Burr's leaving, but nothing was ever said in front of us kids. But before that, he and Earl left American Falls one day in search of horse races and Earl never came back. There! Now that dear boy has part of his story told," Jo finishes with a sigh.

"Thank you for the insight into Earl and your uncle, Jo. There's still one envelope remaining in the express package."

"Oh, yes. That's an article I thought may provide you with some more information. It's in Earl's own words. Earl sent it to Uncle Burr, who forwarded a copy to my father in the 1920s. You can read that yourself after I hang up. Now, if you ever get to Las Vegas, you must stay with me. I have a guest room, there's lots of good restaurants, and plenty to do in Vegas."

"I will, I promise. Thanks again for all the photos you sent and the information you have provided over the phone."

"My pleasure, Dearie."

Brett waits until I replace the receiver and then exclaims, "Wow, you really struck the jackpot there. How fortunate such treasured first-hand memories will not be lost."

I open the last envelope and pull out an October 19, 1925, "Saturday Evening Post" article written by Earl Sande and James R. Crowell in which Earl tells his own story. Brett comes over to the same side of the desk and reads along.

> The opportunity to ride did come when I was fifteen years old, but it was not until several years later that the fascination of the game had so fastened itself on me that I could think of little else. Every time I rode for Burr Scott, a burly Western fellow, the thought took deeper root that I would become a jockey, haunting me in my spare moments and school hours.
>
> I must confess I was actually thinking horse in the schoolroom one day when one of the younger children scribbled a note and covertly passed it to me. It read, "Earl, there's a man outside what wants to see you." I invented some pretext for leaving the room. Outside, I found Burr Scott seated in a ramshackle sheep wagon, to which was tied his entire string of horses—two cold-bloods. I had often ridden these half-breed horses for Scott and knew they could run as fast as any in the vicinity.

"Earl, I'm going upcountry on a little trip and I thought as how I'd stop and see you before I left," Scott said. "I'm taking the two cold-bloods with me."

"Going to race them?" I asked.

"Yes, if I can get any match races. They're in pretty good shape now and I thought as how I might make a nice little clean-up."

"Good luck to you, Mr. Scott. Wish I could go with you."

"Well, that's just what I wanted to see you about. Why not come along with me?"

Scott's suggestion sent the blood through my veins. Here was the chance I had so dreamed about, reposing right at my door-step. But there were insurmountable obstacles. My mother was not in sympathy with all these foolish notions I had about race riding. She would never consent to my quitting school.

"Tain't possible, Mr. Scott," I grudgingly admitted after some meditation. "The family would never stand for it."

Burr Scott was a strapping man who tipped the beam at 210 pounds, and his powers of persuasion were as powerful as his massive frame, his voice almost purred as he said, "You see, Earl, I was figuring they ain't nothing around this neck of the woods what can beat these race hosses, and I says to myself that if I can get Earl Sande to do the riding we might make a pretty good clean-up, you and me."

It was the spring of the year and there was a mellow touch to the air that made you long for the outdoors. My emotions were confused. On the one side a sense of duty to my family and on the other a love of this horse game which wouldn't die. Scott, seeing what was going on in my mind, busied himself with the harness while I fought out the battle within myself.

"How long do you expect to be gone?" I asked.

"Oh, two weeks, maybe three, maybe more and maybe less, ain't no telling. Just thought I'd mosey around and make a nice clean-up for you and me."

"Wait a minute, Mr. Scott," I instructed him as I re-entered the school. In a moment I had returned, with my cap stuffed down deep in my pocket to keep it from being seen. I sprung into the front seat of the sheep wagon.

"It's a bet, let's go," I told him.

"Put it there," boomed Scott's hearty voice. "We're going to make a nice little clean-up, you and me." And we shook hands.

So you see, I embarked on my riding career by running away from school and home. Not a very good example to set for other boys who have the riding notion in their heads, I must admit, and I certainly do not advise them to do the sort. But there is a freedom to the life of the West that makes such an act not as bad as it seems, a spirit of self-reliance inbred in youngsters that enables them to care for themselves. And Burr Scott was a fine type of man, even though some may condemn him for being accessory to a runaway. Within a year and a half I was riding on the big tracks.

Earl rationalized his actions of leaving school, his job at the Fall Creek Mercantile Sheep Store, and his family behind while he pursued his dream of horse racing in the big time. After all, in the papers he followed the career of jockey Johnny Loftus, who recently won the Travers and Withers Stakes races on Spur and the Kentucky Derby on George Smith with a record time of 2:04. However, his leaving American Falls without as much as a goodbye to his family left his mother devastated and sick with worry over the fate of her elder son. The July 29, 1916, issue of the "American Falls Press" Fairview News reported, "Mrs. Sande was ill a few days this week but is able to be up again." This was followed up with a note on August 3, 1916, "There was no meeting of the Ladies' Club this week owning to the illness of Mrs. Sande."

Slowly, the Sandes' family life returns to normal. While Earl learns his craft, Lester follows his lead and also quits school before graduating. He

Early photo of a young Earl Sande. Courtesy Sande Tomlinson Collection.

travels to Butte, Montana, and Boise, Idaho, to obtain instruction in telegraph and comes back to American Falls to work in the railroad depot. The Ladies' Club elects Mrs. Sande treasurer and the group raises money to aid suffering caused by the hostilities in Europe. Helen and Frances help in their small way by purchasing war saving bonds and thrift stamps. Eva moves to the Emmit house in town to attend school. She also continues singing at Women's Club functions.

Mrs. Sande receives a letter from a Doc Pardee, who assures her, "Earl is being well looked after, I have him in my own special care and Earl is not exposed to the temptations that so often beset jockeys. My wife, Edith May, is looking after his feeding and he won't go wanting in that department. Earl is a fine lad."

Part 2

Taking the Reins

Chapter 4

The Idaho Hot Potato:
The Outlaw Circuit

Burr Scott bites off a plug of tobacco and hands Earl Sande a fistful of hard candy as his wagon lumbers down the dusty road. He looks the young boy in the eye and gives him a wink.

"Stick to the candy, son. Tobacca is the devil's work."

"Yessir, Mr. Scott."

"Now that you and me are officially pardners, call me Burr, Earl."

"Yessir, Mr. Scott, I mean Burr."

Over the next few months, the two racing adventurers make their way through the county fair circuit and main street races of western towns in Utah, Wyoming, Colorado, and New Mexico before ending up in Prescott, Arizona. Earl quickly earns the reputation as "The Idaho Hot Potato" for his racing skill and ability to outsmart his opponents with horsemanship and a bit of trickery.

Burr pulls his wagon up to a stone building with a "Doc Pardee's Pony Restaurant Feed and Livery" sign hanging over the doorway. He surveys the newly constructed building. Its space and layout provide ample room for storing large quantities of feed and other supplies. Corrals adjoining the livery give horses and stock freedom to roam and exercise. Burr dismounts; Earl follows suit and starts to trail him into the livery. Burr signals

Earl to wait outside while he enters. Inside he sees a large man shoeing a horse. He finishes his work before looking up at Burr.

"By the looks of this place, you've made a nice little clean-up with your business, Doc."

"Well, if it ain't Burr Scott! You know, anyone can make money if they work. I never had trouble makin' money, but I was not very astute at the savin' end of things. You still runnin' those rag horses of yours around the country, Burr?"

"Sure am, Doc. Did right good this year. Got myself a darn good jockey to treat those county fair boys to a trail of dust." Burr nods toward Earl standing beyond the livery doors.

Doc sizes up Sande. "Kinda lanky for a jockey if you ask me. But you say he can ride?"

"Without a doubt he can ride, but better 'an that, this boy's got it, Doc, honest-to-goodness hoss sense. Never saw a jockey with such gentle hands; they almost speak to the hoss. To top it all off, he even sings to the hosses as he drives them to victory. He asks and they respond. He's a natural if I ever seen one, Doc."

Outside, Earl moves over to the horses tied to the hitching post and starts talking to them and giving them a gentle rub behind the ears. They look at him as if understanding what he is whispering to them.

Burr lowers his voice. "Here's the hitch, Doc. I have to get back to Idaho in order to tend to my road construction business, but ain't no sense this young lad going back home. He ain't ready for the big time yet, but with the right kind of tutoring it won't be long. I've done all I can for the kid. I thought as how you could sure help him along with your knowledge of hosses and racing experience. How 'bout it, Doc?"

Doc scratches his head and then throws another glance toward the boy. He kicks some straw with the toe of his cowboy boot.

"That'd be like takin' on a son. Me and the wife don't have kids. Don't know if I'd rightly know how to care for him."

"Don't worry about that, Doc. The kid's a self-provider, good worker, polite, and never any trouble. Judging from the hard work you put into building this livery out of river rock, Prescott will be your home for a spell. I've been looking over your operation. I says to myself, you could use a hand shoeing, cleaning up, and working with the hosses."

"You're right about that. Sure am not gettin' any younger. I leave chasin' the rodeos to the young bucks nowadays. Put my hand in it here now and then, but not like the old days. I guess I'm more cut out to be the announcer with my boomin' voice. Burr, you drive a hard bargain. About needin' help at the livery, I could see addin' a hand if he could double as a jockey for my racehorses. Not that you would sell me a pig in a poke, Burr, but how about we put him on a horse and see what this boy's made of?"

"You're on, Doc."

Burr and Doc walk outside and approach Earl, who continues to gently stroke the horses. Burr puts his hand on Earl's shoulder and says, "Earl, this here's C. W. 'Doc' Pardee. A real legend in the Wild West. Done everything from bronc busting to making movies with Tom Mix."

"Pleased to meet you, Mr. Pardee."

"Everybody calls me Doc. Understand you like to ride horses and have burnt up the outlaw and leaky roof circuit with Burr's mules. Would you mind ridin' one of my real horses for me? Like to see what it has in it. That all right with you, son?"

"Sure, Doc, love racing. I'll get on a horse any chance I get. I like to know who I'm riding. What's his name?"

"Tick Tack. He's in the back stable, far left. Saddle him up and lead him out."

Earl readies Tick Tack and brings the horse out of the livery. He mounts and guides the horse over to Doc and Burr.

"Why do you call him Tick Tack, Doc?"

"He's a half-breed or cold-blood horse. He used to pull a milk wagon. I bought him after the milkman's young son tried to ride him, and the horse just took off with a burst of speed. When the frightened youngster got off the back of the horse, he described his experience by sayin' that the horse started runnin' and went 'tick-tack' all the way back to the stable. That's the gosh honest truth of how a milk wagon horse named Tick Tack got into the racin' game."

"Look's like he's more suited to racing than milk wagon pulling to me, Doc."

"Well, let's go and see how you feel after you've ridden him. Burr and I will ride the wagon out to the racetrack. You can follow on Tick Tack."

Earl spurs on Tick Tack and trails Burr and Doc. The sun beats down hard and he shields his freckled face with the brim of his hat. He pulls the reins and stops Tick Tack alongside the wagon at the edge of the fairgrounds track.

Doc instructs, "Take Tick Tack around once easy and then let the horse loose for a fast gallop, openin' with all he's got in the final stretch."

Earl puts Tick Tack into a lope on the first lap and then urges the horse to give a bit more speed. As Earl maneuvers the first turn, Doc watches with interest. He and Burl lean against the top rail while Doc studies how Earl crouches in the stirrups and nearly floats by after the first lap. With his hands, Earl guides Tick Tack to a full gallop on the second trip around and then into a final burst of speed as they pass Burr and Doc standing at the edge of the track.

"What I tell you, Doc?"

"Well, the kid still needs a lot of polishin.' Yet I've never seen anybody get that much out of Tick Tack before. Without anyone breathin' down his neck, at that. Think what he could do with other horses and riders challengin' him. Burr, I know I found myself a new stable hand, and more importantly, a good jockey."

"I thought you'd see it that way. Let me break it to the kid. We haven't talked this over, and it will be a shock to him."

"No problem. I'll ride Tick Tack while you two work it out on the way back by wagon."

Earl slows Tick Tack down to a walk and heads back to Doc and Burr. Along the way, he pats the horse gently and whispers in his ears. He looks anxiously, at Burr and then at Doc.

"You have a fine horse here, Mr. Pardee."

"You turned him around the track just fine, but remember to call me Doc. How would you like to race him in the Prescott Frontier Days horse races? Things start hoppin' around here tomorrow."

Earl turns toward Burr, who nods his approval. A wide grin spreads across Earl's face.

"You bet, Doc. We've been to a lot of small county fairs and town races over the past few months so this will be a new challenge. But who will ride Burr's horses?"

"My mules, as Doc calls them, can't compete against the quality of Doc's hosses and others in the Frontier Days races. Go for it, Earl."

"Good. It's settled then," Doc says. "I have an errand to do, so I'll ride Tick Tack back to town. Catch up to you and Burr at the livery later."

Doc rides off, leaving a trail of dust. Burr turns to Earl and puts his arm around Earl's shoulders.

Doc Pardee. Courtesy Sande Tomlinson Collection

"Nice job, Earl. You've earned the right to be riding for one of the best all-around horsemen in this part of the country."

Burr and Earl mount the wagon and Burr hands the reins to Earl. He snaps the leather. Dust rolls up from the wagon's wheels as the two rock along in silence. Earl studies Burr's face and finally gathers the courage to speak.

"Not like you to be so quiet, Burr. Are you upset 'cause I'll be riding Doc's horses tomorrow? I can tell Doc that I will be riding for you, no problem. I shouldn't be jumping the fence after all we've been through together. We're pardners."

"Earl, that ain't it. But there's something darn right important we need to discuss now that the time's right. We've done right fine as pardners. I would love to continue racing with you, honestly. Fact is, you've gone beyond what I can teach you. Besides, I need to head back to American Falls to take care of business. You've made your break. There ain't no sense in you going back to Idaho. Your future is hoss racing. Doc has a lot of hoss sense and you can ride for him the rest of the year, and next, if you want. That's the next step you need to take. You have it in you to make it to the big tracks back East. Doc'll know when you're ready, and he'll treat you fair."

Burr pulls up to the livery and says, "I'm shoving off now, no sense prolonging goodbyes. Give my regards to Doc. Bring Tick Tack across the finish line in fine style tomorrow. Win or lose, you'll make me proud. Remember, people judge you on how you take care of yourself and your appearance. We never had much money, but we kept our clothes clean after all the instructions my sister-in-law gave us. We looked like a couple of swells. Keep in touch, Earl."

Earl pulls off his hat and looks Burr in the eye. "I'll never forget what you've done for me, Burr."

Earl bypasses Burr's outstretched hand, gives him a big hug, and then climbs off the wagon. Tears stream down his cheeks.

"That's what a pardner's for," Burr whispers. He snaps the reins and clucks the horses forward down the dirt road. The tracks in front of him blur as he lifts the reins and wipes his eyes with the back of his hand.

Earl watches until the wagon disappears out of sight, then squares his shoulders and enters the livery. He finds Doc shoeing horses. This time Doc stops his work and walks over to Earl.

"Fine man, that Burr Scott. None better in my book."

"He sure is, Doc."

"Come into my office, son. Let's see what type of arrangement we can set our minds to."

Earl follows Doc Pardee to the front of the livery and through the door on the left. Doc maneuvers around the desk and settles down into an oak desk chair on wheels. He rests his elbows on the chair's arms and motions for Earl to sit down across from him.

Tom Mix and Doc Pardee in Prescott, Arizona. Courtesy Sharlot Hall Museum & Archives, Prescott, Arizona.

Earl notices Doc's ornate chair, the arms of which some craftsman fashioned into horse heads. His gaze moves to the wall filled with framed pictures and then back to Doc.

"I see that you like my chair. Only one like it in the territory. Tom Mix whittled it for me as a kinda goin' away present. When Mix pulled up stakes and left to film in Hollywood, the Prescott Frontier Days darned near folded. I helped reorganize the rodeo, bringin' in the first buckin' horses from Juarez, Mexico. I just love that rodeo, guess that's why I'm still here. See that picture in the center of the wall, that's Tom Mix and me. Great man, Tom Mix, a real Westerner."

"Sure is a nice chair, Doc, and that Mix, what a cowboy. Saw him in the movie theater back in Idaho."

"The grunt work goes on out there in the livery, but unless you take care of the business end you'll waste all of your sweat for nothin'. Let's get down to the details. You come well-recommended by Burr. That goes a far piece with me. If you think $20 a month for sweepin' out the stables, milkin' my cows, feedin' the wagon teams, ridin' the horses, and hot-walkin' them sounds fair to you, Earl, then we have a deal. 'Course that comes with all of Mrs. Pardee's good grub you can eat. As you can see from my frame, I don't miss many of Edith May's meals if I can help it."

"As long as I get to ride, I'll do anything you want, Doc."

"That's OK here, son. But when you get out in the real world there are lots of desperadoes eager to take advantage of you. Drive a hard bargain no matter how bad you want something. Take care of business and your hard work will present the right opportunities to you."

"Yessir, Doc."

"Put 'er there then. A handshake seals the deal in my book."

"Mine too."

Doc's large hand swallows Earl's and gives it a good shake.

"We have an extra room back at the ranch, and you are welcome to bunk with us."

"If it's all the same to you, Doc, I feel more comfortable sleeping in the stable with the horses. Gives us a chance to get to know each other better."

"Suit yourself. You can start work tomorrow."

Doc gets up to return to work. Earl glances again at the picture wall.

"Mind if I look at your photos, Doc?"

"Go ahead. No, I'll give you the grand tour. Guess that shoein' can wait. Let me give you a bit of my history. Horses have been my life. Rode my first horse race when I was eight, went into the livery business for myself at fourteen, owned my own travelin' Wild West Show from 1910 to 1912, and traveled the rodeo circuit from Oklahoma to the Calgary Stampede way up in Alberta, Canada."

Doc turns to the wall and points to a picture. "This here one's of me ridin' that ornery Harry Tracy with the saddle strapped on backwards on a bet in Medicine Hat, Canada, in 1912. Here I'm bronc bustin' in Calgary, wrangin' the championship at the 1913 Calgary Stampede. Won $1,000 from show-man Idaho Bill on this horse with the same name in Dewey, Oklahoma. During the rodeo, this horse threw four top bronc riders without wastin' a second. Idaho Bill bet me 1,000 bucks I couldn't ride his namesake. I just happened to have the money, so I put it up. That horse was a spinner and not as hard to sit as many thought. So I got the job done and collected Idaho Bill's money to add to my own. To my recollection, Harry Grammer proved the only other rider to sit Idaho Bill. Fine, smooth rider, one of the best, that Grammer."

"Guess that makes you one of the best, too, Doc."

"I always believe you let your deeds speak for you, son. Do your best and there'll be no need of talkin'. Well, that's all the jawin' we need to do today. We'll get to know plenty about each other over the next months. Take a stroll around town and get your bearings so when I send you out for supplies, you won't get lost. Like to have you drop off this Veterinary Department column at the 'Yavapai Magazine' office while you make the rounds."

"Are you really a vet?"

"Took some courses but never finished. Wasn't cut out for schoolin'. I learned enough to get along. What I didn't get from the books I picked up from hands-on experience with various critters over the years. My philosophy: try to do as little harm as possible with my doctorin'."

"Thanks for the background, Doc. I'll head out now so I can get back to the livery before sundown."

"OK, but before you leave I need to talk one more thing over with you. I took off for myself as a young buck and never looked back, but now that I'm married I see the woman point of view more clearly. Have you written your family since you've been gone?"

Earl looks down at the ground, "Don't rightly know what to say, Doc."

"Well, you do some figurin' on that, and when you're ready, write to your folks back in Idaho. In the meantime, do you mind if I write your mother to let her know you are fine and in good hands?"

"I would appreciate that. Once I make something of myself, I'll set down to do some writing."

The next day Earl rises early in anticipation of proving his talents by riding a good race. Crowds pour into Prescott by horseback, horse-drawn carriages, automobiles, and trains for Frontier Days. By this first day of festivities on July 4, 1916, accommodations prove scarce. Doc's livery serves as a rendezvous for many visiting cow-punchers, seeking a place to bunk while competing in the days' rodeo and racing events.

C. W. "Doc" Pardee serves as arena director, dressed in his well-worn but well-decorated chaps and wearing a tie. H. R. Wood, Grant Carter, and L. P. Tolladay monitor the horse races while Roy Young, Hank Miller, and Nelson Puntenny judge the steer roping contests. The honor of judging the World's Championship Bronco Busting Contest falls to Art Sanders, Elza Brown, and Frank Condron.

Despite Doc's declaration to Burr that he was leaving the rodeoing to the young bucks, he delivers fine performances: he wins first money in bareback riding and divides first and second money with Frank Thompson of Blythe, California, in bronco busting. The judges award the World's Championship Bronco Busting medal to Doc. Clarence Jackson garners first money in steer roping. On the track, Earl drives Tick Tack home to victory in his maiden race for Doc Pardee.

Doc and Earl participate with dozens of other cowpokes in delighting Eastern tourists at Castle Hot Springs Resort. Among the range knights performing riding and cowboy sports feats, noted rodeo cowhands Billy Simon, Bill Wheeldon, Clark Wingart, Bill Shomp, and Walt Cline thrill the spectators. They take on bull dogging, steer roping, steer riding, flag contests, and horse racing in front of enthusiastic fans.

Earl mounts Tick Tack, sets the pace and easily wins several horse races. A special cowpony race through the creek bed sees Mrs. Hyde of Wichita, Kansas, beat out her daughter, while Miss Dutro of Prescott takes third. The resort holds a dance for the cowpokes, with guests and cowboys intermingling late into the evening. The next day, the resort hosts a farewell lunch out on the range in honor of the cowboys. Bill Wheeldon attracts the admiration of several young ladies with his trick-roping exhibition and spends a good deal of time giving personal tutelage to several good-looking gals. When they leave camp, he discovers three of his ropes missing.

Doc chides Wheeldon, "Not a bad trade, Bill. Three ropes for a day of inhalin' parfum."

"Shucks, I would have given them fillies each a dozen ropes for a peck on the cheek," Wheeldon says.

Each evening, Earl and the other cowhands hang out at the livery talking over the day's events, singing songs, and spinning yarns. A newcomer to the West joins them in their revelry.

"Hey tenderfoot, do you know how to handle that six-shooter strapped to your leg? Bet a silver dollar you can't fast draw and shoot this here bean can off the fence," one of the cowhands ribs the greenhorn.

"Put the can on the post and get ready to hand over your money," the tenderfoot retorts.

The cowhands place side bets as the tenderfoot spreads his new boots, hitches up his holster, and tries a few practice draws.

"You gawn' to practice drawin' all night?"

"Hold your horses. I'll turn around at the count of three and shoot that can dead center. Stop your snickering and start counting."

"One, two, three."

The tenderfoot spins on his heels and grabs the six-shooter. The sight catches on the holster and as his finger squeezes, the bullet flies wide right and ricochets off a boulder, striking Doc's livery foreman in the chest. The cowhands quickly head downtown carrying the injured man to the physician's office, while Earl dashes to the ranch on Tick Tack to report the incident to Doc Pardee.

After cleansing the wound and bandaging up the cowboy, the doctor says, "Your man took a bad shot, Doc. He'll be laid up for a spell healing from this lead wound. Another inch and that bullet would have killed him for sure. I better keep an eye on him for awhile, make sure infection and fever don't set in."

After Doc and Earl return to the livery, Doc says, "Looks like Bud's bad luck is your good luck, Earl. I still need a livery foreman. I can raise your salary to $60 per month plus your split of the race proceeds. You up to the task, son?"

"You bet, Doc. You won't be sorry."

Doc and Earl make the rounds of the Arizona horse race circuit throughout the rest of 1916 and into 1917. Sande advances from "bug boy" (apprentice jockey) to Doc's star rider. At the fairgrounds in Tucson, Sande and another jockey, Jesse James, race down the track while a military artillery unit performs maneuvers nearby. Without warning, the artillery horses cross the track, pulling cannons. The artillery unit bowls over both riders, sending them to the hospital.

"For a while there, I thought I would be shippin' a broken-up jockey back to Idaho," Doc says, as he and Earl head back to Prescott.

"Just a few scratches, Doc. Nothing to worry about. I'll be fine."

Before races begin at Springerville, Doc points out Charley Thompson, one of the best jockeys in the West.

"I've got you inked in for twenty plus match and two purse races today. You don't have to win them all, just enough to cover the expense of this trip. You'll see Charley Thompson a lot today, Earl. Watch him and study how he operates. He's back in the bush leagues but has raced on just about every major racetrack in the East. He's gearin' up now for another run at the big time, and you can learn from his experience. Charley tends to his business and takes his job seriously. A lot of these riders use dirty tricks to get ahead, but Thompson knows how to counteract them and beats them with skill. Not that he doesn't try a fast one now and then."

"I'll sure keep on eye on him, Doc, and learn what I can from Thompson, but I'm still going to try to win all the races I can."

"Horse racin' involves more than just makin' your horse go fast. You need to know the pattern and style of your competition. Watch the other riders to see where they've lost the race by failin' to commit, or when they make their move to leave the pack in the dust. Study the other horses to see how they respond to their jockey's lead. You also have to pace your horse so that you have enough in reserve to catch and pass the horses in front of you. Judgin' pace is one of the highest expressions of natural horsemanship. Develop the knack of timin.'"

"I'll work on that, Doc. Thanks for the advice. I want to understand all the skills I can about this racing game."

"Remember, each horse is different. Tick Tack likes to get the lead and stay there. If you let him get too far ahead, he starts to slack off and can lose the race in the homestretch. On the other hand, Vanity Fair's a slow starter, but if you keep her close to the pack, she'll give her all from the final turn to the wire. She may lose, but you know you have gotten everythin' out of her."

"They're both fine horses once you know their peculiarities, Doc."

"It's been proven that the greatest distance any racehorse can run at top speed is around three-eighths of a mile. Beyond that, the horse must either slacken his gait or drop dead tryin.' It's your job as the jockey to know when the limit has been reached and not push your horse too far. That's where an acute knowledge of pace separates the great riders from the good riders."

"There's a lot to remember, Doc, but I'll do my best."

At the end of Springerville racing, a tired Sande collapses in the back of the wagon. A hand nudges his shoulder, and he looks up at a smiling Charley Thompson astride a horse.

"You coulda let someone else win at least one race today. Winning twenty-three races in one day, a great feat for a bug boy. Looks like I'll be seeing you in the big leagues, Earl." Thompson spurs his horse and leaves Sande in the dust for the first time that day.

Besides hitting the dirt tracks of small towns, Doc and Earl also run Doc's horses in Phoenix. Sande jumps to an early lead on Vanity Fair and maintains it to the finish. Queen of Hearts never closes within neighing distance of Vanity Fair over the three-eighths of a mile run. Each owner wagered $760, and Doc Pardee walks away with $1,520 in his pocket. Ironically, the "Prescott Journal-Miner" reports that Queen of Hearts won the race and reprints a correction the next day, after Doc Pardee points out the error.

Days later, back in Prescott, Earl enters Doc's office carrying the "Prescott Journal-Miner." A grin lights up Sande's face from ear to ear. "Seems like you're the center of controversy, Doc. Let me read you this account of the rodeo. 'About Doc Pardee. There was criticism yesterday that this paper favored Pardee in its report of bareback riding. Possibly so, for the 'Journal-Miner' always attempts to favor the man who has it coming. Furthermore, it was said that Doc might have paid something for a favorable report. This is ridiculous. The writer has lost four bits on one of 'Doc's tips' on the cowpony race.'"

Doc responds to the accusations. "Bribery, hogwash, 'ain't my style. 'Twas like this. I drew Big Sid for the finals. At first, the cayuse stuck to the chute and refused to play. Then he wandered out into the field, made a few little back jumps as a curtain raiser, and then opened up. I don't mind tellin' you I had my hands full and didn't have much thought to payin' attention to the position of my feet. I rode that bronc as best I could. The judges called the horse back after the ride and examined him to see if I had scratched. Evidently they found no marks to their likin', for they disqualified me. I have no argument with the judges, nor do I have an argument with a writer who sees it another way. It was time for a new champion anyway."

"My money is still on you, Doc."

"Enough of that. We've got more important things to talk about." Doc motions Earl to follow him out of the office and into the shop. They stop in front of a mass of wires, an electric motor, and metal arms.

"Been tinkerin' with this contraption for months now and hope I finally have all the bugs worked out. What do you think?"

"What in the world is it, Doc?"

"Son, you are the first to see a genuine Doc Pardee electrically driven hot-walker. These compartments separate the horses and the motor does all the work. It's kinda like turnin' a merry-go-round for horses. It cools off the horses without takin' up valuable time of my hired hands."

"Looks like you're trying to work me out of my job, Doc."

Doc motions to a hay bale, where he and Earl take a seat. Doc removes his hat and wipes his brow with a red neckerchief. He shuffles his feet a bit before he starts to speak.

"Been meanin' to talk to you about that, Earl. I think it's about time for you to try your hand at the major racetracks. There's no more competition around here to bring you up to the next level. I know you've been hangin' around out of your sense of duty. I sure hate to lose a good hand and the best jockey in these parts, but it's in your best interest to move on."

"Do you really, think I'm ready for the professional track, Doc? Where should I go?"

"I'd bet my money on it, Earl." Doc reaches into his vest and retrieves an envelope. He shifts it from hand to hand before placing it in Earl's pocket.

"You take this letter to New Orleans and look up an old horse tradin' friend of mine, Joe Goodman. He'll see to it that you get your chance to ride with the big boys in this racin' game. There's also an extra $100 in your pay this week to help out with your travel expenses. Going to miss you, Earl. You've been like a son to me and Ma. She's especially goin' to miss you eatin' her homemade ice cream. You sure could pack it in. You'll need to watch your weight more closely from here on out."

"Burr said you would tell me when the time is right. I guess that time is now. I'll clean up and head out on Sunday. You'll get a full week's work for your pay. Besides, I still have some chores to finish and then want to take one last dip at Granite Dells before leaving. I'm sure going to miss you and Mrs. Pardee. Thanks for everything, Doc. I appreciate your giving me the opportunity to ride for you and what you have taught me."

"Don't mention it, Earl. Just doing my part in helpin' to hone a natural talent. Besides, it was fun winnin' all those races and showin' up my friends on the outlaw circuit."

"We had some grand times and great races, didn't we, Doc?"

"Sure did. There's one more bit of Doc Pardee advice to carry with you. Not all the horse owners back East are horse people, if you know what I mean. They own horses, but they're not horse people as you and I know them out here in the West. Remember, it's a business to them, plain and simple. A matter of dollars and cents, but doesn't always make good sense. Trust your judgment about who you deal with. Make sure to look out for yourself."

"OK, Doc. You've always given me solid advice, and I'll remember this as well."

"Don't forget your friends back in Arizona. We're here any time you need us."

"I'll never forget you and Mrs. Pardee. Thanks."

Chapter 5

E. Sande, Jockey:
Donning the Silks

In full stride, the young man throws his pack into and then hurls his body through the slight opening of the moving boxcar. He regains his feet and brushes off his pants. From the dark, a voice warns, "This car's spoken for, don't you try and muscle in here. Best you find another car."

Earl's eyes adjust to the faint light and make out a middle-aged hobo hunched in the corner, holding a two-by-four tight in his right hand. A pair of crutches rests next to him on the boxcar floor.

"Sorry, mister, I didn't know anyone occupied this car. No need to worry about me. I don't mean any harm. Just want a place to bunk while I make my way across the country."

"That mean you're alone? No more of you coming aboard?"

"Traveling by myself. I won't be any bother."

"Well, guess there's plenty of room in here for the both of us. Set yourself down over there. Seeing as I'm sharing my accomodations with you, it's only fair that you share with me. Got any grub?"

Earl unwraps some of the Edith May's homemade muffins and hands two to his bunkmate. The man's eyes lock on Earl as his left hand grabs the muffins. As he bites into the first muffin, his other hand releases the two-by-four, and it drops softly into the straw covering the boxcar floor.

"You won't find any better muffins than that."

The man gobbles down the remaining muffin. Earl settles into the box-car, opposite of the man.

"Where you headed, son?"

"New Orleans. I'm going to ride racehorses."

"Lots of ties to roll over before you get to Nor'lins. As for me, I get off at Santone. You say you're going to ride racehorses? Used to hang around the racetracks a bit myself when still in the money. Those days are gone, forever, I imagine."

"Yessir, I plan to ride racehorses in New Orleans."

"Always thought jockeys were on the small side. I'd say you're about six inches too tall for a jockey. I wouldn't bet money on your getting into the race racket at your size."

"I think I can compensate for my size by my riding ability. I did all right riding in Arizona, despite my height."

"Let me know you name, son. Just in case you beat the odds and break into horse racing and I ever fall into a stake."

"Sande, Earl Sande."

Riding the rails preserves the $500 Earl saved while working for Doc Pardee. He arrives in New Orleans late in 1917 and begins searching for Joe Goodman at the Fair Grounds Race Track. Not finding Goodman, he tries for days to secure a riding job with other stables. He approaches a horse rubber about the chances of getting hired as a jockey.

"I wouldn't advise that you try here. We have several boys riding and a big lad like you ain't got a chance."

Sande next tries trainer John Lowe, who looks Sande over and asks, "How much do you weigh, son?"

"Under 100 pounds."

"I doubt that! You look more like 125 pounds to me. You're close to five foot six and if you don't weigh that now, you will when you fill out by spring racing season. Why don't you try picking up work as an exercise boy? You look better suited for that kind of work."

Discouraged, Sande approaches Al Clopton, who handles the Whitney stable horses, for a job as an exercise boy.

"Don't have any opening now, kid. I will remember you if anything comes up. Keep coming around, somebody usually needs a hand around here from time to time."

After several days, Sande finally succeeds in tracking Goodman down in a seafood restaurant. He hands Goodman Doc's letter and waits for a response while Goodman finishes his oysters.

"I appreciate the letter, but you're awfully tall for a jockey, and weight will be a problem as you get older and start putting on the pounds."

Goodman looks up at Sande's crestfallen face and continues, "Seeing though that you came this far, and Doc Pardee highly recommends you, I'll give you a tryout tomorrow. I'll put you up on my filly, Adelina L., and see what you can show me. You might be worth a chance if you can gallop like Doc says you can. Meet me at the Fair Grounds in the morning."

Sande arrives bright and early, checks out Goodman's stable, and locates Adelina L. He gently brushes the horse and talks to her. Goodman arrives and signals Earl to saddle up and lead the horse out of the stall. He puts his foot into the stirrup and swings his frame up onto the horse with ease.

"Take her up the track, break her off at the three-eighth pole, and breeze her for a half a mile."

"You got it. But before I do, could you explain what a three-eighth pole is, Mr. Goodman? We didn't have poles at the racetracks where I raced out west."

Goodman shakes his head and then gives Sande a quick instruction on poles. Sande guides the horse onto the track per Goodman's instruction. He takes a deep, long breath before spurring the horse into action. Goodman watches as the long-legged kid hunches low over the saddle in faultless style and guides the horse through a smooth performance.

"I'd have bet against it, kid, but you've earned yourself a job. You'll start as an exercise boy. Once you know the ropes around the stable, I'll work you into the racing lineup."

"Don't worry, Mr. Goodman, I know my way around a stable."

"Reckon so, if you worked for Doc Pardee. Return Adelina L. to the stable and then come to my office to sign a contract. This provides for a salary of $20 a month, riding silks, and bridles; a winning fee of $25 and a losing fee of $10 per race. You are responsible for buying everything else, including your saddle. It's dated December 1917, but I have to file the contract with The Jockey Club before it's effective. You can't ride until after it gets recorded."

"That's OK. I need some time to study this barrier starting system anyway. It's sure different from the lap-and-tap start we used in Idaho and Arizona." Earl thinks, "It isn't much money. In fact, less than I made working for Doc Pardee in Arizona, but I'll be racing on a major track for the first time. I'm on my way!"

"Work with my former jockeys Casey Jones and Dick Watts. Both are solid riders and they'll show you the ropes. Search out Frankie Robinson also. He's a strong, vigorous rider but never gives an impression it's hard work, makes it look easy. Good jockey to pattern yourself after, if you ask me. You might also want to talk to and study Albert Anderson, Frankie Keogh, and Bill Obert. They've been around and know the ropes. With Robinson, they're the top jockeys at the Fair Grounds so far this season. The heavy betters around the Fair Grounds consider them the 'money riders.'"

Robinson tells Sande, "You're lucky. The Fair Grounds serves as a great training ground for new jockeys. It attracts top jockeys from major tracks in Kentucky, Maryland, and New York to its winter racing. Its history traces back before the Civil War. The New Orleans Jockey Club formed in 1880 and this beautiful white arched building we are sitting in was built in 1882. Tod Sloan rode his first race here in 1889. Ed 'Snapper' Garrison won many an exciting race at the Fair Grounds. Outlaw Jesse James's brother, Frank, worked here as a betting commissioner in 1902. Now it's our turn to try to make history here."

Sande's day begins around 5:30 a.m. with a sparse breakfast of toast, fruit, and coffee, but no sugar and milk, which result in weight gain. The Fair Grounds teems with activities of trainers, exercise boys, rubbers, valets, jockeys, and track staff performing their respective duties. Jockeys school younger horses at the barrier, gallop the entire stable string, work out horses scheduled to race that day, and pilot mounts of other owners arranged through agents. Sande participates in roadwork to harden his leg muscles and take off excess weight.

By 10 o'clock the track clears for harrowing, and jockeys grab some rest before returning back at 1 o'clock to the Clerk of Scales. Each jockey reports his afternoon riding engagements and equipment to be carried including whip, spurs, blinkers and/or breastplate. Horses inclined to loaf, and those that run better when they don't see other horses in the field alongside of them, require blinkers. Some jockeys favor breastplates to keep their saddle from slipping back.

Dick Watts comes into the Goodman's stable, where Sande is working, at the end of the day. He tells Sande, "Goodman wants you to get the corner post key from the Clerk of Scales at 1:15 p.m. tomorrow and bring it to the track steward."

"Sure thing."

The next day, Sande arrives promptly at the Clerk of Scales. Jockeys, readying to ride, stand in a long line waiting to get weighed.

Sande walks up and says, "Mr. Goodman asked me to retrieve the corner post key from you."

"I can't hear you. Please speak up."

Earl repeats the request loud enough for everyone in line to hear him ask for the corner post key. The jockeys break out into uproarious laughter.

Frankie Robinson chimes up, "Make sure you also get a left-handed monkey wrench, Earl. You can't turn that key without it."

Sande takes the good-natured ribbing in stride. His initiation into the ranks of professional jockeys begins. There will be much to learn over the next months and years.

He picks up all the riding tips he can from Jones, Watts, Robinson, and other Fair Grounds jockeys. Watts watches as Earl trains on Goodman's horses.

"You ride like a Westerner with your toes pointed down. Point them up and you'll have better balance and positioning to get the most out of your horse, Earl."

"OK, Dick. I'm also having trouble getting the younger horses going at the break. What solution do you have for that?"

"Let's see what you're doing that may be the cause of the problem. Take one of the young mounts from the barrier. Casey has been taking this young horse away from the barrier like lightning. You try it and see what happens. Maybe we can pin this thing down."

Earl takes the mount to the barrier and the horse breaks slowly. "See what I mean?"

"I think I know what's causing your problem. When you break, you drop your left hand down along side of the horse's neck. That doesn't bother the older mounts and they go about their business of taking off. But the younger horses are more skittish and your hand passing by their eyes bothers them. They hesitate, trying to figure out what is going on instead of breaking fast from the barrier. Control your hand from dropping and you won't have any more problems with the younger horses breaking."

"Thanks, Dick. You certainly figured out the answer."

"One more piece of advice. Make a horse your friend, not your foe. Horses are much like humans. You can kid them into running for you if they like you. When they are not afraid of you and know they can trust you,

A young Earl Sande in silks. Courtesy Sande Tomlinson Collection.

they keep their attention on racing and won't have one eye on you and the other on the track. You can accomplish more by treating them with respect than you can by growling at them."

Robinson takes to calling Sande "Long Back" because of Sande's height compared to other jockeys. Sande's first official race on a recognized track takes place on January 5, 1918, at the Fair Grounds.

Goodman tells Sande, "You've earned the right to pilot Liberator by figuring out how to handle him at the barrier. The other riders take hold of the reins and Liberator reacts by throwing his head in the air and breaking slowly. You give him loose rein and he feels more comfortable, breaking with the field. Good job, Earl."

Before the race, Sande asks the rubber to grab several printed programs listing E. Sande as the jockey on Liberator. He plans to mail those to his family, Burr Scott, and Doc Pardee. Sande dons riding silks for the first time and admires himself in the mirror. Strict track rules require the jockeys to stay in the jockey room until their engagements have been completed for the afternoon. Track rules prohibit visitors to the jockey room.

Sande readies himself for his debut professional race. The humid New Orleans weather creates sweat on his brow. As he mounts Liberator, the squeak of leather reaches his ears. Puffs of dust rise from the hooves of the mounts in front of him as they approach the barrier. His legs rest against Liberator's sides. The horses line up and his heart pounds with anticipation. He tells himself, "It's just like every other race." He doesn't believe it.

He gets off with the leader. Throughout the race, Sande keeps a loose rein and Liberator runs easy. He sets his position just outside of a horse named Viley. The other jockeys move to the inside of Viley while Sande takes to the open outside route. When Viley begins bearing off to the right, Sande loses much valuable ground. In the turn for home, he whispers into Liberator's ear and hand guides him down the stretch. Liberator responds to Sande's urgings. He lengthens his stride and picks off horses along the way. He continues to gain on Busy Joe, a pretty black filly owned by E. R. Bradley and ridden by Albert Johnson. Sande and Liberator run out of track and finish second a length and a half behind Busy Joe.

Sande sits in the jockey club, disheartened after his first professional race defeat. One of the other jockeys comes in and says, "Joe Goodman wants to see you in his office, Earl."

"I guess this is it, the end of my short jockey career. I better go face the consequences."

On the way to see Goodman, he tries to figure out how to explain losing the race.

"I'm sorry Mr. Goodman, I have no excuses. I made a mistake going to the outside of Viley. If Liberator had no one on his back, he would have won. With me up, he finished second. If you give me another chance, I won't make that mistake again. I promise."

"Nonsense, you did great to even place that platter. He was a 20 to 1 shot and you brought him to the finish line in the money. He paid $8 to place when that horse had no right to even be in the race, much less win. You got more out of him than any other jockey. Don't worry about your job, Earl. It's safe. Remember, bugboys get to make their mark on long shots. Don't expect to ride a string of favorites until you prove your worth."

"The Times-Picayune" reports in its Hoofbeats column, "E. Sande, who rode his first mount of the meeting yesterday, was unfortunate enough to be outside Viley when that mare ran to the outside, and Liberator, Sande's mount, was carried nearly to the fence. But for that, Liberator might have won the race, Sande is under contract to Joe Goodman and shows signs of developing into a good boy."

"The Racing Form" comments, "Liberator, probably best, suffered from much interference and was forced to race wide all the way, but came fast in the stretch and finished gaining."

Days later, four jockeys suffer injuries and two horses die in spills at the Fair Grounds. Apprentice jockey Arthur Johnson receives bruises when his horse, Poppee, falls in the second race at the half-mile post and dies. That afternoon, J. Cruise, J. Williams, and W. Kelsay get bruises when their mounts collide and fall in a tangle at the six-furlong post. Checks, Williams's mount, dies in the accident.

Goodman warns, "It's a tough business out on that track, Earl. Protect yourself."

Another tragedy strikes the Fair Grounds on January 19 as Pan Zareta, winner of seventy-six races and termed "Queen of the Turf," dies of pneumonia in her stall and is buried in the infield.

Over the next week, Sande pilots a series of horses for a variety of owners with odds as wide as 20 to 1 and 50 to 1 before placing in the money again, with second place on Liberator for the second time. Recognizing Sande's riding ability, bettors push down the odds on Goodman's horse to 10 to 1 for this outing. The next day Sande scores another second-place finish on 15 to 1 Korfhage.

On January 21, Earl officially earns his first win, breaking his maiden on 8 to 1 shot Prince S., beating out well-respected jockeys Larry Lyke on Trentino and Albert Johnson on Jack Reeves.

In the jockey room, Johnson and the other riders, douse Sande with a bucket of cold ice water. "Welcome to the ranks of winning jockeys, Earl."

Dripping wet, Sande says, "Sure feels great to enter the winner's circle for the first time as a professional jockey. Thought it would never happen."

"The Racing Form" writes, "Prince S. running in vastly improved form over his last previous race, despite an inexperienced rider, raced well from the start and came away in the last seventy yards." The same day, Sande also guides 9 to 1 Acheron to a third-place finish in a race Frankie Robinson wins on Astec, and Sande delivers 50 to 1 shot Caro Nome to fourth place in a field of seven, in a race won by Obert.

In the stands, Commander J. K. L. (John Kenneth Leveson) Ross watches as Sande beats one of Ross's star jockeys, Lyke. As the owner of the strong horse Cudgel, Ross is intent on building up his stable of fine racing horses and top jockeys. He turns to his trainer, Horatio G. "Guy" Poteet, and says, "Keep an eye on that Sande kid. Looks like a real comer. What do you think of his riding style, Guy?"

"Sande rides as flat as a serving tray. He's much more streamlined and wind resistant than the other jockeys. That's a decided advantage. He buries his face in the mane of the horse, only peeking out from time-to-time around the neck to survey the field. That keeps the sand out of his eyes and gives him a clear view of the track when needed."

"The Racing Form" acknowledges Commander Ross's presence in his white naval uniform. "J. K. L. Ross, the Montreal turfman, is cutting quite a figure in the racing here and the small stable that he has at the Fair Grounds more than holds its own."

The next afternoon, Sande loses four races on two 50 to 1 and two 30 to 1 horses before mounting J. M. Booker's 5 to 1 Dundreary in the last race of the day. Dundreary bursts into the lead at once and shows good speed throughout to win by six lengths and leave the favorite eighteen lengths behind in the dust. Sande places second a day later on Dolina by riding a good race and pressing St. Jude in the final drive.

"The Times-Picayune" Hoofbeats column calls attention to Earl's progress. "Jockey E. Sande looks like one of the most promising apprentice boys developing this season. He is riding better and better with every start and gave Dundreary an expert ride to win the sixth race. Dundreary looked beaten at the last eighth post, but came again and was going away at the end."

Further evidence of Sande's riding ability comes on the following day as he delivers Mary's Beau and F. C. Cole, both long shots, to the winner's circle. "The Times-Picayune" praises Sande,

> Apprentice Jockey Lands Long Shots; E. Sande Is Star. Riding the first race of his career January 5 when he finished second with Liberator, the apprentice jockey, E. Sande, has sprung into the limelight of good race riders with a cyclonic rush, and from now on undoubtedly will be watched closely in all his races.
>
> At the Fair Grounds, Sande brought Mary's Beau, 20 to 1, home in front in the first race, and landed F. C. Cole, 50 to 1, a winner in the sixth. He made a strong bid for victory on Fairy Legend, 12 to 1 in the fourth race, finishing fourth, and in the seventh race finished a bang-up second with Meelicka, against which 10 and 15 to 1 was offered.
>
> The little fellow's ride on Mary's Beau was a gem. He was away in a tangle but kept his mount right on the rail where the best going was to be had because of the extra attention paid to that section of the track by the harrowers. At the turn for the stretch, Mary's Beau moved up on the inside of Dioscoride, which had set the pace, and as Baby Star challenged, Sande went to work on his mount and outrode the veteran, Roscoe Troxler, who was up on Dioscoride, in a terrific ride to the wire.

To say Sande's victory on F. C. Cole was a surprise is putting it mildly. His performance took the spectators off their feet as F. C. Cole was considered the rankest kind of an outsider. But Sande rushed him to the front and rating the gelding perfectly, pulled away from Tarleton P. when the latter challenged in the stretch.

With Fairy Legend in the fourth, Sande loomed up a winner at the head of the stretch but the sturdy gelding, Paddy Dear, well meant and well ridden, would not be denied and he left Fairy Legend and several others fighting it out as he opened up a gap and won easily.

In the seventh, Sande most probably would have come home with another long shot but for being twice cut off on Meelicka. He took the mare to the front immediately but took her up in his lap to save her when Busy Alice challenged at the far turn. Ruvoco, the favorite, challenged at the same time and Sande, evidently determined to make the others take the overland, let Busy Alice get too far ahead, with as a result Busy Alice swerved over and cut off Meelicka. Swinging into the stretch, Sande took a chance and brought Meelicka through on the rail, saving lengths. Then he bent to the task of riding Meelicka and had the winner, Napolean, straight as a string under the wire.

Sande, Happy Buxton, and Albert Johnson divided the riding honors pretty much among themselves. Each of them winning two races. Johnson's riding, while not as sensational, was on a par with the saddle work of Sande.

Jockey Frankie Robinson stops by as Earl changes out of his silks. "Nobody at this track could have ridden those horses better than you did today. Take my word for it, Long Back, you're headed for a big racing stable."

"Thanks, Frankie. I did have a good outing. Your coaching and pointers have sure helped."

"It takes the right combination of talents to make a great jockey. I'd say it's 20 percent alertness at the barrier, 20 percent judgment of pace, 20 percent lightness of hands, 20 percent lightness of seat, 10 percent courage, and 10 percent cool head. Long Back, you've got all of that and more."

"I love the battle of muscle and wits, the thrill of the close finish. This is what I want to do with my life."

"The Racing Form" states that Sande is beginning to learn the ropes on the tough winter circuit.

> Sande Has a Lucky Day. The obscure E. Sande and the crack F. Robinson shared the spotlight in a riding way, the former for his really able riding ability, and Robinson for his luck....Sande started off the proceedings by landing Mary's Beau a winner despite rough tactics from Troxler on Dioscoride and at the end the youngster clearly outgeneraled the veteran and subjected him to as much interference as he received. The judges also took a hand and suspended Troxler for three days.

> Sande was again successful in the sixth race when he showed a rare bit of horsemanship in landing the despised F. C. Cole winner in a close finish from Tarleton P and Al Pierce. In the closing race, he came within a neck of beating Napoleon with Meelicka and but for interference that Meelicka suffered from at the half-mile ground would have won.

"Looks like you're getting more good press, Earl," Albert Johnson says, holding up the day's paper. "Headline reads, 'Jockey Sande Making Good.' It goes on to say you've already won a few races and get an unusually large number of mounts for a newcomer. You're making the rest of us look bad, Earl. The bright spot in this article for the rest of us jockeys is that it quotes knowing trackmen saying you should gain weight soon and no longer be a factor. Let's buy Long Back steak and potatoes after today's races. What about it, boys?"

"Does it mention in there how I'm learning riding skills from you roughnecks and have been suspended for three days? Let's give the complete story, A. J."

"The time off will give you a chance to wash your riding pants. I've never seen any jockey before who changes his pants after each race to look so pretty on the horses."

"I was taught to always look my best. I may only be making apprentice wages here, but I should represent each of the owners the best I can."

Sande burns up the track at New Orleans over the next two weeks, drawing attention from other jockeys, trainers, and racehorse owners. By mid-

February, when the racing closes down at New Orleans, Sande captures a flurry of first-place finishes. He gives Dolina a solid ride to earn first place, outrides Billy Nestlehouse to keep Flapper in the lead and gain the winner's circle, guides Waukeag to a first-place finish, wins driving on Alhena, takes Dundreary to the lead yet again, paces Cobalt Lass behind Orlando of Havana until the last eighth and then takes command of the race, spurs Korfhage to a vigorous finish to win going away, and wins easily on Eagle.

Despite a three-day suspension and missing several days' riding because of an injury suffered from a fall on Stanley Fay II, Sande rides a total of seventy-four mounts at New Orleans. He places in the money thirty times, including thirteen first-place honors.

Goodman congratulates Sande. "You've achieved a highly respectable start for an apprentice jockey, Earl."

A sportswriter praises Sande's craftsmanship to Goodman, "The only reason Sande does not win more races can be accounted for by the fact that some of the camels he rides couldn't get in the money at a pumpkin show. Give him the mounts and he will sure convince. Get busy Joe and get him some real ponies."

By delivering competitive apprentice rides at New Orleans, Sande attracts the interest of racehorse owners Waldo P. Johnson of Chicago, E. H. Kane of California, Commander Ross of Canada, and J. W. Williams of Oklahoma, riding mounts for each of them. Before racing starts at Oaklawn Park at Hot Springs, Arkansas, agent Ben Levy, acting for Johnson and Kane, purchases Sande's contract from Joe Goodman for $7,500. Johnson and Kane raise Sande's salary to $30 per month plus his colors and riding fees.

Goodman explains to Sande why he sold his contract. "Thanks for the ride, Earl. In gratitude for your good jockeying, here's $1,000 from the contract I received from Johnson and Kane. I don't have the caliber of horses that can keep you busy, and they can get you better mounts."

"Thanks for giving me my big break, Mr. Goodman. I'll never forget it."

"No need to thank me, your talent would have shown through before long without my help. You'll still be riding some of my mounts under Johnson and Kane, so we won't be strangers around the winter race circuit."

Sande's racing at Oaklawn Park during early March begins badly as starter Alexander Barrett "A.B." Dade suspends him and W. Obert four days for disobedience at the post. On March 8, Sande comes in seventh on Dirigo and sixth on Justice Goebel in fields of twelve. The next day Sande finally breaks into the winner's circle at Oaklawn with first-place finishes on J. B. Goodman's Kinney and W. C. Clancy's Paddy Dear. Sande saves Kama under restraint two days later, gaining ground on the last turn and wins riding hard. Sande mounts Justice Goebel for a second time on March 12, gets away fast and finishes first. Four days later, Sande comes into his own. In a thrilling first race, Sande again guides Kinney to the winner's circle, places second on Martre behind Larry Lyke on Busy Joe, and hand rides Joe Goodman's Kama into first place.

"The Racing Form" comments, "Jockey Sande was the riding light this afternoon and accounted for half of the card, winning with Kinney and Kama, both owned by J. B. Goodman. The early running of the race was made by Clean Up, with Kinney in the rear, but Kinney moved up with an electric rush."

In two days, Beautiful Morning gives up the lead only to have Sande drive him home first. The following day, Sande and Trusty leave the rest of the field in the dust. Kama comes in second, with Sande going fast at the end but a tad too late, but he regains the winner's circle for the second time that day on Tumble In. A day later, Sande eases up on Scotch Kiss for an easy win, delivers a game Merchant into second place, and guides Flora Finch to the finish line first. Continuing his winning ways later in the week, Sande steers 8 to 1 Gilligan to the inside on the turn and overtakes Dickie W. for the lead and win. In the second race of the day, severe crowding causes Sande to take a bad spill on Sixteen to One. While Sande spends time convalescing, his mount fares far worse and is destroyed.

Levy comforts Sande. "You took a bad spill, Earl. Luckily you're only banged up and suffered no broken bones. The real test of a jockey is how he comes back after a track accident."

"The Racing Form" compliments Sande's Oaklawn riding. "From practically an unknown rider three months ago, jockey E. Sande, has jumped into the lead of the jockeys at Oaklawn Park. He was injured several days ago, but for that, he would have had an excellent chance to carry off the riding honors of the meeting."

Three late March first-place finishes in a row place him on top of the jockey winning list with twenty victories, three wins ahead of Commander Ross's star jockey, Larry Lyke. Sande adds two more victories with Jule and Margaret N., and another pair of victories on Thinker and Ben Levy. Sande wins the tightest finish of the day, with energetic riding on Ben Levy, who rallies with a whirlwind rush after going wide in the stretch. Sande's Oak-

Earl Sande up on Mary's Beau at Lexington in 1918. Courtesy Sande Tomlinson Collection.

lawn racing closes with a solid riding victory on Minnie F for the Oaklawn riding title. Sande scores twenty-five wins versus seventeen for Lyke.

Racing action shifts to Lexington, Kentucky, on April 24, where Sande wins his first Kentucky race on Diamond despite early interference. Sande guides Diamond to the outside and comes even with Diversion at the finish line. The two share first place honors in a dead heat finish. The next day Sande claims sole first place on Martre in the third race. Reunited with one of his first winning mounts, Mary's Beau, Sande delivers another first-place performance.

At Lexington, Sande wins going away on Wald Master over favorite Green Grass; boots homestretch runner Olga Star to victory twice; accomplishes a come-from-behind game finish on American Eagle; and wins with speed in reserve on Kama. He also guides six mounts to second place, and two other horses to third-place finishes.

Kane seeks out agent Ben Levy. "Waldo Johnson and I have talked it over, Ben. We realize we can't keep Sande in the quality of mounts he needs to win the big races. We've decided to sell his contract to a major stable. However, in order to get the best price, you'll need to get Sande into some big races with other owners' horses."

"No problem. I'll get to work on it right away."

Levy arranges for Sande to ride American Eagle for owner T. C. Mc-Dowell in the 1918 Kentucky Derby. Ben and Earl discuss strategy before race time.

"It's time to see how well you do in the big time. Are you up to the challenge today, Earl?" Levy asks.

"As long as I'm riding horses, I'm happy. I can't believe I'm riding in the Kentucky Derby."

The storied history and pageantry of the Kentucky Derby almost overwhelm Sande. While Louisville racing dates back to 1783, the Kentucky Derby comes into existence in 1875. The track doesn't take on the name Churchill Downs until eight years later. In 1913, Donerail becomes the longest shot to win the Derby, paying $184.90 on a $2 win ticket. The next year, Old Rosebud, sets a track record, winning by eight lengths. Now four years later, Sande marvels at the massive crowds, spectators dressed out in their finery, and top jockeys against whom he will be competing.

Sande writes to his family, "I will be riding against the likes of Loftus on War Cloud, Knapp on Exterminator, McCabe on Lucky B, Notter on Escoab, and other fine jockeys and horses. I hope to make a respectable showing."

Thunder and rain greet the Derby crowd and a muddy track gives advantage to mudders. Water drips from Sande's riding cap as he makes his way to the barrier. His eyes scan the wet, cheering crowd and then look skyward to the majestic spires extending above the Churchill Down grandstands. Sande starts May 11 slowly with three finishes out of the money in the races preceeding the Kentucky Derby. In the first race, Sande's mount Bon Tromp exhibits the most speed in the stretch but tires out in the last eighth, coming in fourth. Sande also finishes fourth aboard Courtship after Warsaw gave up the fight early to finish fifth.

In a steady rain with sloppy track, Willie Knapp slips underdog 30 to 1 shot Exterminator through the crowd next to the inner rail and beats Escoba to the wire in the final drive while favorite War Cloud, ridden by Johnny Loftus and hampered by interference, comes in a disappointing fourth place. Sande finishes dead last on American Eagle but has his first Kentucky Derby experience under his belt.

A dejected Sande says, "Did you see what 'The Thoroughbred Record' wrote? 'American Eagle and Jas. Clark also ran below par and might just as well have not started.' Maybe I'm not cut out for the major tracks yet."

Levy consoles Sande. "That will teach you to read your own headlines. You're in the big leagues now competing against the likes of Loftus, Ensor, Kummer, and Lunsford. Don't worry, you'll settle down and compete at their level."

On May 13, Sande gets back to business and pilots home a second-place finish on Lottery and a third-place finish on St. Augustine, out of five mounts. Sande's first Churchill Downs victory comes the next day on Goodman's Mary's Beau, who leads from start to finish. The following day, Sande spurs Sedan to his first victory of the year, ending a five-race losing streak for the horse. He finishes the day with another win, pushing Parr past Sandstone II in the final drive. In a tight May 17 finish, Sande moves Lottery up steadily and passes Kling in the last sixteenth for the win. Sande wears down Gordon Russell three days later to win with a hard-driving Alhena. He follows that with another win on Lottery in the final race of the day.

On March 20, Sande takes both Alhena and Lottery to the finish line first. Later in the week, Levy again puts Sande up on Goodman's Liberator, the mount Sande rode his maiden race on back in January at New Orleans. Sande takes Liberator to the lead early and outstays his opponents. The underdog pays the handsome sum of $18.40 to Sande racetrack faithful. Sande drives Goodman's Kama home to an easy victory with speed to spare. Goodman's Petrovina, with Sande up, wins handily on May 23. Liberator and Sande garner second in the next race. Sande on Captain Rees claims second place in the fifth race. A win on J. Walker follows the next day plus a second-place finish on High Horse. On the last day of Churchill Downs racing, two wins on Kinney and Cheer Leader boost Sande's winning percentage. He ties Lloyd Gentry for Churchill Downs riding honors with twelve victories.

"The Louisville Courier-Journal" writes, "Cheer Leader had plenty of speed, and when jockey Sande came under the wire he was merrily singing that sweet refrain, 'Shoo-fly, Don't Bother Me.'"

Sande takes Loys, his first Douglas Park mount, to second place. He wins in his second race of the day aboard Sedan, and closes out opening day of racing on May 27 with a second-place finish on Kama. Over the course of racing, Sande goes to the forefront at the most successful meeting in Louisville's Douglas Park history with thirty wins, twelve second-place finishes, and six third-place finishes out of sixty-five mounts. The next closest jockey only wins nine races.

Earl Sande up on J. Walker at Churchill Downs, Louisville, Kentucky, in 1918. Courtesy Sande Tomlinson Collection.

Kane stresses to Levy. "Sande's turning into a standout jockey in Kentucky racing, Ben. Keep up the good work getting him fine mounts. We know Sande can win with medicocre horses that don't have a chance under other jockeys but we need some high profile wins. Each strong win adds value to his contract when we sell it."

Earl writes to his parents, expressing disappointment in his last place Kentucky Derby finish. An enclosed picture shows him in the winner's circle astride Major Parke at Douglas Park.

"I made $500 in one day and put the whole amount into War Savings Stamps. I'm headed to Latonia, next. The track's rich history reaches back to 1883 and includes a number of prestigious stakes races. Generous purses attract the top horses and jockeys in the country. Will write more later as I find time. Love to all, Earl."

Across the river from Cincinnati, the Latonia Race Track comprises the third leg of the 3-L Circuit, with Churchill Downs in Louisville and the Association Track at Lexington making up the other two legs. Latonia's large, impressive clubhouse caters to the area's wealthy race enthusiasts. Kentucky's powerful racing syndicate, The Kentucky Jockey Club, later ac-

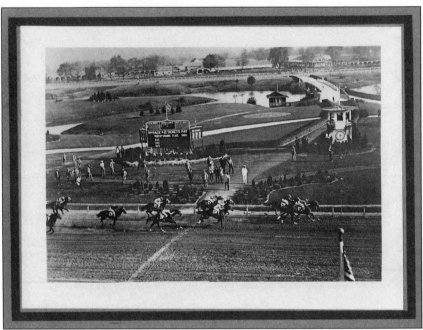

Latonia Race Track. Courtesy Ken Grayson Collection

quires ownership of Latonia Race Track, expanding its holdings to include all three 3-L Circuit segments.

"The Racing Form" declares, "Sande Popular Young Rider. There will be no dearth of good riders at Latonia and the chances are that none will be more popular with the racegoing public than the young apprentice Earl Sande, who has been making good from the day of his first appearance in the saddle at the Fair Grounds in New Orleans in January. Sande appears to be what is described as a natural horseman. There is no jockey here in which the public has greater confidence than this comparative novice. He is steadily winning his share of races and more, day by day. His record for the year stands at seventy-one and represents the excellent percentage of .21, which is remarkable for a beginner and better than that of any other American rider who has had any considerable number of mounts, with the single exception of Lyke, who heads the jockey list for the year to date. Sande stands fourth in the winning list and has confidence enough in himself to believe that he will be the leader before the year is over."

Levy tells track reporters, "You want to know the secrets of Sande's success? He studies the pecularities of the horses he is under engagement to ride, as revealed in their past performances. Every evening he devotes considerable time to reading the charts of previous races in which his mounts for the succeeding day were engaged. He's an exceptional judge of pace for one so new at the sport and generally manages to ride his mounts so well that they leave something in reserve at the end with which to make the final bid for the race."

On Latonia's June 14 opening day, Sande signals other jockeys that he means business by scoring a triple with wins on Kama, Melus, and Major Parke, and a second-place finish on Arriet. On the second day of racing, Sande wins drawing away on Parr and over the course of the Latonia racing season scores another 29 victories including three outstanding rides on Bribed Voter.

"The Cincinnati Enquirer" carries photos of four of the clever young knights of Latonia: E. Sande, E. Poole, L. Mink, and A. Johnson. Sande gets set down for five days for interference of Queen Apple during his win on Sophia Gatewood.

While Sande and Lunsford battle for top track jockey honors, controversy surrounds Latonia. Judge Lew Manson of Covington, Kentucky, fines six Latonia racetrack employees $100 each and sixty days' hard labor for violating the new state law forbidding idleness. The law requires able-bodied men between sixteen and sixty years of age to work at least thirty-six hours a week. Those arrested and convicted include trainers, former jockeys, and clockers.

In handing down his decision, Judge Manson declares, "If gamblers were beaten until the blood ran down into their shoes and they were tarred and feathered, it would be only what they deserve. Men who continue this pernicious business in this time of war, when everybody is doing his utmost to help terminate the strife, have no place in this community. That applies to every handbook crook in this city."

Nationally-recognized former jockey Robert "Tiny" Williams appeals his conviction. Williams's lawyer argues the colored jockey's advanced age and illness prevent him from working full time and wins the case.

During the Latonia racing session, Sande wins the Valuation Stakes on Major Parke. Sande and Lunsford go head-to-head in three races with Sande coming out the winner in all three matchups, two of them on the Williams Brothers Stable's mounts from Oklahoma. On another race, Mooney and Lunsford cross the finish line, pummeling each other with their fists.

The race stewards ask Lunsford, "Were you trying to hurt Mooney during the race?"

"No gentlemen, I was trying to kill the SOB for cutting me off down the stretch."

The stewards warn, "We won't suspend either of you this time, however, both of you jockeys better be on your best behavior in the future."

In the jockeys' room Sande warns, "Don't look back, Lunsford. I'm right behind you."

"Right now I have my eye on Lyke, Long Back. Don't bother me."

"Looks like you had your hands full with Mooney today."

Lunsford and Sande share Latonia riding honors tied thirty-three wins each. The next closest jockey ranks far behind with fifteen wins. For the year to date, both trail Lyke with 117 wins, versus 107 for Lunsford, and 104 for Sande.

"Looks like we will head up to the Empire City track in Yonkers, New York, from here, Earl." Levy says. "A number of big eastern owners are clamoring for your services. Let's give them their money's worth."

"That's good, I hear Lyke will be there too. I've never been to New York before. Should be a thrill."

The sixteen-day Empire City race schedule opens July 17 with Sande placing far out of the money on 20 to 1 Belle Roberts and dead last on James Butler's 30 to 1 Caddie, the next day. Sande earns his maiden eastern victory after three days of racing, on Meadow Brook Farm's Sir Hello.

Levy waves "The Racing Form" in his hand. "These guys really like you, Earl. Says here, 'A good ride by jockey Sande, the youngster who rode so well in Kentucky this spring.'"

"They'll get their money's worth once I figure out these northern riders and their mounts."

Sande puts his words into action. During the last week of July, Sande enters the winner's circle eight times. "The Racing Form" reports, "Sande gave the easterners a practical demonstration of his riding ability in the opening event, when he brought Chillum home a winner over Dundreary in the tightest kind of finish. Dundreary was always in front, and it was only by the most strenuous work that Sande lifted his mount over the wire by a nose margin."

New York papers also take notice. "Sande, on Quietude, searched for an opening on the rail. After discovering the inside track impossible to penetrate, Sande took the overland route. Quietude, with a great burst of speed, swept around the field to enter the stretch with a solid margin."

"The Racing Form" credits Sande's horsemanship with winning the Melrose Stakes on Dorcas, his second winning mount of the day, and winning the Wakefield Handicap on Chasseur.

Ben Levy and Sande arrive at the Saratoga Race Course in Saratoga Springs, New York for August racing. On August 1, Earl Sande mounts L'Infirmier for Crown Stable in his first Saratoga Springs ride. Panaman jumps to an early lead and Sande finally clears L'Infirmier from early crowding. He closes the gap on Panaman but can't regain the ground lost earlier, ending up second on his 20 to 1 mount. W. F. Polson's Billy Kelly wins the third race of the day under the smooth hands of R. Simpson, and Frankie Robinson breaks a track record on Andrew Miller's Roamer while beating Larry Lyke on Commander Ross's Cudgel in the Saratoga Handicap.

Ross's Casino wins an August 2 purse of $600 under the guidance of Lyke's hands. Sande gives a fine riding performance the next day while guiding Solid Rock to first place. Commander Ross offers Polson $25,000 for Billy Kelly. Polson refuses and wins more than $8,800 that afternoon as Simpson brings Billy Kelly to the wire a winner, with a record-equaling time in the United States Hotel Stakes.

On the third, Sande takes the reins of Solid Rock, forces the lead horses to keep up the pace, and wins easing up. Two days later, Sande mounts Wyoming, placing third for owner R. T. Wilson.

Commander Ross puts down the binoculars that are routinely strapped behind his neck. "That Sande looks good even when he loses on some of those plow horses Levy gives him to ride. How does he stack up now against Lyke and Lunsford?"

Ross's trainer Poteet responds. "Lyke still leads with 125 first-place finishes. Sande now has 115 and Lunsford has fallen back to third place with 107."

"That Sande kid gets better with each race. We need the fastest-improving jockey riding for us. Wouldn't he look good on Billy Kelly? I think it's time we talk with that boy's contract owner, Guy."

"Yes, but Polson rejected your offer for Billy Kelly, Commander."

"That was only the first offer. I'll own both Billy Kelly and Sande's contract before long."

"Wait until Billy Kelly loses a race, then make another offer for him," Poteet advises. "In the meantime, I'll talk to Levy about Sande."

Chapter 6

Contract Rider for the Commander: John Kenneth Leveson Ross

Used to having things his own way, Commander J. K. L. Ross makes dramatic decisions and embraces life with a flair. Ross stands more than six feet tall and cuts a handsome figure in his naval uniform as well as the kilted garb of Montreal's Black Watch militia regiment.

In 1914, he donated $500,000 and three large yachts to the Royal Canadian Navy war effort. The Navy converted two of the vessels into destroyers. It rechristened Tarantula as H.M.C.S. Tuna and Winchester II as H.M.C.S. The Grilse. Commander Ross's private yacht, Albacore, transformed into the H.M.C.S. Albacore torpedo boat. Even the Ross family's Cape Breton home got pressed into World War I service, converted first into officers' headquarters and later into an army hospital.

Ross earned his title as a destroyer commander in the North Atlantic with two years service in the Royal Canadian Navy on the H.M.C.S. The Grilse. He received the Order of the British Empire for distinguished naval service.

Commander Ross inherited great wealth from his father, James Ross, one of the founders of the vast Canadian Pacific Railway empire and a major Canadian industrialist with interests in coal mines and the steel industry. In 1892, Ross's father commissioned American architect Bruce Price, designer of the famed Chateau Frontenac in Quebec City, to build a French chateau home on Montreal's Peel Street. This property, as well as the classical style home designed by Montreal architects Edward and William Maxwell for J. K. L. in 1909, later form part of McGill University.

Giving back to the community, James Ross built the Ross Memorial Hospital in Lindsay, Ontario, in 1902, in memory of his parents, and donated money in 1911 to construct the Annie Ross Nurses' Home in honor of his wife. James Ross died in 1913 and left $25,000 to the Ross Memorial Hospital.

Educated at Bishop's College School in Lennoxville and McGill University in Montreal, the energetic young J. K. L. Ross participated in hockey and was a member of the Canadian championship football team. He continued his father's philanthropy with a donation of $150,000 for the construction of a gymnasium at McGill Convocation in 1914 and the addition of a $700,000 Ross Pavilion to Montreal's Royal Victoria Hospital in 1916, to honor his father.

Commander Ross also followed his father's footsteps in the industrial world. He worked as an apprentice in the machine shops of Montreal Street Railway, assistant to the general manager of the City of Birmingham Tramway Company in England, assistant manager of Central London Railway, and commercial manager of Dominion Coal Company in Nova Scotia.

He served as chairman of the board of pension commissioners of Dominion of Canada, governor of McGill University, governor of the Royal Victoria Hospital, governor of General and Maternity Hospitals of Montreal, chairman of the board of Bishop's College School, director of Canadian Pacific Railway, director of Dominion Bridge Company, director of Lake of the Woods Milling Company, director of the Laurentide Company, and board member of Consolidated Mining and Smelting Company.

An avid sportsman, his interests include deep-sea fishing, yachting, shooting, automobiles, and horses. In 1911, Ross lands the record for Atlantic tuna caught with a rod and line at 680 pounds. That catch earns him honorary membership in the famous Tuna Club of Santa Catalina, California. The record stands until Ross breaks it himself, with a catch of 720 pounds. He holds memberships in the Royal Automobile Club, New York Yacht Club, Royal Thames Yacht Club, New York Racquet Club, and he serves as president of the Montreal Jockey Club.

J. K. L. Ross loses interest in the business routine and turns his love of horses and his $14-million inheritance into one of North America's premier forces in the horse racing world. He maintains stables in Nova Scotia and Montreal and purchases twelve racehorses in 1915. He first enters the horse racing business in steeplechasing by hiring Captain W. F. Presgrave of Baltimore, a well-known trainer. Presgrave brings twelve of his own horses to combine with Ross's stable in the spring of 1916. The horses perform well, but the sudden death of Presgrave, and subsequent loss of steeplechase expertise, causes Ross to shift the focus of his operations to thoroughbred racing.

St. Lazarian carries the first Ross black and orange silks that same year, winning several races. After Ross's Damrosch wins the 1916 Preakness and his Achievement places third, the racing world takes notice of the Ross colors and the imposing figure of Commander Ross at the racetrack. He purchases a 2,000-acre tract at Vecheres, near Montreal, as headquarters for his breeding and racing operations and another horse farm near Laurel, Maryland. In 1917, he lures well-known American horse trainer and owner Horatio G. "Guy" Poteet to Canada as the head of his operations. Poteet ranks as the leading trainer in America from 1912 to 1917.

Poteet earned his spurs on the hard knocks racetracks of the West. The son of a horse trainer/trader father, who dragged the family across the country chasing the county fair circuits, Poteet learned about horses early in life. He bulldogged at rodeos and worked as a cowpuncher on the Wyoming range as a teenager. Giving up cowboying around the country, Poteet worked as county clerk in Virginia City, Nevada, for a spell. He opened up a livery in town and gained the reputation of buying broken-down horses and restoring them to good racing form. He was also instrumental in importing camels to Virginia City for a new brand of racing. He often bragged on how he used to ride in four races and drive six harness heats in a single afternoon. Poteet eventually gravitated East, where he became known as a shrewd horse buyer and successful trainer/owner with an uncanny ability to pick good horses and get the best out of not-so-good mounts.

When he goes to work for Ross, he is a hard-hitting, no-nonsense trainer, completely dedicated to his job of winning horse races. Respected by jockeys for his knowledge of how to pace a horse to get the most out of him, he also picks up the nickname "Hard Guy" Poteet for his handling of jockeys. Although a rugged horseman, Poteet looks more the part of a timid county clerk, with a lean build, a sallow face, and hard, beady eyes. In contrast to Commander Ross's immaculate dress and personal habits, Poteet chews plug tobacco, which drips out of the corner of his mouth on

Commander J. K .L. Ross, Canadian racehorse owner, in uniform. Courtesy Keene-land-Cook.

to his shirt. He always turns on mock Southern charm when women visit the stables but uses foul language while addressing his jockeys.

In 1917, Ross's horses place in the money seventy-three times, taking first twenty-two times, second twenty-nine times, and third twenty-two times, winning over $22,000 in total. Not a large amount, but a fine beginning and a foreshadowing of things to come. Determined to build the finest racehorse stable in North America, Ross spares no expense in the process. Ross desires a premier horse to hallmark his new stable.

"I know of such a horse. He's raced only in the West, and not that many people know about him," Poteet says. "I'm sure I could purchase him for the right price."

"Do whatever it takes. I want that horse racing for the black and orange."

Poteet travels to John W. Schorr's stables in Kentucky, where Cudgel now resides, and purchases the horse for $30,000. He then readies him for racing at Saratoga.

Saratoga Springs in 1918 acts as a mecca for the socially and politically connected, who converge on the prestigious Grand Union Hotel, The Casino, Saratoga Spa, and the Saratoga Race Course. Wealthy racehorse owners such as Harry Payne Whitney and Joseph Widener frequent the track. A wide variety of socially prominent people, including opera singer Enrico Caruso, Ziegfeld Follies Poet Lariat and avid horseman Will Rogers, famous Irish tenor Chauncey Olcott, movie star Francis X. Bushman, as well as politicians of city, state, and national renown flock to Saratoga Springs for the festivities and the turf action during race season.

On August 1, Earl Sande mounts L'Infirmier for Crown Stable in his first Saratoga Springs ride. Panaman jumps to an early lead and Sande finally clears L'Infirmier from early crowding. He closes the gap on Panaman but can't regain the ground lost earlier, ending up second. On the third, Sande takes the reins of Solid Rock, forces the lead horses to keep up the pace, and wins easing up. Two days later, Sande mounts Wyoming, placing third for owner R. T. Wilson.

Favored Billy Kelly rushes to the front of a field of eight in the August 7 Albany Handicap after Frankie Robinson on Chasseur beat everyone away from the gate. Schuttinger on Sea Pirate and Robinson on Chasseur make a run at Billy Kelly, all three running neck and neck for a stretch. Billy Kelly shakes them off in the turn but Star Hampton, who got off last with jockey

Ambrose astride, breaks for the inside and pushes through on the rail. A final charge by Billy Kelly comes up short by a length.

Not one to let an opportunity pass by without taking advantage of it, and intent on further strengthening his stable, Ross takes Poteet's advice and seeks out Billy Kelly owner W. F. Polson. At Billy Kelly's stable, Ross looks with disdain at the horse and says, "Billy Kelly didn't fare so well in the Albany this afternoon, W. F.. Too much competition, I guess. My offer of $25,000 still stands if you want to take me up on it, but the offer goes down from here."

"Seeing as Billy Kelly placed second, it will cost you $30,000 to close the deal, Commander."

Without hesitation, Commander Ross whips out his checkbook and says, "We've got a deal, W. F.. Here's my check."

"I noticed the check was already signed, Commander. Were you that sure I would agree to sell Billy Kelly today?"

"Now that the deal is closed, I don't mind telling you that I would have paid $50,000 to see Billy Kelly in the Ross stable."

Many racetrack observers consider the western horse inferior to those bred in the East. One of Ross's friends remarks, "Looks more like a polo pony to me."

"Polo pony?" another scoffs. "You mean a mule!"

Sande dons the Ross colors as a day rider on August 8. Knowing how much horse he has left, he paces Canso to an easy victory. He also places in the money on Goodman's Kama. The next day Clarence Kummer pushes Westy Hogan through the mud to win the Glens Falls Handicap and sets up anticipation for the race between Westy Hogan and Cudgel. Sande then takes second on C. Fellowes's Wonderman, who was run down by a game Thistledon. He earns first place on Ross's Foreground, who begins slowly but catches fire and wins going away. Sande again enters the winner's circle on Cleveland Stable's Scoots.

Commander Ross inquires, "How is Sande taking to your instructions while riding our mounts, Guy?"

"No problems. He listens well and carries out my instructions to the tee. He's improved a lot since New Orleans and Hot Springs. Knows the other jockeys' traits and horses' capabilities and is perfecting his riding style, Commander."

"There's a lot of scuttlebutt around the track that he's the next Tod Sloan. What do you think, Guy?"

Earl Sande in Ross orange and black colors. Courtesy Sande Tomlinson Collection

"He's definitely more low-key, both on and off the track, than Sloan but gets the same results and as efficiently. Riding conditions have changed since Sloan's time. Without a doubt, competition is keener and it takes more all-around talent to ride today. For my money, I'd give the nod to Sande in a head-to-head race."

Amply impressed with Sande's wins, Ross releases star rider Larry Lyke and purchases Sande's contract from Johnson and Kane for $20,000 on August 12, 1918. Commander Ross first offers to pay Sande $60 per month plus his colors and riding fees but then revises the arrangement to have the jockey pay for his own silks.

On Sande's first official mount as a Ross employee the next afternoon, he guides Monomoy out of close quarters in the early running and races past Torchbearer in the final strides. He delivers a tiring Cadillac into second place the following day. He then mounts Commander Ross's newly acquired Billy Kelly for the horse's debut race in the Saratoga Sanford Memorial. Sande gets a slow start away from the barrier on a muddy track with Billy Kelly carrying a weight of 130 pounds. The field of eight includes Larry Lyke on Colonel Livingston, Frankie Robinson on Sketchy, and A. Collins on Sir Barton. Lion d'Or, piloted by L. Ensor, leads by three lengths. In the homestretch, Sande urges Billy Kelly to give all. The bay establishes a lead at the eighth pole and never looks back, winning by eight lengths. The race yields $3,925 to Ross, the initial return on his combined investments in Billy Kelly and Sande.

Commander Ross analyzes the race. "Billy Kelly's known to expend only enough energy to win a race, so the wide margin victory for his first race under the Ross colors impresses me, Guy. Now that's what I call a winning combination."

After Sande dismounts, he says to Commander Ross, "I think Billy just wanted to prove that you made no mistake laying out money for him."

Back in the jockeys' room after the race, Frankie Robinson yells, "Hey, Long Back, looks like you made it to the big time."

A few days later, Sande astride Cudgel challenges Clarence Kummer on Westy Hogan in the Schenectady Handicap at Saratoga. Kummer flashes to the lead in a free-running style and increases his pace as the race goes on. Meanwhile Sande holds back Cudgel, following the leader by two lengths. Westy Hogan increases his lead to three lengths on the far corner and shows no sign of weakening. However, Sande remains calm, waiting to make his move. At the home turn, Cudgel springs to life and starts closing the gap. Kummer takes to the whip as Cudgel narrows the lead to only inches within fifty yards from the finish line. As the surging horses look eye-to-eye, Sande's gentle hands push Cudgel ahead of Westy Hogan by a nose.

Earl Sande up on Billy Kelly. Courtesy Keeneland-Cook.

"Just wanted to make it interesting," Sande yells as he passes Kummer. Racetrack fans give Sande and Cudgel a resounding roar upon their return to the scales.

The Jockey Club handicapper, Walter Vosburgh, considers Billy Kelly practically unbeatable and hands him a weight of 135 pounds for the Grab Bag Handicap. Two other horses in the field of twelve receive weights of 120 and 121 pounds, all the rest carry between 100 and 118 pounds.

Sande again astride Billy Kelly enters the Grab Bag Handicap field of twelve. Top competitors include Larry Lyke on Lord Brighton and Frankie Robinson on Cirrus. Carrying a heavy burden, Billy Kelly trails Sweep On, Ginger, and Stickling all the way to the stretch, working his way up on the outside. When the field straightens out for the run home, Sande gives Billy Kelly his head. The horse responds and passes all but Sweep On by the final furlong. In the final stretch, Billy Kelly responds to an unusual touch with the whip by Sande, surges past Sweep On, and wins by half a length and going away in record stakes time. In the fifth race of the day, Sande also brings home Ross's Valais to the victory circle.

For Billy Kelly's final scheduled season appearance at Saratoga, the Adirondack Handicap, Vosburgh assigns Billy Kelly the extraordinary weight of 140 pounds. Ross meets Vosburgh in the paddock after announcement of the assigned weights. Ross routinely wears his dress whites and Commander's hat to the racetrack and exudes an air of authority. In his own right, Vosburgh carries the weight of his office seriously and takes no guff from anyone, even the imposing Commander Ross.

"That's a terrific weight you have given Billy Kelly, Mr. Vosburgh," Commander Ross booms.

Not one to be intimidated, Vosburgh replies with authority, "Billy is a terrific horse, Commander!"

Ross's face turns red. He abruptly makes an about face and lets the gate slam behind him. That afternoon, Ross scratches Billy Kelly from the race, and the question as to whether the "polo pony" could win carrying 140 pounds forever remains unanswered. Routledge wins the Andirondack Handicap carrying a feather of 111 pounds.

In September, Sande and Billy Kelly move to races at Havre de Grace, Maryland. The city derived its name in 1782 from French General Lafayette who exclaimed "C'est Le Havre!" after noting its resemblance to Le Havre de Grace, France, meaning "Harbor of Mercy." When the House of Representatives voted on the permanent location of the US capital in 1789, The Speaker broke the tie vote between Washington and Havre de Grace.

The Havre de Grace Racetrack, affectionately know as "The Graw," opened on August 24, 1912, under the management of the Harford County Agricultural and Breeders Association. Edward Burke, builder of the Jamaica Race Track on Long Island, funded The Graw. The grandstand holds 6,000 spectators and offers a panoramic view of the Susquehanna flats. Special race trains enter Havre de Grace from Baltimore, New York, Philadelphia, and Washington.

Unlike the gentile atmosphere of Saratoga Springs, Havre de Grace quickly earned the reputation of "Little Chicago" because of the unsavory nature of some of the people who hung around the track. Racetrack fans notch their programs to prevent them from being "lifted" out of their pockets. Free-flowing liquor served on the grounds creates a party atmosphere and the festivities often flow over to Baltimore restaurateur Pink West's Bayou Hotel in Havre de Grace. Ads in "The Harford Democrat" announce "Seven races daily, including steeplechase, Grandstand and Paddock $1.65, Ladies $1.10 (including war tax)."

On September 10 opening day, Sande goes to the front and stays there on McBride's Little Maudie, finishing the race in a canter. In the third race,

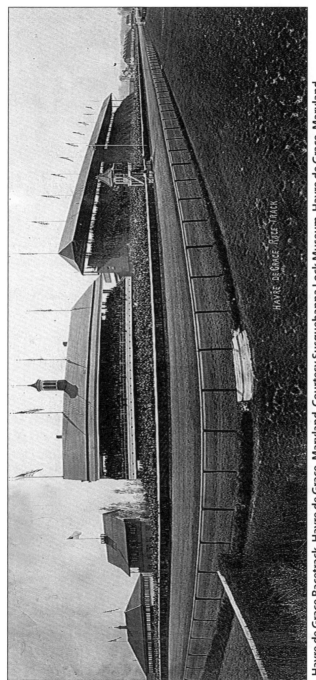

Havre de Grace Racetrack, Havre de Grace, Maryland. Courtesy Susquehanna Lock Museum, Havre de Grace, Maryland.

Sande chases down the leaders on Calumet Stable's Be Frank and gains the winner's circle for the Autumn Junior Purse. On his first Havre de Grace races for Commander Ross, Sande finishes third on Foreground and out of the money on Canso. He salvages the day with a second place finish.

The New York Observer Herald headlines proclaim, "Sande Goes Three-for-Three." The article tells how Sande boots home three winners with St. Quentin under restraint, Dottie Vandiver outrunning her opponents in the Mermaid Purse, and Foreground drawing away on the backstretch in the Fox Hill Purse on September 12.

He follows up that sterling performance by sprinting away on Eddie Henry for the win and three second-place results a few days later. Next, The Hopeful Purse falls to Sande aboard Milkmaid, who teases Mahoney until the backstretch and then pulls ahead, retaining some speed in reserve. Sande scores another Havre de Grace first place aboard L'Infirmier.

Sande starts out the racing with second-place and fourth-place finishes and then takes Billy Kelly to the line at the call to the post for the September 18 Eclipse Handicap. Sande lets Prince of Como show how fast he can run in the slop. Down the backstretch, Sande allows Billy Kelly to run full out and pass Prince of Como in the final strides. Poteet saddles yet another winner in the next race, with Sande boosting Monomoy to the wire first with slight help from the whip. Sande captures another first place on Wood Violet later in the week.

Poteet scratches Sir Barton and Milkmaid because of the September 21 Havre de Grace muddy track. However, Sande up on Foreground manueuvers the horse to the inside on the stretch and wins by a stride. He then mounts Billy Kelly for the Eastern Shore Handicap. Billy Kelly raises a ruckus at the barrier, knocking off the top rail, before the field gets off. Carrying 135 pounds, Billy Kelly follows the pace set by Ambassador III and Bagheera until the turn for home. Down the stretch Billy Kelly takes the lead, but Sande keeps him under restraint until Routledge poses a threat. Sande then releases Billy Kelly, and the horse lunges forward to win by less than a length. The day proves to be a successful one for Ross as he also wins the steeplechase competition with Dramaturge.

Sande brings the crowd to its feet time and time again two days later. On Sweeplet, he follows the pace of Prevariate and Triumphant set early in the race. Sweeplet goes to running and beats Triumphant by less than a length. In the next race, Sande saves ground by going to the rail, and Sybil wins going away. In the sixth race Sande gets cut off rounding the far turn and has

Earl Sande on Milkmaid. Courtesy Keeneland-Cook.

to pour on the steam down the stretch to win with Tootsie's final stride. An easy ride on Lytle gives Sande his fourth first-place finish of the day.

Poteet hands out a rare piece of praise. "Four wins in one afternoon. Nice riding today, Earl."

"Thanks. The Graw's a great track and been kind to me."

Over the next week, Sande wins on Duchess Lace, Lytle, and Refugee. He takes second ten times and third four times. On the last day of Havre de Grace racing, Sande takes True as Steel to a fast pace that he never relinquishes. In the Liberty Handicap, Sande and Cudgel run down Red Sox in the last few strides to eke out a victory. Sande's third triumph of the day comes aboard Billy Kelly as he slips through on the rail and draws away to an easy win, Billy Kelly's sixth in a row.

Sande easily claims top riding honors with twenty-three wins at Havre de Grace, nearly doubling the number of wins of the next closest jockey, with twelve wins. Sande also outpaces the other jockeys in second-place finishes with twenty, versus eleven for his closest competitor.

Commander Ross compliments Poteet, "You sure know how to handle that Sande kid, Guy. First he wins four races in a day and then comes along a few days later with a triple. What a jockey! That's what I call good riding, and good training. Keep up the good work. Let's see what Laurel Park racing brings."

Maryland papers jump on the Sande bandwagon as "The Baltimore Sun" writes, "No jockey within recent years has stood so far above his rivals as Sande, and under the capable handling of Guy Poteet he should continue to land laurels. He has all the earmarks of a great rider and is especially cool under fire. The latter point stamps him as going on to greater rewards."

Racetrack owners and fans follow the progress of Commander Ross's stables led by Poteet. Asked by "The Thoroughbred Record" to explain the reasons for his success, Poteet answers, "I use common sense, that's all. Of course, the fact that no two horses are alike calls for the exercise of judgment. I try to give my horses the same sort of attention that a physician gives his patients. If you keep a horse normal and well, he is bound to respond to training. There is no secret about my methods. I use more cooked feed than most trainers. Every night, unless they are to race the next day, every member of my stable gets a supply of cooked oats with a little corn. This is mixed with bran. I am a believer in hay and keep three kinds before my horses all the time. I like California hay, alfalfa, and mixed clover and timothy. A good hay eater is usually a good racehorse, just as most men who are big eaters of bread are healthy and able to do a good day's work."

Poteet pauses for a while then continues. "Another thing which has contributed to the condition of my horses is there are no doors on the stables, winter or summer. I want all the fresh air possible to reach my horses. They are clothed, of course. I use three or four light blankets in preference to one heavy one, and these are put on and taken off according to the temperature. Particular attention is paid to the feet. Note the fine feet you see on all horses that run the range or are in a wild state. Keep the foot as near nature as possible and you avoid problems."

Asked about the future prospects of Billy Kelly and Cudgel, Poteet replies, "We shall be ready to meet all comers and will fulfill any engagement as long as they are well and fit. I regard Billy Kelly as the best two-year-old in the country. I don't think I have ever seen his equal. As a matter of fact, I don't know how fast he can run, for the little rascal is cunning and won't try unless pressed. I worked him three furlongs with Cudgel and his nose was in front at the pole. No more, no less, just enough to win."

On October 3, A. Johnson takes Billy Kelly to the finish line, beating Mormon and Be Frank at the wire in the Laurel Park, Maryland, Annapolis Stakes. Sande gathers his first win at Laurel Park eight days later by setting the pace early with Sybil, relinquishing the lead to Serenest, and then wearing Serenest down to recapture it and the victory.

The next day Sande begins slowly on Milkmaid in the Quickstep Purse but easily passes the field and wins going away. In the Columbus Handicap, Bulse breaks fast and establishes a lead of several lengths in the first quarter with Sande on Billy Kelly running close behind. As Billy Kelly approaches the lower turn he begins to pick up the pace, leaving Bulse in the dust. On the swing for home, Lunsford on Leochares threatens on the outside, but Billy Kelly rides him out for the victory. In other racing action, Cudgel carries a heavy load of 130 pounds and comes in second to Midway in the Washington Handicap.

"When the season began, you were nothing but an apprentice rider like me, Earl." Lunsford complains. "Now, it seems like everyone is eating your dust."

"Shucks, I just took notice of your riding skill and added a touch of western savvy."

Maryland health officials close the track after the race until further notice because of the spreading influenza epidemic. The track re-opens shortly thereafter. However, Sande sits out racing for a few days due to a bout of influenza.

As Billy Kelly's victories pile up, race fans clamor for a meeting between Billy Kelly and Eternal, who captured the Hopeful Stakes and other important races. Commander Ross and James McClelland, Eternal's owner, agree to a $20,000 purse for the meeting of the two great horses at Laurel, Maryland, on October 28 in the six-furlong John B. McLean Memorial Cup Race. The Baltimore Sun carries photos of Eternal and Sande on Billy Kelly.

Commander Ross boasts, "If Sande and Billy Kelly win, the Canadian Red Cross will be $20,000 richer. If Andrew Schuttinger and Eternal win, the American Red Cross will benefit."

Two days before the matchup between Billy Kelly and Eternal, Sande entertains one of the largest Maryland racetrack crowds ever by winning the Waterloo Purse on Milkmaid and the Dixie Handicap on Cudgel. Sande never uses his whip in either race. Ross's stable also wins the Chevy Chase Steeplechase Handicap with Dramaturge.

A crowd of 12,000 jams into the grandstands to witness the battle for two-year-old supremacy between Billy Kelly and Eternal. Visiting delegations from New York clamor for their Aqueduct favorite Eternal, while

Marylanders cheer on Billy Kelly. Ross, confident of a victory, bets $10,000 at the windows in addition to his $10,000 stakes wager.

Out of the barrier, Sande and Billy Kelly jump to the lead. Schuttinger urges his mount forward. Eternal overtakes Billy Kelly and builds a commanding two and a half length lead. Sande shifts his weight and leans over the horse's head; Billy Kelly springs forward like a jack rabbit. Around the corner Eternal goes a tad wide, allowing Billy Kelly to gain more ground. Sande steers Billy Kelly for the opening along the rail, but Schuttinger deftly closes the path to the inside.

"No opening there, Earl," Schuttinger cries.

In the homestretch, Billy Kelly's nose inches up to Eternal's hip and continues to move forward. At the eighth pole, Schuttinger puts the whip to Eternal's hide repeatedly and drives the horse onward across the wire in front of Billy Kelly, who was closing the gap.

Upon returning to the stands, both horses receive thunderous applause and cheering. Thinking that he had won, Billy Kelly tries to enter the winner's circle before Sande reins him away.

Sande takes full blame for the results and acknowledges the riding ability of his opponent, "I waited too long to break. Schuttinger rode masterfully."

"I congratulate Mr. McClelland and the ride Schuttinger gave Eternal," Commander Ross says. "Of course, I am disappointed. If the race had been a bit further, it may have had a different outcome, for I believe Billy Kelly was wearing Eternal down at the end. Naturally, I would like the opportunity to run the race over again, but no such thing is likely to happen. However, gentlemen, you may quote me, 'If the race took place again tomorrow, Earl Sande would once more be up on my horse.'"

Poteet is less diplomatic and berates Sande while unsaddling Billy Kelly. "You fell for a cheap trick like the novice that you are. Schuttinger out rode you, Earl, plain and simple. You made a fool of the Ross stable and my training ability."

Ross's words gloss over the disappointment Sande feels and Poteet's criticism, although brutal, strikes home. Sande knows in his heart that the experienced Schuttinger outwitted him with the feint of swinging wide around the last corner. Sande admits he made a mistake that cost his owner a big race and promises himself that will never happen again.

Sande tells Frankie Robinson in the jockey room, "Billy Kelly is the only horse I have ridden who never needs the jockey's help. He's always alert at the post and jumps out to a good start. He can measure the strengths and weaknesses of the other horses in the field. If headed by a quitter, Billy Kelly takes his time and does not hurry until the stretch, and he never lets a game competitor take a substantial lead. Billy Kelly was positioned to beat Eternal until I fell for Schuttinger's deception, costing us the race."

"Don't let it get you down. We all make mistakes," Robinson says. "You're young yet, Long Back. Schuttinger's an old pro. You have time to get even."

After the loss to Eternal, Ross scratches Billy Kelly from the Laurel Potomac Handicap. He expands his stable of horses November 1 with the $75,000 purchase of Motor Cop, War Marvel, and War Pennant from A. K. Macomber.

Poteet tells reporters, "Both two-year-olds, War Pennant and War Marvel have shown good form at Aqueduct and Empire City in recent outings. Three-year-old Motor Cop won the Withers Stakes with great speed. These promising acquisitions add great depth to the Ross stable."

Commander Ross reaps a fast return on his investment. Sande mounts Motor Cop in the six-furlong Pimlico Stafford Handicap, only a day after Ross acquires the horse. Sande gets Motor Cop off to a sizzling start and keeps the rest of the field chasing him all the way to the finish line. J. McTaggart on Sam Hildreth's Stromboli finishes second. In the fifth race of the day, Sande aboard Milkmaid trails Larry Lyke on Cirrus and gives the favorite a run for his money down the stretch, coming in second by only a head.

"The Denver Post" reports on the state of horse racing. "Drab predictions for the future of the racing game have come from various quarters from time to time. Yet racing has been more than holding its own. The sport of kings has flourished in the East this season as attendance figures prove. Commander Ross, Sam Hildreth, and others have spent thousands of dollars for youngsters."

"We're gathering a crack stable together in anticipation of a big year in 1919," Poteet explains.

On November 5, Billy Kelly takes to the turf for the first time since losing to Eternal, carrying a weight of 130 pounds. Sande holds Billy Kelly back at the start and then gains steadily on the leaders. He bides his time while Mad Hatter and Over There set a hot pace that cannot be sustained. Down the stretch, Billy Kelly runs down the pair and wins by a length and a half.

Poteet says, "That's how you should have run against Eternal, Earl."

The next day, two wins, aboard Salestra in the Catonsville Handicap and Smart Money in the Roland Park Handicap, add to Sande's winning totals. Poteet saddles War Marvel, with Sande up. He trails the leaders in the early going before making his move entering the homestretch. Under savvy hand riding, War Marvel wins the Driving Park Purse easing up. Closing out racing at Pimlico, Sande scores a victory on Valspar, going wide and charging with a spurt at the end and later in the day running out Hollister to take Boniface to the finish line first.

Commander Ross brings excitement to the racing game in 1918. He earns the distinction of being the first Canadian stable owner to lead the money-winning owners in the United States and uses his influence to bring many of racing's great names to compete in Canada. However, race critics roundly chastise Ross when he buys Sir Barton for $10,000 from John E. Madden after the horse fails to place in the Tremont, Flash, United States Hotel, and Sanford Memorial Stakes.

"Don't worry about the races Sir Barton has lost," Poteet declares. "He's also known as a horse with more than his share of temperament. I guess you'd call it a downright nasty disposition. That just brought his price down. I'll train that mean streak out of him. Look at his parentage. He possesses nerves of steel, which will pay off in the big races. He has the look of an eagle and the mark of a great champion. Sir Barton's poised to be a big winner for the right stable. We're that stable."

Commander Ross agrees with his trainer. "I don't care what anyone thinks. If Guy Poteet sees promise in Sir Barton, we'll make a winner out of that horse."

Eternal leads the money winning two-year-old horses with $56,137, followed by Ross's Billy Kelly with $33,782. The main difference, the $20,000 match race between the two horses. Among four-year-olds, Ross's Cudgel ranks as the top money-winning horse with $33,826. Two of Ross's horses rank among the five highest money winners across all age groups. Commander Ross leads the list of money-winning owners with sixty-four first-place, fifty-two second-place, and fifty-seven third-place finishes for a total of $99,179 in purses, beating out 1917's leading money winner owner, A. K. Macomber.

Only six jockeys ride a hundred or more winning mounts in 1918. Frankie Robinson ranks as the top jockey with the year's most winning mounts of 185, a feat he also accomplished in 1916. Larry Lyke finishes second with 178. Rookie Earl Sande, who spent much of the year on smaller tracks with smaller purses, takes third place with 158 first-place wins. Sande places in the money more than 50 percent of the time. Lunsford follows Sande by three wins and only wins 18 percent of his races. Ensor rounds out the top five with 117 wins but earns only $17,240.

Tragedy strikes the New Orleans Fair Grounds Race Course on December 28, 1918, as the grandstands burn to the ground. Within days, workmen construct a temporary facility in time for the January 1 opening of the winter season.

Top 1918 Jockey Standings							
Jockey	Mounts	1st	2nd	3rd	%	$Winnings	In Money %
Robinson, F.	864	185	140	108	.21	$186,595	.501
Lyke, L	756	178	123	108	.24	201,864	.541
Sande, E.	707	158	122	80	.22	138,872	.509
Lunsford, H.	850	155	167	114	.18	125,708	.512
Ensor, L.	508	117	81	72	.23	17,240	.531

Standings for leading jockeys, according to percentage of races won, rank Johnny Loftus first with 30 percent, while Sande comes in fifth with 22 percent. Beginning in 1919, Johnny Loftus plans to ride under the colors of Samuel Riddle, having signed a contract for the highest salary paid a jockey in many years. It is noteworthy that Johnny Loftus's high percentage was aided by his opportunities to ride the best horses while Pauley's high percentage took place on smaller tracks with less stiff competition. Lyke, Ensor, and Sande were handicapped by having to ride all mounts, good and not-so-good, belonging to their contract employers.

Sande is riding at the top of his game as the 1918 horse racing season comes to a close. "The Times-Picayune" claims New Orleans bragging rights. "Earl Sande is another jockey product of the Fair Grounds. He rode his first mount here in 1918 and before the year closed he had shown the way on so many steeds that he is classed with the stars of the American Turf."

"The American Racing Manual" gives both praise and condemnation to Sande's record and riding style. "An outstanding feature of the horsemanship of the year was the showing of three lads practically unknown to the racing world in 1917, they being E. Sande, H. Lunsford, and L. Ensor. All three rode in great form, their experience considered, and each won in excess of a hundred races. Sande made the best impression, but near the end of the year began to incur suspensions, a sure indication of an exaggerated opinion of his own importance."

Sande feels the sting of the article. He comments to fellow jockey Frankie Robinson, "Too bad that writer can't see what really happens out on the track. I try to make things happen when there's an opening. I can't help it if the hole closes and horses bump each other. I never intentionally engage in rough riding."

"Don't let it get to you. Your skill will show through in the long run, Long Back."

Top 1918 Jockey Standings by Percentage Wins (100 or more mounts)			
Jockey	Mounts	Won	Percent
Loftus, J.	120	37	.30
Pauley, R.	224	56	.25
Lyke, L	756	178	.24
Ensor, L.	508	117	.23
Sande, E	707	158	.22
Humphries, W.	114	25	.22

Part 3

Rising in the Ranks

Chapter 7

World Record at Havre de Grace:
Bitter Disappointment

"Earl Sande, you're skinny as a rail. I know you need to watch your weight for racing, but a few pounds on those bones wouldn't hurt any."

"Don't worry, Mother. I'm eating fine and keep in good shape. Sure is great to see you again. I left in such a hurry we didn't get to say our good-byes. I'm sorry."

"Well, that's behind us now. I took it hard for a spell, before that letter from Doc Pardee set my worries aside. You were lucky to run into such a fine gentleman. After that, we kept track of you in the papers. Sit down and eat some of my cooking."

In the off-season, Sande spends time with his family in American Falls, returning to Baltimore in early January 1919. Idaho is plenty proud of its jockey making good on the big eastern tracks. Sande ranks among the top jockeys in the nation and serves as a role model for three other Idaho jockeys hoping to make the big time: Elmer, Laverne, and Mark Fator.

"The Thoroughbred Record" runs an article on J. K. L. Ross's horses in training and reports that since the war hostilities ended, racehorse owner A. K. Macomber has decided to continue racing. He telegraphs his trainer to contact Commander Ross and offer to re-purchase the three horses (War Marvel, War Pennant, and Motor Cop) sold to Commander Ross earlier.

Macomber orders, "Pay a premium to get them back."

Poteet telegraphs a curt response: "There are thirty-six horses in training in the Ross stable this year, and not a single one of them is for sale."

Commander Ross values his honor. Simply put, a deal is a deal. Nothing illustrates this more clearly than a betting episode involving Commander Ross. The story centers around the meaning of the initials S.P. in the bookmaker world. The traditional definition of S.P. is "starting price," or the price quoted by a bookmaker at post time, as opposed to the "opening price," the figure quoted when bets are first accepted before the race.

Commander Ross wires his New York betting commissioner: "Wish to wager twenty thousand S. P. on my entry second race tomorrow."

The man thinks Commander Ross intends to bet "straight and place" and enters the wager for Commander Ross as $20,000 to win and $20,000 to place. The confusion means Commander Ross stands to lose double what he planned to bet.

Ironically, Ross's horse, Welshman's Folly, wins handily at odds of 6 to 1 to win and 2 to 1 to place. The bookmaker credits Commander Ross with $160,000.

Commander Ross learns of the mistake and instructs the betting commissioner, "Promptly return $40,000 to the bookmaker. I refuse to accept more than the $120,000 I bargained for when I placed the bet."

The race season begins tragically on April 4 with premier jockey Frankie Robinson, dying because of a spill in the sixth race at Bowie, Maryland. Also injured in the tangle, Johnny McTaggart suffers two fractured ribs. Sande takes Robinson's death hard. Besides losing a talented and caring mentor, he misses a good friend on the riding circuit. Out of respect for Robinson, Sande asks other jockeys to not call him Long Back anymore. Millionaire sportsman Harry Payne Whitney offers assistance to Frankie Robinson's nineteen-year-old widow, Lucy, to help settle his $500,000 estate.

An overcast day greets jockeys and race enthusiasts at the April 16 Havre de Grace opening day. Sande starts Dottie Vandiver off fast from the post and keeps the speed on, easing up down the stretch to win going away in the second race. By the time riders mount for the fifth race, clouds open up and torrents of rain prevent race fans from seeing Billy Kelly slog through the goop to win the Harford Handicap. Showing excellent form, Billy Kelly cruises through the track and needs to be restrained by Sande at the end of the race. Ending the day, Sande slips Indolence through a gap on the rail to take the lead and win in a breeze.

The next day, Miss Shackleton runs well enough in the mud to earn a second-place finish under Sande's guidance, and Foreground, with Sande up, sets the early pace and draws away down the stretch to win easily. Billy Kelly and Sande team up again two days later in the Philadelphia Handicap. Havre de Grace's largest crowd ever cheers Sande and Billy Kelly as they emerge from the paddock. Ahead by six furlongs early in the race, Billy Kelly slacks off and wins only by a neck over a hard-driving Charlie Leydecker. "The New York Observer Herald" criticizes Sande for careless handling of Billy Kelly and allowing Charley Leydecker to almost beat him.

In frustration, Sande tells Poteet, "If that writer could get on Billy Kelly, he would see for himself that Billy has a mind of his own."

Over the two weeks at Havre de Grace, Sande delivers wins on Broom Peddler, Ballad, Foreground, Houdini, Jack Leary, Looking Up, Milkmaid, Monomoy, Motor Cop, Murphy, Subahdar, and Widow Bedotte. He also places second on five mounts and third on Jack Leary and Milkmaid.

The racing action moves to Louisville, where track followers consider the May 10 Kentucky Derby a contest between James McClelland's Eternal and Commander Ross's Billy Kelly, with the edge going to Eternal. To date, Billy Kelly had lost three times, while Eternal suffered only two defeats. The two owners exhibit confidence in their own horses by placing a $20,000 side bet with each other.

"I have given my jockey, Sande, his choice of horses for the Derby, and he opted to ride Billy Kelly," Commander Ross tells reporters.

Ross, still stinging from Sande's loss on Billy Kelly to Eternal in the big match race, contracts with Loftus to jockey Commander Ross's other Derby entry, Sir Barton. Leading up to the race, Eternal completes a mile and a quarter at a time of 2:08. Billy Kelly works out with second string Sir Barton, making his three-year-old debut at the Kentucky Derby.

Poteet tells Sande and Loftus, "Our racing strategy is for you, Johnny, to make Sir Barton a pace setting rabbit for Billy Kelly. Once Sir Barton tires out contenders Eternal and Under Fire, it's time for Earl to give Billy Kelly free rein, take the lead, and win the race. This feint will confuse competitors' jockeys into trailing Billy Kelly until he makes his move. By then it will be too late for them to catch up."

Separately, Poteet advises Johnny Loftus, "I don't know which of our horses will win this race. They're both strong contenders. But one of them better beat Eternal to the wire or Commander Ross will be furious. Take the lead early as I instructed and see what transpires. If Sir Barton has it in him, go the distance for the win."

"What about Sande and Billy Kelly, Guy?"

"Don't worry about Sande. I'll deal with him."

A rainy day presents a muddy track for horses, jockeys, and race fans. A record crowd of 50,000 fills the grandstands and infield. Carrying less weight than Eternal, Billy Kelly, and the other horses, Sir Barton shows a burst of speed from the barrier. Loftus keeps the steed in front of Eternal and Billy Kelly in the early going. By the three-quarters of a mile post, the mud gets the better of Eternal and he falls back. In the last quarter of a mile, Under Fire makes a move out of the muck and charges strong, passing horse after horse. However, Sir Barton easily reaches the finish line first, with Johnny Loftus standing in his stirrups. Sande, on Billy Kelly, trails five lengths behind, having passed Under Fire in the homestretch run.

Loftus recounts the race, "All I had to do today was sit steady in the boat and let Sir Barton run. I did not even have to cluck at him, as he was running easily at all times. Never did he show the least signs of distress. He is a much better three-year-old than given credit."

Commander Ross slaps Poteet on the back. "Well, Guy, we did fine today. First time in Kentucky Derby history that a stable captures both first and second place, a Canadian outfit to boot. I'm sure that rankles the Yanks."

"To add icing on the cake, Commander, Sir Barton's $20,000 in winnings today also make Derby history. That gives you considerable bragging rights at The Jockey Club."

"Guy, maybe we moved Sande too fast. He's an excellent rider but still a bit unseasoned." Commander Ross instructs, "Straighten it out with Riddle to have Loftus signed on to ride Sir Barton for us in his major races this year. I don't care how you arrange it. Just get it done."

Sande hides his disappointment of not riding Sir Barton on his win and praises Loftus's accomplishment. "Johnny is as clever a jockey as I've ever seen around the tracks. His bag of tricks contains just about everything a rider needs in his repertoire. He keeps a cool, steady hand and never admits defeat until the finish line has been crossed. He never quits while there is a ghost of a chance."

Sande does not take kindly to Poteet bringing Loftus into the Ross stable of riders. "Why is Loftus getting the rides on Sir Barton? I'm supposed to be your top jockey, Guy."

"I don't think you're ready yet for the big races, Earl. Schuttinger beat you soundly on Eternal and Loftus beat you with Sir Barton as the decoy. Last year when we put you on Sir Barton, you were never in the running in the Hopeful Stakes and finished second to Dunboyne in the Futurity. You'll get your chances, just follow my directions. For now ride the horses I give you."

Sir Barton's win creates controversy over his true character. Critics scoff that the lower weight that Sir Barton carried through the Kentucky Derby mud created his victory, not his speed. Sir Barton and Johnny Loftus put the controversy to bed in the May 14 Pimlico Preakness, beating Schuttinger on Eternal, with each horse carrying equal weight. The Sir Barton victory adds $24,500 to Ross winnings for the year. Sande comes in eighth on Milkmaid but succeeds in carrying out Poteet's instructions to get and keep Sir Barton in the lead. If Sande sees Sir Barton out of the line at the start, his instructions are to break up the general alignment until Sir Barton is in a favorable position. The strategy works and Sir Barton takes an early lead and never relinquishes it.

Two days later, Sande drives Louise V to the front and fends off a late challenge from Quietude to win the fifth race. In the day's final race, Sande guides Thorn Bloom in a late burst to claim another first place. The next afternoon, Sande delivers a solid riding performance on Milkmaid. He keeps Milkmaid under slight restraint in the early stages, staying within striking distance of leader Ophelia. In the last furlong, Sande makes his move and beats the failing Ophelia to the wire, winning the Pimlico Oaks.

Poteet farms out Sande to ride long shots for other stables the rest of the Pimlico racing session. On his lone winner during this stretch, Sande chases Pokey Jane into defeat on board Mlle Dazie.

Loftus and Sande go head to head in the May 22 Belmont Metropolitan Handicap. Lanius, with Loftus up, and Sande on Foreground trail the leaders through most of the race. On the home turn, Loftus takes to the whip and slips into the lead. Urged by Sande, Foreground closes hard but finishes fourth.

At Churchill Downs, Sande continues his string of races for other stables with lower quality mounts. He does bring High Cost from the back of the pack to overtake leader Green Grass for a win. Only two other Louisville wins follow. However, Sande gives his former owner, Joe Goodman, a thrill with a game finish on Bribed Voter for second money.

Not until the last day of racing, on May 31, does Sande get another Ross mount. Eager to prove his worth as a jockey and win back his position as star Ross rider, Sande waits for an opportunity to break through with Milkmaid. Tommy Murray, on Lillian Shaw, employs the same strategy but moves first. Lillian Shaw jumps to the lead and starts drawing away. Milkmaid charges ahead. Delico gets caught in a jam and tumbles to the ground. Murray sets his whip to work and Lillian Shaw edges past Milkmaid for the winner's circle. Race stewards question Sande's actions on the track.

Sande pleads, "I acted in the excitement of seeing an opportunity to win the race and did not plan to interfere with other mounts. It was not intentional, however, I apologize for my actions."

Other jockeys tell their versions of what happened. Sande receives an unprecedented two months suspension.

"The Louisville Courier-Journal" comments, "Jockey Earl Sande established one record during his stay here. He received the longest definite suspension ever given to a rider in Kentucky. Many have been indefinitely suspended and others ruled off, but never before has one been set down for so long a period as sixty days. His work at grabbing Lillian Shaw's bridle was crude, it could be seen with the naked eye from the grandstand."

"I guess there's no need for further debate on who's our top rider, with Sande's suspension putting him on the sidelines, Guy."

"I was leaning toward Loftus anyway, Commander."

An upset and stern Poteet berates Sande. "I don't care what you do out there on the track to win, Earl, just don't get caught. We can't afford to have you sit around the stables while your horses are out there racing."

"That's all right, you have Loftus for the big races."

"Like I said before, you'll get your chance again soon enough, if you earn it back."

Clarence Kummer tells reporters, "Having apprenticed on the outlaw circuit, Sande knows all the tricks of the trade. Without film patrols and only a few judges watching the action, jockeys use whatever they can to gain an edge over other riders. They often swerve their horses in front of another, grab the jockey alongside to prevent them from passing, and lock legs to slow down the other jockey. Sande's the master leg locker by far. His long legs reach out and clamp onto your leg like a hammerhead latching

Johnny Loftus up on Sir Barton. Courtesy Ken Grayson.

onto a nail. There's no getting away from Sande when he's got a mind to stop you."

Sande holds up the next day's newspaper. "Thanks for giving away all of our secrets, Clarence."

Sir Barton continues his dominance of the tracks with an American-record-winning pace of 2:17 2/5 for one and three-eighths miles in the Belmont Withers Stake, beating Eternal again. Following the race, John E. Madden offers to re-purchase Sir Barton for $50,000 as soon as Ross retires him from racing. Commander Ross promptly turns him down.

On June 11, Sir Barton and Johnny Loftus emerge as the first horse racing team in history to win the three top American races -- The Kentucky Derby, The Preakness, and The Belmont -- with a victory over Sweep On and Natural Bridge. Despite a poor start, Sir Barton wins easily, setting an American track record with a time of 2:17 2/5 for a mile and three sixteenths. The horse who did not win a penny in his first six races comes on strong in 1919.

Loftus moans, "Too bad we don't have a triple crown title like they do in England. I won the toughest three races in America and there's no recognition."

"I agree," Sande says. "Even more upsetting, I wasn't up on Sir Barton in those three races as the stable's top rider."

Loftus hurls a towel and hits Sande in the head.

"Hey, is that any way to treat your riding partner?"

With time on his hands, Sande heads for American Falls, where his family is selling the homestead. "The American Falls Press" carries a quarter page ad for the Public Sale of five horses, one pony, nine cows, eight heifers, one young bull calf, one registered Holstein bull, ten shoats, fifty chickens (mostly reds), and machinery including a truck wagon, hay rack, Acme binder, McCormack mower, John Deere rake, Jackson four-tine fork, hay derrick, walking plow, sulky plow, cream separator, four wooden pulleys, steel harrows, and manure spreader belonging to John C. Sande, one of the early farm irrigation pioneers.

"Sure hate to see you sell the farm, Father. You put a lot of hard work into making it a go."

"Time to move on, Son. Oregon's the future now. Besides, we have relatives there."

John Sande sells the farm property to E. D. Colson for $140 an acre. Earl helps pay off the mortgage and assists with the family's move. John Sande takes a job as a yard foreman for the Spalding Mill near Salem. After visiting his family, Earl leaves to resume racing.

A rusty Sande leads Milkmaid to victory August 2, this time in the Saratoga Kenner Stakes. He also pilots War Pennant home for a win, while Johnny Loftus triumphs on Man o' War in the United States Hotel Stakes.

On Sande's next few Saratoga outings, trainer Poteet takes more revenge, placing him on also-rans for other stables. Disheartened, Sande finishes far out of the money with nine mounts. Riding some Ross horses over the next few days, Sande turns in respectable showings with second and third-place finishes. He also wins the Plattsburg Handicap on Assume.

Jockeys across the country vie for new racetrack records. The August 14, 1919, "Denver Post" features a photo of jockey P. Martinez on Art Rick. The Cheyenne jockey nearly makes it into the record books when he brings home five winners in one day, one short of the world record.

Johnny Loftus and Sir Barton. Author's collection.

Poteet taunts Sande, "I see this backwater jockey just missed tying the world record. Maybe he ought to ride for Ross. He could teach you a thing or two, Earl."

"Bet he's not given broken-down nags to ride," Sande replies as he leaves the jockey room.

Not until four days later does Poteet give Sande a top horse to ride. Billy Kelly gets caught in tight quarters. By the time Sande steers him clear and makes a rush for the finish line, it is too late. He comes in a disappointing third. A day later, Sande mounts J. E. Widener's Damaris. He trails the leaders until the final eighth and then wins going away. Poteet saddles Sande on Ross's African Arrow in the Galaway Selling Handicap. African Arrow takes the lead on the backstretch, sets a good pace but tires at the end, barely saving the victory from a fast-charging Tailor Maid.

Several days later, Cudgel starts out slow and runs dead last after making the first turn where he is bumped and thrown off stride. Cudgel keeps gaining on the leaders but is forced to go wide as Exterminator and Sun Briar hug the rail. Cudgel accepts Sande's challenge, and with head down, blows past Sun Briar and wears Exterminator out at the end. Sande delivers a win on Cudgel against Clarence Kummer on Star Master and Johnny Loftus on well-regarded Exterminator.

Sande confides to Loftus. "It's nice to ride a real racehorse again instead of the mules Poteet has been putting me on lately."

"We jockeys don't call him 'Hard Guy' Poteet for nothing."

At Belmont Sande goes too wide on Cudgel and fails to close the gap, coming in third. In the next race, Queen of the Sea snakes through on the rail with Sande's guidance but tires in the final drive to earn a second-place finish. Two days later, Sande regains his form, taking John I. Day to an early lead, widening the gap and winning in a canter. On the next afternoon, Sande gains the winner's circle riding two Ross mounts, Constancy and War Marvel, plus delivers Billy Kelly to a second-place finish behind Naturalist. The following day, Milkmaid comes from behind to win with a spurt to the finish line under Sande's guidance.

Sande re-teams with Billy Kelly for the September 11 opening day at Havre de Grace Race Track. In the Hip Hip Hooray Handicap, Billy Kelly breaks fast and opens daylight. Sir Barton recovers and takes the lead on the rail. In the closing strides, Sande lifts Billy Kelly to the forefront and the win. Sande also places first on Pilsen during the day's outings. The following day Sande drives Bathilde across the wire first and finishes third on 10 to 1 Wisest Fool. Commander Ross's steeds make a clean sweep in the Potomac Handicap at Havre de Grace the following day with Sir Barton, Billy Kelly, and Milkmaid taking first, second, and third, respectively. In addition, Ross's Constancy defeats a field of two-year-olds at six furlongs. Johnny Loftus takes first place at Aqueduct on majestic Man o' War.

The next day, Sande wins handily on Boniface and takes second place on both Billy Kelly and N. K. Beal. Meanwhile, Loftus and Man o' War win the Belmont Futurity Classic easily.

Sande mounts favored Cudgel at Havre de Grace but turns in a disappointing showing of third place. Cudgel trails throughout most of the race, and when Sande calls on him to make his move, the horse fails to respond with his usual speed.

"I tried to get him to take over the race. He just didn't have it today," Sande explains to Poteet.

"Maybe you didn't have it today, Earl."

"The Thoroughbred Record" describes the race. "There was an eclipse of a star in the thoroughbred firmament at Havre de Grace when Midnight Sun crossed the path of Cudgel, the J. K. L. Ross constellation, and dimmed his light with dazzling speed. The eclipse was complete; also sudden and surprising....Cudgel was last to be off....He was not the Cudgel that is always coming at the end with his head down and with long swinging strides. He seemed to be going with his head in the air and looking skyward.... Those who had been watching Cudgel and expecting him to come on with that belated stretch run realized he was not going to show anything."

Sande rebounds with a superb race to win the September 16 Havre de Grace Highweight Handicap. Despite carrying 133 pounds, Billy Kelly charges to the forefront, once released by Sande, and wins by a length going away over Leochares. Johnny Loftus finishes fifth on Startling.

Still intent on getting the most out of his jockeys and keeping them under his control, Poteet schedules Sande for all seven races at Havre De Grace on September 17.

"I'll show Hard Guy Poteet who can race," Sande confides to Loftus.

The first race of the day features a five-furlong race for maiden youngsters. Rapid Traveler, piloted by Johnny Loftus, fails to get a quick break away from the barrier and loses the race to Flying Welchman. Sande comes in a distant sixth on Runnyean.

Loftus sidles up to Sande as he dismounts and whispers, "So much for your showing Poteet who's the star jockey."

"The day's not over yet."

That's when Sande starts his coup de grace at Havre de Grace. In the second race, Sande comes from fourth on 8 to 1 El Mahdi to beat out the tiring General; in the third race of the day, Sande guides Wodan to the victory circle; in the fourth, it's Sande winning the Parkway Purse on African Arrow, after passing three horses down the stretch.

The crowd cheers wildly as Sande approaches the barrier for the fifth race Bouquet Handicap on Milkmaid burdened with 125 pounds. A slow start puts Milkmaid in third place, but Sande holds the horse under slight restraint until the final turn. He then releases Milkmaid, who claims first by a nose. After the fans quit screaming wildly, they clamor to the betting windows to place bets on Sande for the next race.

"Sande in the sixth, Sande in the sixth," runs through the grandstand and at the betting windows.

Sande takes the early lead in the sixth race on Sunny Hill. He drops back and lets Schuttinger, on Jack Mount, set the pace. Down the homestretch, Sande bends low over Sunny Hill's head and massages the horse's cheeks. As if one, the fans rise from their seats and scream at the top of their lungs,

Havre de Grace September 17, 1919, first race card. Courtesy Susquehanna Lock Museum.

"Go Sande!" Sunny Hill pulls next to Jack Mount and then moves ahead to beat him to the wire. Fans again race to the betting windows to place another wager on Sande and obtain souvenirs tickets should Sande succeed in winning six races in a row.

Runyon yells across the press box, "Hang on to your hats, boys. You're about to experience racing history. If Sande wins this one, he ties the world's record with six straight wins."

In the seventh race, Sande paces Bathilde in third place. On the backstretch, he takes over second from Milbrace despite efforts from Musgrave to keep his mount in the race. On the homestretch, Bathilde heads Kirstie's Cub and sends the fans into pandemonium. Hats fly into the air and race fans hug each other as Sande wins his sixth race of the day. Track reporters frantically place telephone calls to report their lead stories as fans overwhelm security and rush on to the track and surround Sande.

Sande earns recognition as the fifth American jockey to win six out of seven races, and the fourth in the world to pilot home six winners, in a row in one day. Colored jockey Jimmie Lee set the mark on June 5, 1907,

Havre de Grace September 17, 1919, second, third, and fourth race cards. Courtesy Susquehanna Lock Museum

TRAIN SERVICE
DIRECT TO COURSE

PENNSYLVANIA RAILROAD

Leaves Philadelphia, Broad Street, at 12.54 P. M.; West Philadelphia, 12.38 P. M.; Chester, 12.56 P. M. and Wilmington, 1.19 P. M.

Leaves Baltimore, by Pennsylvania Railroad, at 12.30 P. M. and 1.05 P. M.

Leaves Washington, by Pennsylvania, 12 o'clock noon. Special train direct to course.

Music Program
BAYSIDE CORNET BAND
CHARLES MYNAR, Director

MARCH—"The Lambs".....................Sousa
SELECTION—"So Long, Letty".............Carroll
WALTZ—"Humorous Humoresque".........Roberts
BARCAROLE...........................Offenbach
OVERTURE—"Stradella"..................Flotow
ONE-STEP—"Dreaming of Home"..........Hanley
WALTZ—"I'm Forever Blowing Bubbles"....Kolette
"Maryland."

SIXTH RACE

Claiming. For Three-Year-Olds and Upward. Non-winners Twice Since July 1, 1919. Purse $1,065.21, of which $200 to the second horse and $100 to the third. Weights: Three-year-olds, 108 lbs.; others, 114 lbs. Non-winners of three races in 1919 allowed 4 lbs. Horses to be entered for $800.

One Mile and a Sixteenth

POST TIME 5.10 P. M.

Mutuel Ticket No.	Owner		Trainer
	W. J. Press		G. B. Cochran
	Blue, Gold Sash and Stripes on Sleeves, Gold		
8801	1 HUBBUB	110	
	M. F. Foley		J. Carroll
	Orange and Black, Thistle Green Sleeves and Cap		
8802	2 JACK MOUNT	110	
	G. B. Miller		
	Red, White and Black		
	3 SUNNY HILL	110	
8809	4 KATIE CANAL	107	
	Winona Point Stable	W. M. Sheedy	
	Blue, Large White Star Front and Back, White Cap		
8803	5 HONG KONG	104	
	F. Musante		
	Brown and Purple Stripes, Purple and Yellow Striped Sleeves, Yellow Cap		
	6 JOAN OF ARC	101	
	B. Chapman		
	Green, Red Bars on Sleeve, White "C" on Back, Red Cap		
8806	7 BOGART	*109	
	Lawrence	W. Short	
	White, Green Swastika Front and Back, Green Cap		
8804	8 SCOTCH VERDICT	*99	
	G. W. Foreman	William Short	
	Blue and White Blocks, White Sleeves and Cap		
8805	9 PUTS AND CALLS	*105	
	G. W. Foreman	W. Short	
	Blue and White Blocks, White Sleeves and Cap		
8805	10 CORA	110	
	E. G. Vivell	A. H. Vivell	
	Cherry, Old Gold Sash, Old Gold Hoops on Sleeves, Old Gold Cap		
8807	11 ARBITRATOR	110	
	J. L. Donahay	C. K. Moore	
	Royal Purple, White Collar, Sleeves and Cap		
8808	12 BEAUTY SLEEP	101	
8805	† G. W. Foreman Entry		

* Apprentice allowance of 5 lbs. each claimed for Bogart, Scotch Verdict and Puts and Calls.

Mistakes must be rectified before Race at Pari-Mutuel Office.

SEVENTH RACE

Claiming. For Three-Year-Olds and Upward. Purse $1,065.20, of which $200 to the second horse and $100 to the third. Weights: Three-year-olds, 110 lbs.; others, 115 lbs. Non-winners of two races since July 30, 1919, allowed 3 lbs.; twice since June 1 allowed 5 lbs. Horses to be entered for $500.

One Mile and a Sixteenth

POST TIME 5.40 P. M.

Mutuel Ticket No.	Owner		Trainer
	G. W. Griffin		Owner
	Black, Red Belt and Sleeves, Red Black		
8812	1 BATHILDE	112	
	William Walker	Helen O'C.	
	Cerise, Orange Blocks on Sleeves, Orange Cap		
8813	2 DON DODGE	110	
	E. Sietas		
	Blue, Orange Sleeves, Black Hoops on Sleeves, Blue Cap		
8810	3 MILLRACE	107	
	Samuel Louis	W. A. Burttschell	
	Red, Blue Stars, Red Cap		
8819	4 FRANK SHANNON	105	
	H. Dernham	J. Arthur	
	Green, White Sash, Brown and Green Striped		
	5 COMANCHE	*105	
	F. McGinty	W. Hickman	
	Orange, Green Hoops on Sleeves, Green Block on Back, Green Cap		
8818	6 PLANTEREDE	105	
	O. Chaney	J. Dale	
	La Polena		
8819	7 KIRSTIE'S CUB	110	
	James Arthur	Owner	
	Green, White Sash, Green and White Cap		
8814	8 EDITH BAUMANN	*102	
	F. Polk	Owner	
	Blue, Yellow Stars, Yellow Sleeves, Red Cap		
8819	9 HIGH OLYMPUS	*105	
	Robert Goodloe	F. Harrington	
	Cerise and Green Stripes, Gold Sleeves and Cap		
8819	10 DIADI	*105	
	M. Smith		
	Navy Blue, Old Gold Cross Sashes, Cerise Cap		
8819	11 CAPITAL CITY	110	
	L. Loughlin	Owner	
	Burnt Orange, Burnt Orange Stripes on Purple Stripes, Purple "B" Front and Back		
8819	12 COL. HARRISON	110	
	W. C. Westmoreland	C. H. Sprague	
	Yellow, White Sleeves, Red Sash, Yellow Cap		
8816	13 TRANBY (Imp)	110	
	Bay 5, Irish Lad—Priestle		
	M. E. Thompson	F. McCollum	
8817	14 FREEMANTLE	110	
	Blue, Gold Sash, Brown Sleeves, Brown and Gold Cap		
	B. L. Smith	B. B. Rice	
8815	15 GRASMERE	110	
	T. H. Wilson	W. B. Wilson	
	Green and Old Gold Stripes, Black Sleeves, Red Cap		
8811	16 GOLDVALE	*97	

ALSO ELIGIBLE TO START

	C. W. Gasser	Owner	
	White, Green Hoop and Sleeves, White Cap		
8819	17 KEZIAH	107	
	F. Musante		
	Brown and Purple Stripes, Purple and Yellow Striped Sleeves, Yellow Cap		
8819	18 JOAN OF ARC	102	
	FIELD		

* Apprentice allowance of 5 lbs. each claimed for Comanche, Edith Baumann, High Olympus, Diadi and Goldvale.

When Bell Rings in Mutuel Building, Machines Will Be Closed

FIFTH RACE

THE BOUQUET HANDICAP

Handicap for Fillies and Mares Three Years Old and Upward. By subscription of $5 each to the winner for horses declared by 10.30 A. M. on Tuesday, September 16, with $2,555.21 added, of which $400 to the second horse, $200 to the third and $100 to the fourth. Closed with 7 nominations, of which 1 declared.

One Mile and Seventy Yards.

POST TIME 4.40 P. M.

Mutuel Ticket No.	Owner		Trainer
	Com. J. K. L. Ross		
	Black, Orange Hoops, Orange Sleeves and Cap		
8790 8795	1 MILKMAID	126	
	B.f. 3, Peep o' Day—Nell Odin		
	Seagram Stable	J. Brinsley	
	Black, Yellow Sash		
8793	2 BELLE MAHONE	113	
	B.m. 6, Ypsilanti 2nd—Irish Lass 2nd		
	A. B. Morris	R. J. Walden	
	All Scarlet		
8791	3 QUIETUDE	109	
	Br.f. 4, Pailhouse—Tabulator		
	A. B. Morris	R. J. Walden	
	All Scarlet		
8791	4 IRENE	106	
	B.f. 4, Trap Rock—Bouncer		
	Mrs. R. L. Miller	W. Short	
	Cerise, Green Cross Sashes, Green Bars on Sleeves, Cerise Cap		
8792	5 DUCHESS LACE	*103	
	Br.f. 3, Fair Play—Dragnet		
	Ogden Stable	S. M. Henderson	
	White, Black Hoop, Black Hoops on Sleeves, Black and White Cap		
8794	6 MADGE F.	103	
	B.f. 3, Voorhaus—Salvatrix		
	8791	† A. B. Morris Entry		

* Apprentice allowance of 5 lbs. claimed for Duchess Lace.

TICKET NUMBER

Be sure that the number on your Mutuel ticket corresponds with the Mutuel number opposite the horse's name on the program. In the event of an extra ticket being necessary, the number will be posted.

Havre de Grace September 17, 1919, fifth, sixth, and seventh race cards. Courtesy Susquehanna Lock Museum

at Churchill Downs, and Herman Phillips tied the record on July 5, 1916, at Reno, Nevada. In their six wins, each swept the card. Other American jockeys with six winners in one afternoon include colored jockey Monk Overton at Washington Park, Chicago, on July 10, 1891, and Clarence Turner with nine straight wins in Charleston, South Carolina, three on one day and six the following day, April 9, 1912 -- before losing the last race of the day.

"The Baltimore Sun" headline proclaims, "Equals Riding Record, Earl Sande Pilots Six Winners in Row at Havre de Grace." The writer comments, "The beautiful part of Sande's exhibition is that he did not have a mount that went to the front and remained there. He used some great pace judgment and easily deserved all the honors that were thrust upon him."

"The Denver Post" declares, "Ross Jockey is on Six Winners: A parlay of $2 on El Mahdi, Wodan, African Arrow, Milkmaid, Sunny Hill, and Bathilde ridden by Sande would have netted the player about $2,200."

"The Louisville-Courier," which had roundly criticized Sande months earlier for his riding in the Kentucky Oaks, poured on praise. "While Gen. John Pershing was marching up Pennsylvania Avenue in Washington, at the head of a division of the victorious army, jockey Earl Sande, Commander Ross's rider, was riding to triumph in the racing world at Havre de Grace. Sande achieved a feat today that has not been equaled in many years, when he rode six straight winners, the last six on the programme of seven races."

Back in the jockeys' room, Johnny Loftus concedes. "Guess I spoke too soon, Earl. Congratulations to a great jockey. One of the best."

"Thanks, that means a lot coming from you, Johnny."

Over the next few weeks at Havre de Grace, Sande exhibits a dazzling display of horsemanship, bringing home seven first-place finishes, ten second-place finishes, and four third-place finishes.

In a number of these races, Sande competes against an up-and-coming jockey, Phil Musgrave. Andy Schuttinger wins the first September 26 race with Musgrave coming in second. Schuttinger gains second place in the third race, and wins the Picadilly Purse in the fifth race, with Musgrave taking third. During the running of the sixth and next-to-last race, a pack of horses race along the backstretch. Schuttinger's mount, Dolina, crosses her legs and hits the turf while running well up in the field. Silk Bird, with Musgrave up, Artist, ridden by Bernard, and Cain Spring, with Obert in the saddle, tumble over the downed Dolina. One of the flying hoofs strikes

Musgrave in the head. Despite doctors' valiant efforts for forty-five minutes, Musgrave dies of his injuries in the infield. Schuttinger suffers a broken leg and severe bruising as Dolina rolls over him. Cain Spring's leg is broken, and track officials destroy the horse.

"Lost another good man today," Sande bemoans.

In October, Sande continues his fine riding at Laurel, Maryland, placing first on Billy Kelly and Orestes and scoring two second-place finishes and two third-place finishes. Laverne Fator wins the Latonia Championship, taking Sam Hildreth's Mad Hatter ahead of the field on a muddy track.

On November 1 at Pimlico, Poteet assigns Johnny Loftus to ride Billy Kelly and puts Earl Sande on Constancy. In the first race of the day, Sande brings Donnaconna home a winner in a field of ten. In the fourth race, Sande boots Constancy into a flying start on a muddy track and maintains a two-length lead until Billy Kelly comes on strong in the homestretch and wins with a final surge across the wire, ahead of Constancy. Sande closes out the day in the seventh and final race with a win of the Arlington Purse on Boniface over Clarence Kummer riding Fairy Wand. Sande ends the 1919 Pimlico season with nine first-place, four second-place, and two third-place finishes.

Commander Ross again shuffles his jockeys and hires Clarence Kummer to ride Sir Barton in the Pimlico Fall Serial Weight-for-Age Race No. 2. Sir Barton takes the lead and goes to the rail on the first turn. In the backstretch, Laverne Fator spurs Lucullite to within a nose of Sir Barton, but quickly fades after the far turn. It's Porter's turn to make a run at Sir Barton and pull ahead for a brief period, until Kummer urges Sir Barton to shoot ahead, claiming victory. Sande, on Billy Kelly, never poses a threat.

Sir Barton, Billy Kelly, and Lucullite rematch again on November 11 with the same results. Kummer, on Sir Barton, paces the field of three, winning with ease. Commander Ross's strategy of bringing Clarence Kummer on board pays off with Sir Barton wins.

Commander Ross repeats as top winning owner in 1919, with $209,303 in purses. Sir Barton, with $88,250, leads all three-year-olds. Ross's jockeys also gain top honors. Placing first in big stakes races, and on 37 percent of his mounts, ranks Johnny Loftus as the leading money-winning jockey with $252,707 even though he only crossed the finish line first sixty-five times. Earl Sande's $126,042 ranks considerably lower, obviously hampered by his two-month suspension. He completes the year winning 23 percent of the time and landing in the money more than 59 percent of the time.

Idaho jockey Laverne Fator's first year in big time racing ranks him third in national standings, with 129 first places and purses of $213,051. During 1919, Fator moves from the racetracks in Havana, Cuba, to American tracks, and fans take notice. So do racehorse owners. Trainer Sam Hildreth pays Laverne Fator $15,000 to sign a contract with Harry F. Sinclair's Rancocas Stables for the 1920 racing season.

Top 1919 Jockey Standings							
Jockey	Mounts	1st	2nd	3rd	%	$Winnings	In Money %
Robinson, C.	896	190	145	126	.21	$201,282	.515
Murray, T.	832	157	103	109	.19	140,562	.444
Fator, L.	606	129	105	83	.21	213,051	.523
Lunsford, H.	639	100	84	80	.16	96,384	.496
Thurber, H.	722	85	110	88	.10	107,098	.391
Kummer, C.	399	82	59	61	.21	137,809	.506
Sande, E.	346	80	67	58	.23	126,042	.592

Top 1919 Jockey Standings by Percentage Wins (100 or more mounts)			
Jockey	Mounts	Won	Percent
Loftus, Johnny	177	65	.37
Sande, Earl	346	80	.23
Fairbrother, C.	172	39	.23
Schuttinger, A.	220	49	.22
Fator, L.	606	129	.21
Kummer, C.	399	82	.21
Robinson, L	896	190	.21

"The Thoroughbred Record" carries an article on Commander Ross's jockeys. "The four jockeys that will come to Havre de Grace track in the first week of April with the forty odd thoroughbreds of various ages and kinds that will prepare here for racing in the East, in Canada and in Kentucky under the silks of Commander J. K. L. Ross of Montreal, are Sande, Nolan, Wessler, and Veitch. They are at the Ross farms in Howard County, Maryland, helping H. G. Poteet get the Ross thoroughbreds ready by shed exercise for real training in the open and they are already in condition for riding. Sande will be the star rider of the stable and Sande's conduct over winter might well have been emulated by every other jockey in the United States. Sande has not missed a day. He lives at the Ross farms, exercises his own division of the string and never goes to town without permission."

Commander Ross assesses the prospects for 1920. "I have a lot of faith in our stable of horses, my trainer Guy Poteet, and top jockeys like Sande. We look forward to another great year in 1920."

Neither the article nor Commander Ross mention Johnny Loftus or Clarence Kummer, nor the use of these jockeys in place of Sande in key races during 1919. Because of an infraction of The Jockey Club rules, Johnny Loftus is denied a 1920 license to race. Faced with that reality, Commander Ross and Guy Poteet are forced to reinstate Sande as the leading stable jockey.

Determined to recapture his status as star Ross jockey, Sande launches the 1920 season with three great rides. Although a train strike cancels special train runs to Havre de Grace on April 16 opening day, the fans who make it to The Graw enjoy a day of exciting races. Commander Ross's horses win three of the feature events. In the Toggery Purse, Milkmaid, with Sande aboard, breaks slowly and gets boxed out along the inside. He guides Milkmaid to the outside and handily passes the interference. Fruit Cake uses up energy breaking away from Constancy, and Sande easily passes both, beating Fruit Cake by a length. The win puts $1,167 into the Ross coffers.

"Milkmaid is a great horse, game as they come. Despite being squeezed out early, we went wide and made up much lost ground. Once Milkmaid got within striking distance of the leaders, she ran them down and came away a winner," Sande says.

In Sande's second outing of the day in the five-and-a-half furlong Chester Purse, King Thrush goes to an early lead and builds it up to four lengths. Sande wins easily as he crosses the winning line with King Thrush under restraint. The race adds another $1,017 to Ross winnings for the day, with King Thrush taking first and his stablemate, Irish Dancer, coming in third.

Sande scores a hat trick with a win in his third outing of the day in the six-furlong Harford Handicap. Billy Kelly jumps to the front and never relinquishes any ground. However, a hard-charging Star Master gives the crowd a thrill as he pulls within striking distance down the stretch. Billy Kelly adds a purse of $3,850 to the Ross winnings. In total, Ross gathers in

$6,234 on opening day with the addition of $200 won by Intrigante in the maiden two-year-old race.

Ross's good fortune on opening day does not carry through to the next day. In the first race, Ross's two-year-old Donegan, with Sande up, gets cut down so badly that the horse, for which Ross paid $7,100, probably will never race again. In the six-furlong Aero Purse, Ross's Motor Cop, ridden by Sande, goes lame and gets beaten by Pickwick, while War Pennant finishes third. In the Edgewood Purse, Sande on Boniface brings a brief respite in the run of bad luck with a victory over Bullet Proof on a muddy track. In the Classic Handicap, Blazes, wearing the Ral Parr silks, beats a field of five, including two Ross horses. Faisan Dore, with Sande up, finishes second, and His Choice trails last with Kummer in the saddle. Finishing the day, Sande comes in third on Welshman's Folly.

Things look a little better in the Belair Handicap. Billy Kelly, carrying 132 pounds, sets a great pace at the outset of the race and beats War Mask by a length and a quarter. Sir Barton, with Clarence Kummer up, gives a game race but tires down the stretch, coming in fourth.

For the remainder of April at Havre de Grace Sande delivers first-place finishes on Boniface in the Delaware Handicap and in the Melbourne Handicap, Damrosch in the Perryville Purse, Foreground in the Pennsylvania Purse and another race, King Thrush in the Princeton Purse, Star Voter in the Advocate Purse, and War Pennant in the Fort McHenry Purse. He also scores four second-place finishes, one with Billy Kelly, and four third-place finishes, including mounts on Billy Kelly and Sir Barton.

Moving to Pimlico races, Sande raises the stature of Boniface by winning the May 1 Merchants Handicap. Three days later, Sande notches two big wins for Commander Ross. Intrigante establishes a large lead he never relinquishes, and Sir Barton forces a fast pace before taking the lead in the stretch turn. The next day Sande and Boniface enter the mile-and-a-sixteenth Pimlico Spring Handicap. Boniface rounds the far turn accelerating. He passes Star Master, with Clarence Kummer up, in the last eighth and wins his fifth consecutive race easing up at the wire.

On May 6, Sande drives home King Thrush in a mile-long sixth race, winning easily. The next day Sande delivers two mounts in the money out of three races, with a first-place victory on King Herod in The Pikesville Handicap. Other notable early Pimlico May wins include first-place finishes on Assyrian Queen, Little Nearer, and Thorny Way, and second-place finishes on Boniface in the Belvidere Handicap, and Billy Kelly in the Equity Handicap.

Commander Ross lowers his binoculars and says, "None of the three-year-olds are performing up to the standards of a Kentucky Derby horse, Guy."

"No, sir. We'll have to pass the Run for the Roses in Louisville this year, Commander."

Sande and five-year-old Boniface team up again for the May 15 Churchill Downs Clark Handicap. Boniface enters a heavy favorite, having won five of his first six 1920 starts. He and Sande don't disappoint the fans. After a long delay at the post, Boniface shoots to the front and presses his lead to six lengths in winning a purse of $7,500. Two days later at Pimlico, Sande takes Jeg to the inside and slips through to gain the lead and win going away.

In the May 18 Preakness, Sam Riddle's Man o' War breaks to an early lead from the outside, while Sande, on Ross's King Thrush, gives chase. King Thrush mounts a brief challenge to the leader but quickly fades, ending seventh. Poteet saddles Sande on Jacobina for his next victory, over a week later.

Ross brings excitement and talent to Toronto's Woodbine starting May 27. Sande keeps Baby Grand under restraint throughout the second race and still wins easily.

In the fifth race, Sande on Boniface gets crowded out early, is forced to go wide late, and delivers Ross another purse, despite giving up a hefty nineteen pounds to the next competitor.

Back in the States, Poteet opens the Belmont meeting with Sande on His Choice, who easily outgames Gloria France for the victory. In the third race, Sande on Damrosch chases down leader Sunflash II in the stretch but doesn't have enough to finish the task, coming in second.

Poteet enters Sande on Milkmaid in the June 3 Ladies Handicap against W. R. Coe's Cleopatra, with McAtee up, coming off a victory at the Pimlico Oak. Sande settles down a restless Milkmaid at the barrier after several false starts. Milkmaid and Lady Gertrude break together with Cleopatra two lengths back. On the far turn, Milkmaid pulls ahead. Cleopatra passes Lady Gertrude and challenges the Ross horse. Jockey McAtee whips Cleopatra, while Sande gives Milkmaid a light lash or two and lets the horse do the rest. Milkmaid wins by a length.

Ral Parr's Paul Jones enters the June 5 Belmont Suburban Handicap, having recently won the Kentucky Derby. Sande challenges on Boniface in a field of five that also includes the 1918 Kentucky Derby winner, Exterminator. Foul weather causes owners to scratch Donnaconna and several other horses. Torrents of rain and a muddy track do not dampen the spirits of the crowd.

Paul Jones takes the lead at the outset, followed close behind by Thunderclap and Exterminator. By the first turn, Upset noses in near the rail and Exterminator drops back. In the stretch, Exterminator makes his move and edges out Upset. On the outside, Boniface displays a burst of speed and passes both Upset and Exterminator and sets his sight on a tiring Paul Jones. Boniface gains ground with every stride. Schuttinger responds by laying the whip on Paul Jones's hide and wins by half a length over Boniface.

"The American Falls Press" claims, "Leading Jockey of U.S. Is Our Own Earl Sande." In the article, retired fighter and sportswriter James J. Corbett declares, "Sande is the best in the field. Sande's jockeyship has almost been as responsible for many of the victories of Billy Kelly, King Thrush, Sir Barton, Milkmaid, and the other Ross horses as have the horses themselves."

Sande turns in three good June 14 Jamaica performances, coming in second on Sacajewea in a competition for two-year-old fillies, first on Boniface in the Excelsior Handicap, and third on Lion d'Or in the Richmond Highweight Handicap. Fifteen thousand people see Sande and Boniface establish a new track record of 1:45 1/5 while winning the $6,000 Excelsior Handicap purse.

Milkmaid sinks under a load of 130 pounds in the Aqueduct Gazelle Handicap, with Sande bringing the filly in second, behind Laverne Fator on Pen Rose. The next day Sande takes 7 to 1 Sundial II to the finish line first, while placing third on both Rockland and Flibbertygibbet.

Commander Ross ships Sande and Star Voter to Latonia Race Course for the July 3 running of the Cincinnati Trophy Race. A hard rain before the race creates a quagmire much to the liking of Ross's Star Voter. Sande gets Star Voter off to a good start and increases his lead over the field of eighteen without any trouble. Star Voter crosses the finish line under restraint and five lengths ahead of Black Servant. Ross picks up winnings in excess of $8,000, the largest Cincinnati Trophy purse in Latonia's history.

"The New York Observer Herald" writes, "Jockey Sande, who has come to Latonia to ride Star Voter and other of the Ross horses that will campaign in the next few days, sent his mount to the front with the break and, after opening up a gap of two lengths, was never in danger."

Back at Aqueduct, Sande mounts Billy Kelly for the horse's first race since opening day of the local season. Carrying a top weight of 136 pounds in the Highweight Handicap, Billy Kelly gains the lead at the head of the stretch and holds on to win by a neck against a game Fruit Cake from the A. K. Macomber Stable.

Other July Aqueduct Sande triumphs come few and far between, with a first-place finish on Lion d'Or, two second-place, and three third-place finishes. Especially frustrating were third-place finishes on Billy Kelly in the Iroquois Handicap, Boniface in the Empire City Handicap, and thirteen out-of-the-money races.

Meanwhile, Commander Ross fumes as he watches Man o' War win race after race and set track and world records. He itches to reclaim some of the racing spotlight that has shifted from his stable to Man o' War and Sam Riddle.

Sande once again mounts Sir Barton in the August 2 opening day Saratoga Handicap against Exterminator and three other contenders. The field breaks nearly even, then Sande urges Sir Barton to take a lead, which he never relinquishes while establishing a new track record of 2:01 1/5 and winning by three lengths over Exterminator. Commander Ross picks up another $5,200 to his stable's winnings from the race. Sande boots home three winners the next day with another impressive victory by Lion d'Or and wins by Rockland and Dinna Care.

Commander Ross's turf winnings total nearly $500,000 since his stable's debut on the racing circuit in 1917. Ross earned more than $209,800 in 1919 and $151,483 in 1920 through early August. Man o' War's earnings also draw race fan attention. The horse earned $117,590 to date in his racing career. Sam Riddle's Man o' War looks to add another $4,700 to that total in the August 7 Miller Stakes at Saratoga. Earl Sande gets his first and only chance to ride Man o' War as the result of a broken shoulder suffered at Aqueduct by Riddle jockey Clarence Kummer.

Riddle cautions Sande, "Don't let Big Red out more than necessary to win the race by a comfortable margin."

Sande mounts Man o' War for the Miller Stakes in front of 35,000 cheering Saratoga race fans. Man o' War breaks into the lead immediately, and for all practical purposes, the race is over. With masterly handling of Man

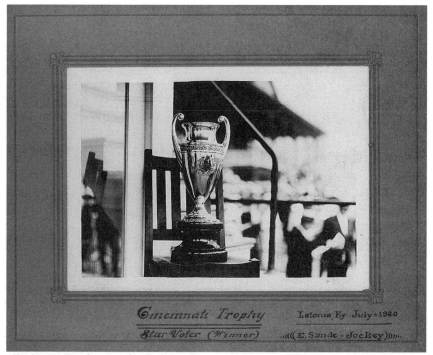

Cincinnati Trophy

Star Voter (Winner)

Latonia Ky. July–1920

(((E. Sande – Jockey)))

Cincinnati Trophy won by Earl Sande on Star Voter at Latonia in 1920. Courtesy Sande Tomlinson Collection.

o' War, Sande makes the exercise look like a real race and still wins easily by six lengths.

"The most powerful horse I've ever ridden. He has a flawless stride. Man o' War won by five or six lengths and he never extended himself. Wish you would have let me give him free rein, Mr. Riddle. We would have set a track record today."

In other Saratoga racing action, Sande brings Nightstick home a winner, comes in fourth on Registrar in the $10,000 United States Hotel Stakes, and finishes eleventh out of thirteen on Servitor. On August 10, Boniface earns the moniker "Iron Horse of the Ross Stable" as Sande and Boniface easily win the Delaware Handicap and a $2,000 purse by defeating J. E. Widener's odds-on favorite, Naturalist, on a muddy track.

Commander Ross and Guy Poteet ship Sir Barton to Fort Erie in Ontario, Canada, to compete in the $10,000 Dominion Handicap run at a mile and a quarter. Sande gets the nod to ride Sir Barton. Carrying 134 pounds, Sir Barton takes the lead early and hugs the rail throughout. Bondage makes

Saratoga 1920.   Man O' War   (start)

Earl Sande winning the Miller Stakes on Man o' War. Author's collection.

his move on the far turn, gaining on Sir Barton with every stride. Despite Bondage's effort, Sande hand rides Sir Barton to another victory.

Back at Saratoga, Milkmaid, with Sande up, breaks badly and trails the field in the August 13 Salem Handicap. Despite conceding much weight to the field, the horse steadily gains on the pack and wins going away. In the Hudson Handicap, Sande and Donnaconna race neck and neck with Dinna Care throughout the backstretch but lose ground on the homestretch, finishing second.

In the sixth and final race of the day, Sande rides Intrigante, a heavily played favorite in the field of twelve. As the horses approach the turnout of the backstretch, Sande senses trouble as several horses bear down on him. They bump his mount and she stumbles, hurtling Sande into the air. He lands close to the rail, allowing the riders behind to swing out and miss running over the downed jockey. The judges claim rough riding the cause of the spill but cannot determine who is at fault, so no action is taken against any of the riders who bumped Sande.

Earl Sande on Man o' War at Saratoga. Courtesy Keeneland-Cook.

"The New York Observer Herald" reports, "Jockey Earl Sande, who is by many regarded as the best rider in the country, had a narrow escape from serious injury if not death."

Sande and Milkmaid team up again on August 20 in Saratoga. This time Milkmaid staves off the challenge of War Marvel and Sennings Park for the victory.

Sande returns to Fort Erie, this time to ride Boniface in the August 18 Edward W. Maginn Memorial Handicap. Boniface concedes sixteen pounds to Midnight Sun and twenty-nine pounds to Kings Champion. Sande keeps Boniface behind Midnight Sun until the homestretch and then releases the horse into a solid lead and crosses the wire easing up.

On the next day at Saratoga, a dry, fast track helps jockey Turner and Yellow Hand establish a new track record for seven furlongs in the third race by beating the previous 1910 record by a fifth of a second. While it took ten years for the record set by Priscillian to be broken, Sande lets the new record stand less than a day before eclipsing Yellow Hand's time by three-fifths of a second on Milkmaid. Sande finishes second on Milkmaid

MILKMAID SANDE UP
WAR MARVEL
SENNINGS PARK
SARATOGA AUGUST 16 1920

Cook
Photo N.Y.

Sande aboard Milkmaid in August 16, 1920, race against War Marvel and Sennings Park. Courtesy Sande Tomlinson Collection

a week later in the Berkshire Handicap and adds two more second-place finishes to close out the day.

Sande and Sir Barton establish a new world record for a mile and three sixteenths at Saratoga in the August 28 Merchants and Citizens' Handicap, despite carrying a heavy weight of 133 pounds. Sir Barton beats Gnome, ridden by Frank Keogh, in a close race with a time of 1:55 3/5, breaking the record set by Commander Ross's Cudgel in 1918 and equaled by Cleopatra several days before.

With both Man o' War and Sir Barton setting world and track records on a regular basis, the racing world clamors for a match race between the two thoroughbreds. Canadian Abram Michael (Abe) Orpen's $75,000 purse and a $5,000 Gold Cup outbids tracks in Chicago, Kentucky, and New York to host the "Race of the Century." Orpen orders the Kenilworth Gold Cup made for the October 12, 1920, one-and-a-quarter-mile match race at Windsor, Ontario's Kenilworth Park. The two owners agree that the match race will be run as a weight-for-age event, with Sir Barton to carry 126 pounds compared to 120 pounds for Man o' War.

Owned by Samuel Riddle and trained by Louis Fuestal, Man o' War achieves a remarkable record of winning nineteen out of twenty races between 1919 and October 1920. Big Red leads all horses in money won in 1920. Johnny Loftus rides Man o' War to victory eight times, but also accounts for Man o' War's only loss, in the 1919 Sanford Stakes, where he finishes second. Man o' War sets records for the mile, 1 1/8 miles, 1 3/8 miles, half mile, and 1 5/8 miles, in Belmont, Dwyer, Lawrence Realization, and Withers stakes races and for purses won.

Riddle's Clarence Kummer rides Man o' War to victory in eight outings, including prestigious races such as the Belmont, Dwyer, Jockey Club Gold Cup, Preakness, and Withers. Kummer leads all jockeys in the amount of money won in 1920, with more than $290,000. Riddle keeps Man o' War from entering the Kentucky Derby because he feels the race comes too early to ask a three-year-old to carry weight over a mile and a quarter. This decision probably costs Man o' War the distinction of being the second horse to win America's top three races.

A lot of controversy surrounds the period leading up to the race. Samuel Riddle hires twenty-four armed guards to prevent his horse from being drugged by gamblers trying to affect the outcome of the race. Rumors spread that Sir Barton is training poorly and that his notorious tender feet will not fare well on Kenilworth's cement hard turf.

To discount the rumors about Sir Barton's condition, Poteet responds, "Sir Barton is doing all I have asked him in his work for the race. He is ready to run as fast as he has in the past and I look for him to render a brilliant account of himself. I make no predictions, but I believe Sir Barton will not disgrace himself in the most pretentious effort of his successful turf career."

"The New York Observer Herald" reports, "Both Man o' War and Sir Barton are to be ridden by capable riders. Clarence Kummer, who has had the mount on the Riddle colt in nearly all of his races this season, will again ride the three-year-old champion. Earl Sande, who is the stable jockey for Commander Ross and one of the best riders in America will, of course, ride Sir Barton."

However, behind the scenes Commander Ross and Guy Poteet discuss Earl Sande and Sir Barton. Sande's position as the lead jockey for the Ross stables, his brilliant world-record-setting ride on Sir Barton, an astonishing fourteen stakes wins, and 102 first place finishes in 355 trips to the post in 1920 speak well for Sande's qualifications to ride Sir Barton in the match race.

Commander Ross announces to the press, "Sande will be my jockey."

Sir Barton and Sande prepare for the big race at Ross's Laurel, Maryland, stable. Five days before the race, Sande takes Sir Barton for his final trial run before being shipped to Canada. Loaded with 126 pounds, Sir Barton cruises through the mile-and-a-quarter test. Newspaper reporters write that Sir Barton turned in a decent time but did not appear as sharp as in recent races. Poteet and Sir Barton head for Ontario while Sande plans to join them on October 10 after he completes scheduled races.

Poteet works Sir Barton with Carroll Shilling in the saddle. Schilling holds Sir Barton hard all the way. Sir Barton completes an excellent run and emerges in fine shape.

Commander Ross exhibits his faith in Sir Barton. "I know Riddle considers Man o' War invincible, and he has certainly proven himself worthy on the track these past two years. On the other hand, Sir Barton is a fine horse in his own right and worthy of the challenge. He will give Man o' War the race of his life, and with the right conditions we could win this race, Guy."

Under the strain of preparation and dealing with the press, a haggard Poteet responds, "Great workout yesterday, Commander. I guarantee you, Sir Barton will be in his top form. I'm less worried about Sir Barton than I am about Earl. The boy cost us the Eternal/Billy Kelly match two years ago. I don't want to repeat that scenario. That's why I arranged for Frankie Keogh as a backup in case Sande can't ride. Keogh reported to the track officials and is listed as an alternate. We can make the switch at any time. I strongly recommend substituting Keogh for Sande."

"But Sande beat Keogh in a big race not long ago," Commander Ross argues.

"Sure, he beat Keogh on Gnome, but Sir Barton was the better horse and Keogh kept pushing Sande and Sir Barton into making record time. I'm telling you the kid's not ready for a race of this scope. He's inconsistent, especially in the big races. Let's go with Keogh, a seasoned veteran having a great comeback year. Don't forget, Sande said Man o' War was the best horse he ever rode. He doesn't deserve to ride in this race."

Commander Ross and Poteet continue their discussion of Sande's riding merits versus those of Keogh late into the night. Poteet always ends his argument with, "He cost us the Billy Kelly/Eternal race."

"Let me sleep on it and see Sande work out with Sir Barton in the morning. This isn't a decision to be made in haste."

Just before Sande readies Sir Barton for a final trial run, Poteet approaches him. "I'd like to have you give Sir Barton his usual workout but don't push him too hard today, Earl. By the way, I talked with the Commander about this race. We think we might go with Frankie Keogh on Sir Barton tomorrow. We brought him in as a backup just in case."

Sande's face turns red. "What do you mean?"

"I mean you may not be ready to run this race, Earl. It's as simple as that."

"You've been riding me hard since I lost that race on Billy Kelly against Eternal. That's two years ago! I've come a long way since then and have earned the right to ride in this race. I've ridden every mule you threw at me and turned many of them into winners. I've ridden Man o' War and know his tendencies. I can keep Sir Barton in this race. I'm the only jockey with the experience to give him a shot at beating Man o' War."

"It's too late, Earl. The decision's as good as made in my book. It's Frankie on this one, if I have anything to say about it. Now, take Sir Barton for his workout. You can stay around if you want, the decision's up to you."

"I'll do the workout and then you can find yourself a new boy. If I don't ride Sir Barton in the match race, I don't ride for the stable."

Poteet slams the tack he holds onto the floor. "It's settled then. I'll tell the Commander to release you."

"No. You tell the Commander I asked to be released."

Commander Ross leans against the rail. He watches as Sande puts Sir Barton through his paces. Guy Poteet approaches and leans close to Ross. "I wouldn't talk to the Sande kid if I were you, Commander. I've never seen him so skittish."

Commander Ross looks at Sande's face and sees a pained look. He turns to Poteet and says, "Guess your right, Guy. Inform the track officials that Keogh will be our boy on Sir Barton."

Commander Ross calls a press conference an hour before the race. "I have determined to substitute Frank C. Keogh for Earl Sande on Sir Barton in today's race for the reason that my boy is not in good form, as his recent performances show. My action is taken without prejudice to Sande, and in making the change I am only exercising my prerogative as owner of Sir Barton. I would rather win this race today than all the other races in which Sir Barton may participate. Keogh is at the top of his form at present, and I want to take advantage of it so there will be no excuse after the race is won or lost. I have the utmost confidence in Sande, but feel I would be doing myself and Sir Barton an injustice if I did not send him to the post with every avenue safeguarded."

Rumors fly that Sande's removal as Sir Barton's jockey for the match race resulted from the ride put up by Sande earlier in the week. Poteet and Commander Ross felt Sande hesitated at a crucial moment, costing Ross the victory. They feared Sande might be too nervous in the big Sir Barton/ Man o' War race and make a critical mistake.

Sande enters the jockey room before the race. Trying to hold back tears, he gives Keogh some last minute pointers on what to expect from Man o' War and Clarence Kummer, and how best to handle Sir Barton at the barrier. "Pace him by using your hands, he responds well to hand riding. Use the whip sparingly, Sir Barton does not react favorably to continual whipping. Good luck out there, Frankie."

"Thanks. A lot of jockeys would have held a grudge against me because I got the mount in this big race. Thanks for your advice, it means a lot to me. You're a real gentleman, Earl."

"You would have done the same for me, Frankie."

The two embrace for a second, and then Keogh leaves Sande alone.

Sportswriter John Day witnesses the heart-breaking scene and captures the poignancy of the moment. "Alone at the top of the jockey room while the race was being run, stood a boy who felt keener pangs of disappointment than could have come to any other at the track."

Thirty-two thousand fans arrive to see the great race between Man o' War and Sir Barton. Famed photographer Edward Muybridge strategically places fourteen cameras around the track to record the race for later showing in movie theaters throughout North America. Poteet instructs Keogh to take Sir Barton to an immediate lead and hold it the length of the race. Sir Barton draws the inside position and jumps off to the lead but after 200 yards Man o' War quickly gains the advantage. Keogh takes to the whip early but Sir Barton does not respond well and seems to shorten his stride.

In his private box, Commander Ross remarks, "Sir Barton's not himself. I think his feet are hurting him, but he certainly is game."

Man o' War easily wins by seven lengths, breaking the track record by six and two-fifths seconds. After the race, Samuel Riddle pours the champagne out of the $5,000 gold trophy cup and refills it with water, which he gives to Man o' War.

Commander Ross congratulates Riddle. "Man o' War, what a marvel. It is strikingly amazing. This performance of Man o' War is absolutely remarkable. Man o' War is really a super-horse."

"The New York Times" comments, "As the race was run, the Canadian Sportsman might just as well have entrusted the ride to Sande."

Sir Barton retires after thirty-one starts, finishing in the money twenty-four times and earning $116,857 for Commander Ross. Ross puts the first horse to win America's top three races out to stud at the end of 1920.

Commander Ross takes the loss to heart. "I'm disappointed in myself that I allowed you to persuade me to change jockeys at the last minute, Guy. More importantly, I'm disappointed that Sir Barton was not in prime condition for the competition. We lost the race, we lost our best jockey, and now it's time for us to part company. I believe we did Sande a real disservice when we switched jockeys at the last minute. Our action was not very sportsmanlike. Under the circumstances, I see the need for a trainer to instill new life and integrity in this organization."

Chapter 8

Riding for Rancocas: America's Top Jockey

"It was a matter of integrity. I had to quit." A dejected Sande returns from Canada in mid-October, unsure about the future of his racing career, having left one of the most prestigious stables in North America.

Poteet tells reporters, "If you ask my opinion, the racing public makes too much of jockeys and too little of trainers, who are primarily responsible for a horse's performance. Sande is a little squarehead who couldn't ride if allowed to use his own judgment. Even so, we cancelled his contract out of fairness to the lad."

When asked about Poteet's comments, Sande replies, "I'll let my riding speak for me."

Clarence Kummer continues his winning ways with a first-place finish on Ten Lec and second place on Prince of Como on October 14. Frankie Keogh returns to the States to race at Laurel, Maryland, the next day, coming in second on Superwoman. Sande misses the $50,000 Latonia Championship and hires out as a freelance rider at Empire City while considering his options. On October 18, Sande rides five mounts for a variety of owners. In his first race after leaving the Ross stable, the Empire City race crowd treats Earl to a royal reception with a standing ovation and rousing cheer. He shows his appreciation by booting home a winner on Berlin. The crowd cheers even louder as he passes the judges' stand. He then places second twice and third twice to close out the day.

Rumors abound as Harry Payne Whitney and a number of other stables offer Sande riding positions. After Commander Ross and Poteet part company, Commander Ross swallows his pride and offers Sande $10,000 if he will remain with his stable until next season. Sande refuses.

Meanwhile, trainer Samuel C. Hildreth works hard to convince his boss, Harry Ford Sinclair, to hire Sande before another stable picks him up. Sinclair started with nothing and amassed a great fortune in oil ventures, while vertically integrating his company from wildcat drilling to refining and marketing. Before World War I, Sinclair's holdings grew to more than $50 million. By 1919, the Sinclair Holding Company net worth exceeds $100 million and operates out of New York offices in the Equitable Building and the eight-story Sinclair Building in Tulsa, Oklahoma.

As a diversion from the business world, Sinclair dabbled in professional baseball, investing $500,000 in the Federal Baseball League. Ever the shrewd businessman, Sinclair obtained the rights to many of the Federal League's baseball stars for his investment. When the Federal League folded, Sinclair sold the players' contracts to recoup his investment and turned his attention to thoroughbred racing.

One day at the tracks, baseball park and racetrack caterer Harry M. Stevens introduced Sinclair to Sam Hildreth. As he often did, Hildreth marked race programs of many friends with potential winners. Hildreth extended the same courtesy to Sinclair. Sinclair accepted and was delighted when five of the six horses that Hildreth picked won. The scene repeated several times over the next few weeks before Sinclair asked Hildreth to meet him for lunch. A race partnership resulted from that meeting.

Sam Hildreth grew up on a farm near Independence, Missouri. His father kept a string of quarter horses he raced on western dirt tracks. The young Hildreth raced as a Parsons, Kansas, jockey until his weight got the better of him. By 1883, he worked as a trainer for $40 per month and moved to the eastern tracks in 1887. Hired by W. C. Whitney in 1898 to train his expensive stable, Hildreth won the 1899 Belmont Stakes with Jean Bereaud.

During one six-month stretch, Hildreth earned more than $250,000 in bets and purses with his own stable of horses. His horse Joe Madden won the 1909 Belmont Stakes. Hildreth headed the list of winning owners in America in 1909, 1910, and 1911. After the legislature closed New York racetracks in 1911, Hildreth took Charles Kohler's horses to race in France. While overseas, Kohler died and Hildreth returned to the United States. His success attracted the attention of August Belmont II, who hired Hildreth as trainer for Belmont's stable, The Nursery Stud. Under Hildreth's tutelage, Belmont's Frair Rock won the 1916 Belmont Stakes and Hourless won the 1917 Belmont Stakes. After leaving Belmont, Hildreth trained his own horses until 1920, when Harry F. Sinclair and Hildreth went into a fifty-fifty partnership on bets and a pool of racehorses.

Sinclair and Hildreth purchase Grey Lag for $69,000 and the horse wins eight consecutive victories. Sinclair convinces Hildreth to jointly purchase the 1,244-acre Rancocas Farm developed by Pierre Lorillard near Jobstown, New Jersey. Sinclair uses his unlimited funds to refurbish Rancocas, rebuild the six-furlong track, add a three-furlong track, and construct numerous barns and fences. Not able to keep up with Sinclair's lavish spending pattern, Hildreth sells his interest in the operation to Sinclair and remains as general manager and trainer.

"Sande's a nearly flawless rider, Mr. Sinclair. Despite his height, he hunches down lower in the saddle than any other rider today. He's like a streamlined locomotive; no part of his body sticks up to resist the wind and slow down his mount. And once that boy gets the lead, he's the best herd rider around."

"But I don't want any hot-headed kid working for me," Sinclair argues. "I hear he outright quit Commander Ross's outfit. The owner has the absolute right to choose which rider mounts his horses. What kind of oil business would I have if my workers had the right to determine who would do what job?"

"If Ross and Poteet did to you what they did to him, you would have blown off a little steam too. Sande's no hot-headed kid, believe me. No matter what happens, he always remains cool. He's cool in the saddle and polite off the track. You treat Sande with fairness and he'll deliver for you. We have good horses and are winning decent races, but Sande can make them great horses. He's that talented. Ensor's been doing fine for us, but we only have second call on him. We need Sande to ride the Rancocas green and white silks to victory."

"You know horses and jockeys. I'm convinced. If you vouch for him, that's good enough for me. Make Sande an offer, Sam."

Hildreth approaches Sande. Earl ponders the numerous riding positions from various stables, both in the U.S. and abroad."

Samuel C. Hildreth, Rancocas Stable general manager and trainer. Courtesy Ken Grayson Collection

"What kind of an owner is Sinclair?" he asks Hildreth.

"Sinclair's the kind of man, who, if he thinks you know what you are doing, gives you a free hand. If you don't, you won't be with him long. I think you know my reputation as a trainer, Earl."

"That's fair enough. Let's sign the papers."

Sande agrees on October 19 to ride for Harry F. Sinclair's Rancocas stable and signs a $15,000-a-year contract with Samuel C. Hildreth, Sinclair's star trainer. Sande retains agent Frank Hackett to handle his outside riding engagements. That afternoon, Sande mounts Mavourneen for owner J. J. Murphy. Mavourneen breaks from an outside post position and rushes to the rail. During his drive, Mavourneen bumps Pouch, who broke from the rail position. The action forces jockey Buxton to pull up Pouch and drop from the race. From there on, Mavourneen sets a good pace until Quecreek, with Mooney up, closes fast on his heels. Quecreek makes his move and wins by a length; Mavourneen finishes second.

After the finish, race stewards remove the first two numbers from the finishing position board and call Sande on the carpet. After review and much argument between the stewards, they reinstate Quecreek as the winner and disqualify Mavourneen. They hand Sande a rough riding suspension to prevent him from riding the balance of the week.

Hildreth complains to reporters. "Makes no difference whether I buy a horse or a jockey, something bad happens right away! First Purchase and Lucullite break down, then my $100,000 investment in Inchcape goes for naught this year after that horse first comes down with a skin disease and later wrenches an ankle. Now we are hit with suspension of our new rider. There is no getting rid of the jinx."

Intervening with the steward on Sande's behalf, Hildreth pleads, "I've just hired the kid to ride Cirrus for Rancocas on Saturday, here at Empire City. Ensor is already scheduled for the Latonia Championship in Kentucky and can't take the Empire City mount. This suspension is a severe handicap for our stable."

The race stewards confer and agree to reduce Sande's suspension by one day so he can race for Rancocas on Saturday. However, they issue a stern warning. "Tell your boy to watch the rough riding because we'll be watching him."

On Saturday October 23, Sande once again faces Mooney on Quecreek while riding Dry Moon for R. T. Wilson. This time Quecreek sets the pace, with Dry Moon chasing his tail. Sande saves Dry Moon in the early going, gains ground on the far turn, and moves up on Quecreek. A final at-

Sande in Rancocas silks. Courtesy Sande Tomlinson Collection.

tempt leaves Dry Moon wanting, and Quecreek rebuffs the challenge for the win. In other racing action, Sande comes in fourth on Needam before he mounts Cirrus for his maiden Rancocas ride. Cromwell breaks fast and exhibits good speed in the early going. Cirrus trails the leader closely for the first three-quarters but fades in the backstretch, coming in second in the three-horse Pelham Bay Handicap. Sande finishes out the day riding for other stables with a win on The Wit and a third-place finish on Lady Algy.

Two days later, Sande takes Krewer to the lead early in the Hillside Handicap, determined to hold on for the win in his first victory under the Rancocas colors. Sande starts the day's racing on October 27 aboard Flambette with a solid win. He then captures second on Ace of Aces and third on Lord Brighton, before winning the final race of the day by a hair's-breadth on Machine Gunner.

At Louisville on November 6, Sande mounts Grey Lag for a run at the $23,695 Kentucky Jockey Club Stakes purse. Frank Coltiletti, on Harry Payne Whitney's Tryster, establishes an early lead. Behave Yourself makes a run at Tryster but tires out on the stretch turn. At this point, Sande makes his move and drives Grey Lag hard in the stretch. The horse passes Behave Yourself but falters, never getting closer than one and one half lengths to Tryster, coming in second and earning $1,500 for Sinclair.

Two days later at Pimlico, Sande rides 11 to 1 Jadda to a third-place finish. He then mounts Sinclair's Mad Hatter for the $10,000 Bowie Handicap. Ironically, the field of nine includes Commander Ross's Boniface ridden by Frankie Keogh, a horse Sande knows well and a rider Sande experiences a burning desire to beat before the capacity crowd.

An unruly Boniface delays the start of the race. Boniface and The Porter jump to an early lead, with the rest of the field trailing through the first quarter. Not to be denied, Mad Hatter makes his move, passing both steeds, and leads by two lengths going through the backstretch. As if teasing Keogh, Sande puts Mad Hatter under light restraint and waits for Boniface's final thrust. Keogh makes his move, and the two horses race down the homestretch and cross the wire head to head at near record time. The crowd cheers wildly for Sande as he rides Mad Hatter back to the judges' stand. Sande cherishes the victory and moves his horse alongside Keogh.

"Ask Commander Ross how he liked that race, Frankie."

Sande boots home another winner on board Carpet Sweeper in the Catonsville Handicap, staying ahead of Andy Schuttinger on Rubidium and favored Enfilade. Two days later, Commander Ross stacks the deck and enters both Sir Barton and Billy Kelly, Sande's former mounts, against Hildreth's rider on Mad Hatter in the Pimlico Serial Weight-for-Age Race No. 3.

Sande on Mad Hatter gets a poor start at the break, while Sir Barton takes an early lead. Making a bid, Sande brings Mad Hatter up from last on the outside. By the backstretch, Mad Hatter moves up fast and takes the lead. However, Billy Kelly challenges and Mad Hatter has nothing left to counter. Billy Kelly pulls away easily to win, and Frankie Keogh on Sir Barton edges out Mad Hatter with the last stride for second place.

Keogh moves alongside Sande and says, "I think the Commander likes today's race better."

Sande does score a first-place finish on Fallacy in the sixth race Country Club Purse. On November 11, Sande brings in five horses in the money, including first-place finishes on Lord Brighton and Carpet Sweeper. Sande and Lord Brighton win the Linstead Handicap, slipping through on the rail and beating Enfilade to the finish line.

The next day, Sande brings four out of five horses home for victories, but in the important race against Ross's Boniface and Kilmer's Exterminator, Sande struggles aboard Mad Hatter for a fifth-place finish. A day later, Sande guides Tippety Witchet home for a first-place finish ahead of Wyoming.

Clarence Kummer closes out 1920 as the leading money-winning jockey with $292,376 in purses for his owners, ending 25 percent of his races in first place. Sande achieves a competitive record, with 29 percent of his mounts winning first place, and garnering purses of $228,231. In addition, Sande places an astonishing 67 percent of his mounts in the money. Considering that Kummer rode Man o' War for many top prizes, Sande's 1920 record is outstanding. Buddy Ensor also establishes an enviable 1920 record, earning $192,244 while winning 31 percent of his races. Man o' War leads all three-year-olds with winnings of $166,410 for owner Riddle.

The hiring of Sande loads Rancocas with Idaho-bred jockeys, as Earl joins Laverne and Mark Fator at Jobstown. Hildreth holds the young jockeys captive with stories of racing in his youth.

"I was the greatest jockey the turf has ever known, boys."

Laverne Fator asks, "What was your record for straight winners?"

"I never lost a race."

"How many races did you ride?" Sande asks.

"Two hundred forty-eight and a half and never lost a race!"

Mark Fator queries, "Can you find it in the record books?"

"Maybe, if you could find the record books. Say boys, I don't know if I like the way you three are laughing about my great riding record. I'm trying to impart some wisdom to you young bucks and you laugh in my face."

Sande and the Fators smile at each other.

Top 1920 Jockey Standings							
Jockey	Mounts	1st	2nd	3rd	%	$Winnings	In Money %
Butwell, J.	721	152	129	139	.21	$216,742	.582
Ensor, L.	372	116	77	42	.31	192,244	.632
Coltiletti, F.	665	115	132	101	.17	195,910	.523
Rodriguez, J.	706	114	126	107	.16	170,581	.492
Lyke, L.	489	111	81	62	.23	175,464	.519
Kennedy, B.	604	110	106	99	.18	140,874	.522
Carmody, J.	541	106	88	82	.20	77,306	.510
Sande, Earl	355	102	80	56	.29	228,231	.670

Top 1920 Jockey Standings by Percentage Wins (100 or more mounts)			
Jockey	Mounts	Won	Percent
Ensor, L.	372	116	.31
Sande, E.	355	102	.29
Ambrose, E.	225	64	.29
Kummer, C.	353	87	.25
Keogh, F.	153	38	.25
Lyke, L.	489	111	.23
Thompson, C.	330	72	.22

"Well, if you don't like those stories, let me tell you one that is true as my sitting here. Back in the Midwest I used a very interesting fella as my betting agent. The man was straight as a string when I made his acquaintance. There were plenty of chances for him to cheat me, but he never did. I remember once when the books opened Khaftan at 4 to 5 odds, expecting me to come along and back him off the boards. But when they didn't see my money, Khaftan's price went up to 4 and 5 to 1, and it was then that my betting agent went around dropping small bets here and there that added up to a nice-sized wager. It would have been easy enough for him to have told me that some of my money had gone down at the short price. But that wasn't his way. He brought the tickets along to show me what odds he received, all at the top of the market. Now there's an honest man for you."

Hildreth gets up and makes ready to leave the stables while the young jockeys ponder the story. As he starts to exit the doorway, the Fators and Sande ask in chorus, "Who was your betting agent?"

"None other than Frank James. Heard he had a brother named Jesse."

The Fators and Sande spend the winter working the horses and performing other tasks at Rancocas. One day as Sande brushes and sings to one of the horses, a small figure quietly moves close to the stall.

"Do you always sing to the horses?"

Earl turns around to find a pretty, young, red-haired girl.

"Just a habit of mine, find it keeps them calm."

"Seems like it works."

"Mr. Hildreth's mighty particular about who visits the horses. Does he know you're here?"

"You mean my Uncle Sam?" With that, the girl turns away. After fifty paces, she yells over her shoulder, "My name's Marion Casey, what's yours?"

"Earl, Earl Sande.'"

"See you around, Earl Sande."

Primed and ready for the Kentucky Derby, Hildreth ships Grey Lag to start the 1921 racing season in Louisville. The horse suffers a stone bruise preparing for the race and Hildreth has no choice but to withdraw him from the Kentucky Derby twenty-four hours before race time. Sande watches as Colonel E. R. Bradley's Behave Yourself beats his stablemate, Black Servant, by a head. The one-two Kentucky Derby finish matches the feat accomplished by Commander Ross in 1919 with Sir Barton, ridden by Johnny Loftus, and Billy Kelly, ridden by Earl Sande.

On May 13 at Pimlico, Commander Ross's gelding Billy Kelly wins his fourth consecutive race of the season, with Fairbrother up, while Sande captures first on Sammy Kelly at Jamaica. Two afternoons later, Sande and Fator finish first and second in the Colorado Stakes on Kai-Sang and Little Chief, respectively. The next day, Sande does not compete in the Preakness but boots home two winners, first on Sammy Kelly and then on Valor in the Auburndale Handicap.

At Jamaica, Sande guides Dominique to the winner's circle in the May 17 Rainbow Handicap, ahead of Clarence Kummer on Audacious. The rest

Mark Fator, Earl Sande, and Laverne Fator at Rancocas Stables. Courtesy Keene-land-Cook.

of the month Sande lands in the money with first-place finishes on Biff Bang, Budana, Cirrus, Cum Sah, Quecreek, Regal Lodge, Rose Brigade, Thunderclap, and Whimsy; eight second-place finishes, including one on Mad Hatter; and seven third-place finishes.

Moving to Belmont, Sande notices Marion Casey in the stands with Mrs. Hildreth. Marion waves to Earl and he returns her greeting with a tip of his cap. He takes the first May 28 race on Krewer. Fifteen thousand fans cheer as Sande races Mad Hatter to the lead in the $5,000 Metropolitan Handicap and burns up the track on the backstretch to claim victory.

The next day, Sande claims the $1,200 Hempstead Handicap in the third race, while Laverne Fator on Penrose wins the Ladies' Handicap. Sande scores a hat trick with three May 30 first-place wins with Grey Lag in The Freeport Handicap, Stromboli, and Main Mast.

Earl Sande up on Grey Lag. Courtesy Keeneland-Cook.

Noted sportswriter Damon Runyon pens his first of many poetic tributes to Sande in "The New York American:"

Tryster's a Race horse, Tony
So is that big colt Snob.
But Grey Lag's a real good pony
When Sande is on the job.

Maybe there's better jockeys
Somewhere on land or sea,
But gimme a handy guy like Sande
Riding the mount for me.

The following afternoon at Belmont, Sande brings home Grey Lag a winner despite giving up twenty pounds to his closest competitor. Two days later, Sande starts out the day with a first-place finish on Lord Brighton, and then scores a second-place finish on Stromboli, before mounting Grey Lag for the Withers against Schuttinger on Leonardo II and Kummer on Sporting Blood. Although considered the favorite, Grey Lag breaks sluggishly. Leonardo II takes the early lead and crowds the rail four lengths in front at the first turn. Sande works Grey Lag up to second but gets beaten by Sporting Blood and barely captures third over a hard-charging Touch Me Not. Sande secures a June 3 double, with wins on Pillory and Beach Star.

In the fifty-fifth running of the $8,100 Suburban Handicap the next day, 30,000 race fans witness a riding duel between Clarence Kummer on Audacious and Earl Sande on Mad Hatter. Audacious breaks away at the start, but Mad Hatter overtakes the leader by the backstretch. Sennings Park scoots into second place, running three lengths behind Mad Hatter. Audacious regains second and begins to challenge Mad Hatter around the turn and into the homestretch. At the sixteenth pole, Audacious catches and passes Mad Hatter. Sande urges Mad Hatter forward, and for a brief moment the steed pokes his nose in front of Audacious before running out of gas. Audacious wins by a head, driving hard.

Sande recovers with four horses in the money June 6, with first-place finishes on Stromboli and Tom McTaggart, a second-place finish, and a third-place finish. He follows that with several days of in-the-money finishes including wins with Fantouche, Jock Scot, and Muskallonge.

Five days later, Sande does not get a good send off on William A, breaking last from the post as the horse receives a kick from one of the other mounts. Despite the injury, Sande coaxes William A to the lead and wins the Keene Memorial. Hildreth unsaddles William A with joy over the win and concern for the horse. The kick bruised William A on the inside and outside of the stifle, one of the most damaging places a horse can be injured.

"I don't know how you brought this horse on to win, Earl. He won't be running anymore for a while."

Hildreth then saddles Sande for the running of the Belmont Stakes on Grey Lag. Sande rates Grey Lag along and saves him for a drive after he rounds the turn into the stretch. Spurred to action, Grey Lag comes from behind and gallops home, four lengths in front of the nearest competition, setting a new track record for the distance. Grey Lag's win evens up the score for his earlier loss to Sporting Blood and Leonardo II in the Withers and earns Sande his first Belmont Stakes win. Sande finishes out his day with a third win on George D. Widener's filly Last Straw. Over the next week, Sande wins on Biff Bang, Flambetta, Polar, and Top Sargeant. He also places second twice and third twice.

On June 17, Rancocas Stables purchases two three-year-olds, Knobble and Playfellow, for $25,000 and $115,000 respectively. Rancocas's jockeys waste no time in making the investment start to pay off. The next afternoon, Sande mounts Knobble in the Aqueduct Carlton Stakes, while Laverne Fator takes the reins on Playfellow, in competition with well-regarded Harry Payne Whitney's Broomspun, winner of the Pimlico Preakness. The race starts off badly as a kick to the shoulder ends Broomspun's chances. Within a few strides the horse's leg snaps and dangles. Clarence Kummer dismounts and leads the horse off the track, where he is destroyed. Meanwhile, Sande leaps to a lead of two lengths on Knobble, where he remains for the entire race. Playfellow captures second for a one-two Rancocas finish. Closing out the day, Sande comes in fourth on Dick Deadeye in the fifth race and wins the maiden fillies' race on Vivian.

Sande finishes in the money in three out of four June 19 races. Sande and Lord Brighton cross the finish line for a win in the first race. Then Sande takes second on Sennings Park in the Hanover Handicap behind Yellow Hand, and second in the fifth race on Dorcas, behind Edward Kummer on Rockport. Around the far turn and heading home, Dorcas has a length lead and looks like a solid winner. A hundred yards from the finish line, Rockport zooms past a surprised Sande for the win.

"The New York Observer Herald" criticizes Sande's riding at Aqueduct. "It was a rather peculiar circumstance that Sande, who is probably the best rider in the country right now, should make two mistakes in quick succession, when earlier in the day he had given one of the best exhibitions of riding seen in some time. However, in the fifth race Sande lost with the odds-on choice, Dorcas, which was defeated by a nose by Father Bill Daly's Rockport, a 15 to 1 shot, and the outsider in the field of five…Sande appeared to be winning easily, keeping an eye on Salute and entirely overlooked Rockport. The younger Kummer suddenly slipped upon the favorite and Sande found himself going to the whip, but it was too late."

Other June racing at Aqueduct shows Sande booting home winners with Budana in the Clover Stakes, and Valor in the Rockaway Stakes. On June 23, Sande appears headed for an easy win with a comfortable margin on Tom McTaggart, when Sir Grafton makes his move. Sande urges his horse on, but his tired mount has no more to give and finishes second. Later in the day, Sande scores a first on Montara. After the races, the track judges set down Sande for two days on a charge of reckless riding after jockey Mooney complains that Sande interfered with his mount, Devil Dog, who finished fourth. The ruling prevents Sande from riding Mad Hatter in the Queens County Handicap. On the next day, fellow Rancocas jockey Laverne Fater gets set down for five days for being too anxious in getting away from the post with Modo in the first race. "The Thoroughbred Record" June 25 cover carries a photo of Grey Lag with Sande up.

Back in the saddle, Sande takes Rose Brigade to an early lead and easily draws away from the pack, winning under restraint. He scores a second-place finish on Valor in the June 27 Myrtle Selling Stakes and another win on Thunderclap in the Africander Handicap. Two days later, Sande gains the winner's circle on Leghorn.

In early July at Aqueduct, Sande turns in some uncharacteristically poor performances with out-of-the-money finishes on Ultimata and Top Sergeant, but recoups with a first-place finish on Valor, five second-place finishes, and four third-place finishes in stakes races.

During the last two days of racing at Aqueduct, Sande scores a stunning quartet of wins on Budana in a walk, Mad Hatter in track record time, Little Chief, and Grey Lag. Grey Lag's victory in the Dwyer Stakes earns $7,000 for Rancocas and breaks Man o' War's world record for a mile and a furlong, with a time of 1:49 flat. The next day, Sande racks up two more first places on Sennings Park in the Domino Handicap and Surf Rider, plus a second-place finish on Valor.

Reporters corner Sande before the racing at Empire City. "We understand that those in the know in the racing world have discarded the 'dope' and just 'play Sande.' How do you explain the secret of your success?"

"There isn't any, except perhaps that I think I know horses pretty well. As a rule, I receive very little instructions from trainers as to how they want their horses ridden. They leave it to my judgment. That's sound thinking, I believe. Sometimes I get orders enough to ride a three-mile race. No one can tell you what will happen once away from the barrier. You have to think fast and react even quicker or the race will be over before you've made up your mind. In short races, the break generally decides the race. In the longer races, the main thing is to keep out of interference without losing any more ground than you can help. Simply put, I just ride my mounts the best I can, and let fate figure out the rest. That's all a square-headed kid from the West can do."

"How do you get ready for racing, Earl?"

"The Fator boys and I exercise the Rancocas horses every morning, which means two or three hours of work. To help keep the weight down,

I watch my diet closely and visit a Turkish bath two or three times a week. Reducing, but keeping strength, is the jockey's toughest task."

"What interests do you have away from the track?"

"A great many things. The theater, baseball, and boxing. Unfortunately, jockeys seldom have any time to devote to them. I do love the major operas and have memorized all of them. I often sing to my horses during the race."

"Do you think your singing to them makes your mounts run faster, or are they running faster to get away from your voice?"

"I guess you'd have to ask them. Well, it's time to don my silks and riding boots. Thanks for stopping by, boys."

Sande places first on Thunderclap in the July 9 Rialto Purse and second on Aknusti and Jock Scot. He is due to ride Grey Lag in the Empire City Handicap, but the assignment of a high weight causes Hildreth to withdraw the horse from the race. Instead, Sande mounts Mad Hatter, who finishes third behind Yellow Hand and Audacious. Two days later, Grey Lag carries a weight of 130 pounds, giving up twelve pounds to Quecreek, and still wins the Bryn Mawr Purse, with Sande up. Sande also wins on Sammy Kelly but finishes a distant sixth on Rose Brigade.

In other July racing at Empire City, Sande wins the Melrose Sellings Stakes on Valor. Other quality rides include first-place finishes on Collinga and Sammy Kelly, a second in the Van Cortlandt Purse with Lord Brighton, and another second-place finish on Cum Sah.

Pen Rose, with Sande up, strikes out with a flash of speed on July 22 and sets a torrid pace. Although tiring in the end, Pen Rose withstands Elected II by a nose to win the Pocahontas Handicap. Sande completes a double with a victory easing up on Pickwick in the fifth race. The following day, Sande urges Sunflash II to an early lead in the Rye Purse, but a game The Boy runs Sunflash II down and wins with a final thrust to the finish line. In the next race, Sande paces Mad Hatter under restraint and wins the Cosmopolitan Handicap, with much in reserve. Carrying 135 pounds and conceding twenty-seven pounds to Careful in the Knickerbocker Handicap, Grey Lag, with Sande at the reins, wins with a pace only two-fifths of a second slower than the track record. Another double falls to Sande June 25 with wins on Apple Jack II in the Moderate Purse and Purchase in the Bronxville Handicap. In the next week, Sande and Grey Lag triumph by seven lengths in the Mount Kisco Stakes.

At Canada's Devonshire Park, Thunderclap gives Sande his all in a final thrust to the finish line but fails to beat Slippery Elm. In the next race, 15,000 fans cheer wildly during the running of the July 30 $20,000 Devonshire International. Sande and Grey Lag come from behind in the stretch to defeat Colonel Bradley's highly-regarded Black Servant, ridden by Larry Lyke. In the process, Grey Lag establishes a new Canadian record for one and one-eighth miles. The Devonshire International win marks Grey Lag's eighth consecutive victory over a host of top quality racehorses, including Exterminator and Mad Hatter. However, an injury suffered in the race causes Hildreth to terminate Grey Lag's 1921 racing.

Damon Runyon weighs in on Grey Lag and Sande. "There is not a horse in America today that can be named in the same breath with Grey Lag. Horsemen have to go a long way back to think of a handicap horse as good, or near as good, as Grey Lag. He stands out over anything we have seen in years and brings back memories of some of the famous thoroughbreds that used to fight it out in the big handicaps in the good old days. There is no jockey in the United States who can be compared with Sande. While you are having this mental picture of the horses that made turf history years back, think of any of the past generations of jockeys that had anything on Earl Sande as an all-around horseman. This lad has the qualities of a number of the old stars all in his makeup."

For the August 1 Saratoga opening day, Sande boots home three second-place finishes and a third-place finish. Sande and Mad Hatter battle Yellow Hand to the wire in the Saratoga Handicap but come up a nose short. The next day, a jury acquits seven former Chicago White Sox players, including Shoeless Joe Jackson, of an alleged conspiracy to defraud the public by throwing the 1919 World Series games.

Sande leads Harridan to the wire August 2, in front of Laverne Fator on Pierre Qui Roule, and later Sennings Park in the Lake George Handicap, ahead of Fator on Thunderclap. The next day, Chicago White Sox owner Charles A. Cominsky, arbitrator Judge Landis, and American League President Ban Johnson declare the acquitted Chicago White Sox players barred from baseball for life.

"Another example of big business taking advantage of sports figures striving to make an honest living," Jack Dempsey says to Sande.

"I agree. You can't convince me that Shoeless Joe Jackson took a bribe. It's not in his nature."

Sande mounts Thunderclap for a slew of thrilling August victories. The team captures the Hudson Handicap, after Sande kicks Thunderclap along to overhaul Smoke Screen down the homestretch. Sande and Thunderclap add the Watervilet Handicap to their string of victories with a display of demonic riding that spurs Thunderclap to overcome Frankie Keogh and Knot by an inch. Sande's masterful riding gets Thunderclap over the finish line by a neck, in front of Routledge, to win the Warrenburgh Highweight Handicap.

Hildreth praises Sande. "Nice riding today, Earl. If you don't have any plans tonight, why don't you join me and Mrs. Hildreth for dinner? Our young niece is in town and she would like to meet that cute freckle-faced jockey. So I guess that's you."

"It would be my pleasure, Mr. Hildreth."

Hildreth leaves and the Fator brothers crowd around Earl.

"Hey cute freckle-faced jockey, would you like to babysit me? Would you like us to chaperone?" Laverne chides.

"I guess they figure their niece would be safe with you, Earl. The closest you've ever come to a female are those fillies you ride," Mark adds.

"Just leave me alone. I'm not going out on any date. Fact is, if it weren't Mr. Hildreth asking, I wouldn't be going out at all. He's the boss and you've got to keep him happy. If that means babysitting some gawky-eyed school-girl then that's what I'll do."

"There's a candy store down on the corner. You can get her a lollipop or some bubblegum."

"Thanks for the advice, boys, but I don't see the girls chasing either of you two Idaho hayseeds around the track."

Earl dresses in a white shirt, vested suit, silk tie, and black shoes. As he leaves the jockey club, Laverne and Mark follow close behind. Mark holds a camera in his hand.

"Where do you two clowns think you're going?"

"Thought we'd get a photograph of you and the schoolgirl. Don't forget, curfew is nine o'clock for young children," Mark says.

"Don't embarrass the poor girl. She's probably scared to death to meet Rancocas's top jockey as it is. You notice she didn't ask to meet either of you two."

"OK, Freckles. You can go alone, but we want a full report tonight when you get back to the stables."

Outside, Sam Hildreth and his wife stand near the grandstands. Earl approaches, straw hat in hand, and says hello to Mrs. Hildreth. Slightly behind her stands the pretty redhead with dark, bashful eyes and a fleeting smile. She wears a fashionable long coat trimmed with a wide fur collar. Her hair is rolled into a bun, while a lock curls down and rests on her forehead. A lace dress shows beneath the opening of her coat. Her dainty hands fidget.

"Earl, this is my niece, Marion Casey from Cambridge. She just graduated from Notre Dame Academy," Mrs. Hildreth says.

"Believe I had the pleasure to meet Miss Casey briefly back up at Jobstown last winter."

Earl stands about two feet away from the girl and stretches out his arm to shake her hand. They awkwardly touch without eyes meeting.

With the formalities out of the way, the Hildreths turn and walk toward their car for the drive into town for dinner at the Grand Union Hotel. The young couple falls into place behind Mr. and Mrs. Hildreth. A sideways glance tells Earl that this is no longer a young schoolgirl. She's almost a woman. Mr. Hildreth opens the front door of the car for his wife and Earl follows suit with the back door. Marion enters and Earl slides into the seat beside her. Since she has only moved partially across the car seat, the sides of their legs touch.

After dinner, the couples stand outside the hotel, waiting for the valet to bring the Hildreths' Packard around. A cool evening breeze slightly moves the lock on Marion's forehead.

"Earl, why don't you and Marion walk back to the stables. We would like to pay our respects to some friends in town. We can pick Marion up later," Sam Hildreth says.

"If that's all right with Miss Casey."

"I would love to walk back. It's such a beautiful night."

The Hildreths leave while Marion and Earl watch a chauffered purple Marmon limosine pull into the Grand Union Hotel driveway. Gold letters on the door spell out F. X. B. A rush of people crowd the car as a man with a long white cigarette holder in his mouth exits one side of the car and a beautiful lady in sequined dress exits the other side.

Ladies swoon as Francis X. Bushman takes the arm of his wife, actress Beverly Bayne, and gracefully enters the hotel amid a flock of admirers.

Earl looks at the limosine and says, "I'm going to have a chauffer someday."

Marion smiles and says, "I'm going to look beautiful some day like Miss Bayne."

"She has nothing on you, Miss Casey."

Marion blushes and the two walk along in silence for the first few blocks. They pass a school and at the playground, Marion stops.

"Earl Sande, do you like to swing?"

"Sure do. Besides riding on a horse with the wind blowing through my hair, it's the next best thing. Let's swing. I'll get you started with several good pushes and then I'll catch up," Earl says.

"Just like you do on the racetrack, Earl Sande, come from behind just at the right moment to win."

"Something like that. By the way, call me Earl, not Earl Sande."

He gets Marion swinging high before mounting the adjacent swing. He pumps his legs to get in motion. For a while, she swings out while he swings back so he has ample opportunity to study her graceful legs. After their fill of swinging, the young couple returns to their walk.

"It's like heaven. All the stars, bright moon, and cool air. I hope you don't mind my asking Uncle Sam to introduce us. I'm usually not so forward. It's not proper, you know."

"I don't get to spend much time with regular folks. It's nice. I'm glad you asked."

"Do you really live at the stables?"

"Yes. The track is my home, my life. Where else would I live? I haven't lived in a home since I was an early teen back in Idaho. Even then, I sometimes slept on the daybed of the man I raced horses for. On the road we slept in boxcars, back of the wagon, in stables, wherever we could drop our weary bodies. Guess I got used to it."

"Isn't it uncomfortable to sleep on a hard floor?"

"Not if you outfit yourself with a Soogans."

"That's a funny name. What's a Soogans."

"Soogans is the name for the cowboy bed. They are kind of like quilts. When I worked for Doc Pardee back in Arizona we spent many nights on the road, far from any town. Soogans make more sense than a mattress because they can be moved easy when on horseback, and they double as a place to store your gear during the day. For comfort, I'd match my soogans against any bed in a fine hotel."

"I'm convinced."

"Besides, it's nice being close to the horses. You fall asleep listening to their breathing and neighing. Nothing better in the world."

"Guess it sure beats the automobile traffic in town and the noisy revelers in the hotel hallways."

Before long, they arrive back at the stables. Earl stands with his foot up on the lower fence rail and looks out at the track. Marion looks at Earl.

"You love racing, don't you?"

"Nothing else like it in the world. Do you like horses? Would you like to see Mad Hatter?

"Sure would, Earl. I love horses."

"He's one of the best in the Rancocas string. Never have I ridden a more temperamental horse. He's the most difficult to handle. He cost me and the owners a couple of races before I figured out how to treat him. He's a big, strong fella with a will of his own that he's not afraid to assert every step of the way. For some reason, he doesn't like the rail and sticks to the center of the track and sometimes likes to bear out at the finish of a race. I learned after several trips around the oval that it would be a question of whether he or his rider is the master. He thrives on the battle between himself and the jockey. Once he figures out you are the boss, he gives his all, and he has plenty to give."

"Do all of the jockeys know so much about the horses they ride?"

"If they want to win they should, Miss Casey."

"Please call me Marion, Earl."

Marion moves closer to Earl. He reaches out to touch her hand, and they lightly lean against each other in silence as the clouds drift past the moon.

"Thanks for a nice evening, Earl. I feel very comfortable with you."

"I'm not much on knowing how to behave with women, Marion. I'm more comfortable with horses. Give me time to get used to the idea. Will you be coming to the track again?"

"I'll be visiting my aunt and uncle for several weeks. Would you like to see me again?"

"Yes. I would love to!"

The Hildreths arrive and Marion leaves with them. Back in the stables, the Fator brothers await news of the evening from Earl.

"Did you kiss her?"

"That's none of your business, boys. She's no gawky-eyed kid. She's beautiful, and she's going to be my wife!"

"Hold on there, Earl. You don't even know how many other horses there are in this race. How do you know if you even have a chance?" Laverne asks.

"Let's just say I know a sure thing when I see it."

Earl and Marion date over the next few weeks and plan to marry on September 14, 1921. While preparing during the week before the wedding, Sande wins on Georgie in the September 9 Cedarhurst Handicap. He also places second and third in other races. The next afternoon, Sande wins a $10,000 purse on Mad Hatter in The Jockey Club Gold Cup. He wins one more race and places second in his last ride of the day. Two days later, on a slow track Sande comes in second on Wrecker. A day before the wedding, he takes second place on Donnacona in the Great Neck Handicap and third place on Elected II in the Bellair Handicap. Sande takes the day of the wedding off from racing. However, his best man Laverne Fator places three horses out of five in the money.

Marion Hildreth Casey and Earl Harold Sande exchange vows in an evening ceremony at St. Mary's Church in Jamaica, Long Island. Laverne Fator and Marion's brother, T. Childs Casey, serve as ushers, and Marion is attended by her friend May Gallagher and cousin Florence Casey. Following the wedding ceremony, Mr. and Mrs. Samuel C. Hildreth host a dinner party at the Waldorf-Astoria in New York City. Among the twenty-five guests at the Waldorf-Astoria are the Hildreths; Marion's parents, Mr. and Mrs. T. Harry Casey; Marion's aunts and uncles, Mr. and Mrs. Frank Taylor and Mr. and Mrs. Herbert Casey; and horse breeder John E. Madden.

After a brief honeymoon, Sande once again dons the Rancocas silks at Belmont and mounts Dunboyne for the third race. He rides out onto the track for his first race as a married man and receives an ovation from the crowd. Sande on Dunboyne is content to follow the lead and pace set by Mercury through most of the race. In the stretch, Mercury tires and Sande takes his advantage, driving Dunboyne to the forefront. Dry Moon then mounts his attack. Sande holds him off by riding Dunboyne hard to the finish. Sande earns a double with another first-place finish on Story Teller in the sixth race of the day. As he leaves the track, he tips his jockey's cap to Marion in the stands. The next day, Sande wins on St. Henry and comes in third on Elected II.

The young couple settles in Brooklyn while Earl continues racing for Rancocas at Aqueduct and Jamaica, and then they move to a cozy cottage in Saratoga Springs. They socialize with the Hildreths but spend most of

A dapper Earl Sande and fashionable Marion Casey. Courtesy Earl Sande Family Collection by Marion Jensen.

their time with fellow jockey Clarence Kummer and his wife, Marion. Af-

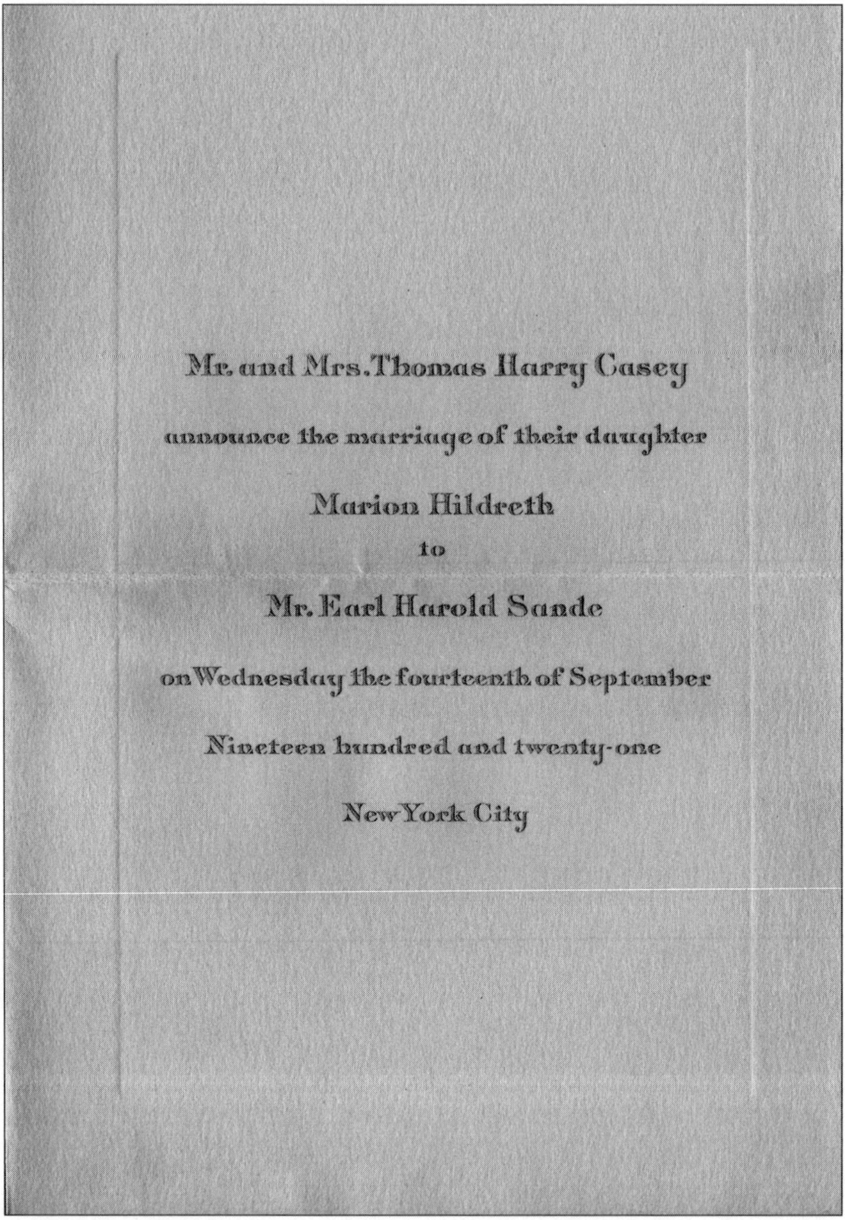

Mr. and Mrs. Thomas Harry Casey

announce the marriage of their daughter

Marion Hildreth

to

Mr. Earl Harold Sande

on Wednesday the fourteenth of September

Nineteen hundred and twenty-one

New York City

Marion Casey and Earl Sande wedding invitation. Courtesy Sande Tomlinson Collection.

ter two out-of-the-money finishes by Sande, Laverne Fator remarks, "By the look of your riding Earl, I'd say you have more on your mind than horses since you've been married."

For the October 15 Jamaica Continental Handicap, Sande and Thunderclap join forces once again to defeat Benny Marinelli on Donnacona. Sande enters the November 2 $2,000 Pimlico Stafford Handicap on Knobble, facing a field of fourteen, including Laverne Fator on Dominique and Commander Ross's Oriole. Rancocas jockeys have not scored a victory since the race scene shifted from Jamaica with the close of the season there. Rancocoas Jinx rumors fill the racetrack.

The race starts and Carmandale breaks fast, ahead of all the horses in the early going. Sande urges Knobble to the front, with Oriole close behind and Laverne Fator on Dominique on the outside. Both Oriole and Dominique go after the leader. They don't have enough to catch Knobble and Sande wins by two lengths, ending the jinx. In the next race, Sande breaks Northcliff swiftly and asks him to run. Northcliff keeps the field at bay for the remainder of the race, winning in a canter.

Racetrack rumors indicate Commander Ross plans to retire from racing. Commander Ross sends Sande a message that he would like to speak with him. Sande joins the Commander for lunch in his private dining room.

"Earl, I know there's some bad feelings over that Sir Barton/Man o' War match race. I take full responsibility for everything that happened. I knew deep in my heart Sir Barton never had a chance against Big Red but let my emotions and pride get in the way of clear thinking. Likewise, I never should have let whatever went on between you and Poteet affect my judgment over who jockeyed Sir Barton that day, but it did. I'm a big enough man to admit I made a mistake, a big mistake. I can't undo what's already been done. I just wish you can accept my sincere apology."

"That's over with, Commander Ross. You were the owner of Sir Barton and had every right to decide who should ride your horse. I only wished I would have been able to tell my side of the story before you made your decision. I accept and thank you for your apology."

"Good, I'm glad that's behind us. Now, for the other reason I wanted to have this little chat with you. I'll be entering Boniface in a number of key races in November and would like you to jockey him. I know you're the man we need. In fact, my new trainer, Henry McDaniel, specifically requested you. I've talked it over with Sam Hildreth and he approves but the final decision has to be yours. I will pay a good price. What do you say?"

"I know your money's good, Commander Ross. To tell you the truth, if Poteet still ran your stable I would flatly refuse, no matter what you offer. I know that Frankie Keogh will be riding Gnome, and it would be nice to beat him again. With no hard feelings between us, I will be honored to ride again under the Ross silks. Only this time, you pay for them."

"It's a deal," Commander Ross says as he offers his large hand to Earl.

In an ironic twist, Earl Sande mounts Commander Ross's Boniface to compete in the November 7 Bowie Stakes. Only a year ago, Sam Hildreth's Mad Hatter nosed out Boniface, ridden by Sande under the Ross colors. This year, Sande faces Lewis Morris on Harry Payne Whitney's Damask and Frankie Keogh on Admiral Grayson's Gnome, in a field of ten.

Bit of White sets the pace for about a mile. Bunga Buck, Dark Horse, Polly Ann, Boniface, Damask, and Gnome trail. As Bit of White rounds the lower bend and starts lagging, Sande, Morris, and Keogh urge their steeds to a faster pace. They pass the rest of the field and head down the stretch. Sande bends to the task and Boniface wins by a head in front of Damask, and Gnome comes in a close third. In the process, Sande reclaims the Bowie Stakes, clips three-fifths of a second off the track record and adds $10,000 to Commander Ross's race winnings.

"I knew Sande was the jockey to ride Boniface to victory," Commander Ross tells reporters. "I would like to congratulate Earl Sande for his riding ability and his actions as a true gentleman."

Laverne Fator catches Earl in the jockey room. "Looks like you have a new nickname, 'Gentleman of the Track.' I guess it pays to wear impeccable, tailored clothes."

"It doesn't take a gentleman to agree to ride a great horse to victory. That's what we get paid to do. As for the clothes, I believe there's an old saying that the man makes the clothes, not the other way around."

"The Racing Form" writes, "Boniface came fast when called on into the lead and, standing a hard drive gamely, won because best ridden at the finish." "The Throughbred Record" adds, "And here, in the stretch run, Sande showed his superiority over Morris. He was in the lead, but Morris had Damask running well, and the Whitney horse came through the straightaway from fourth position to pass the others and challenge the leader. Sande on Boniface saw Damask coming and there he showed his cunning. He pretended to whip Boniface, and it is probable that Morris thought he had the horse beaten, for he never raised his whip, while Damask was getting closer and closer to Boniface. Then Sande quit hand riding in the final

Earl Sande taking a rare break. Courtesy Sande Tomlinson Collection.

few strides, while the great crowd was urging him to come on, and went to work with his whip. Also Morris went to work with his whip, but he was too late. Boniface restored himself to popular favor with the Marylanders this afternoon when he won this race, but to Earl Sande, who rode him, should go the credit of winning. It was the superior riding of this premier jockey that won over Morris on Damask."

Five days later, Sande rides Boniface in the Pimlico Cup Handicap. Exterminator sets the pace in the field of three, with Sande close behind. Sande rides with restraint until the last quarter and then makes his move, bringing Boniface close to Exterminator but never able to close the distance.

In its inaugural year of horse racing, Rancocas ranks as the biggest money-winning stable at the end of 1921, with a total of $263,500. Rancocas's Sam Hildreth leads the trainer ranks by saddling eighty-five winners during the year. Champion of the three-year-olds, Grey Lag, wins nine of thirteen starts and earns $62,596, while stablemate Mad Hatter wins several big stakes races. Rancocas's jockey Laverne Fator turns in a respectable year, winning 25 percent of his races and purses totaling $223,948. Rancocas's top jockey, Earl Sande, leads all American jockeys with winnings of $263,043. During 1921, Sande comes in first an astounding 33 percent of the time and in the money 71 percent of the time. Frankie Keogh, who replaced Sande on Sir Barton in the Man o' War match race, only wins 21 percent of his 1921 races and $134,118.

Top 1921 Jockey Standings							
Jockey	Mounts	1st	2nd	3rd	%	$Winnings	In Money %
Lang, C.	696	135	110	105	.19	$161,047	.502
Penman, L.	708	128	116	95	.18	173,216	.479
Marinelli, B.	625	126	114	95	.20	100,830	.536
Sande, E.	340	112	69	59	.33	263,043	.705
Fator, L.	438	110	100	63	.25	223,948	.623
Hinphy, W.	468	108	71	55	.23	54,840	.498
Taylor, E.	649	101	74	79	.16	68,480	.391

Top 1921 Jockey Standings by Percentage Wins (100 or more mounts)			
Jockey	Mounts	Won	Percent
Sande, E.	340	112	.33
Fator, L.	438	110	.25
Hinphy, W.	468	108	.23
Marinelli, B.	625	126	.20
Land, C.	135	135	.19

"You're on top of the racing world, Earl. I'm so proud of you," Marion says.

"Thanks for all of your encouragement. It's great to see you in the stands with the Hildreths as I emerge from the paddocks."

In the off-season, Earl and Marion visit Earl's family in Salem, Oregon. Mrs. Sande invites friends and neighbors to honor Earl and meet his new bride. Among those present are Mr. and Mrs. John Sande, Miss Frances Sande, Miss Ruth Edwards, Lester Sande, Mr. and Mrs. Lyman Sundin, and Mr. and Mrs. Sidney Seime. The happy couple spends pleasant evenings playing mah-jongg and cards and singing.

On May 5, 1922, Sande delivers four out of four Jamaica mounts to in-the-money positions, including a third place on Edgar Allen Poe. The next day, Sande guides Title to victory over Marinelli on Picnic and Clarence Kummer on Gem. In the Kings County Handicap, Clarence Kummer breaks fast on Audacious. As the four-horse field makes the clubhouse, Sande trails in second place on six-year-old Mad Hatter. Larry Lyke on Sennings Park runs third, and Yellow Hand trails the pack after being pinched off the rail. On the backstretch, Sande patiently settles into second, a length and a half behind Audacious. As the field approaches the turn, Yellow Hand makes a move toward the inside but is blocked. Meanwhile, Sande breaks for the outside and draws in front of the pack. In the stretch, Sennings Park closes on Mad Hatter and the two sweep past the judges, striding hard. Mad Hatter wins by a head.

After the day's racing, Sande and Clarence Kummer meet their wives. At dinner, Kummer turns to his wife and asks, "How did you do in wagering today at the track? I did place in the money several times, so you must have won some money."

Marion Kummer blushes and her eyes avoid meeting Clarence's while she says, "I did fine, I guess."

"I can't believe it. You bet on Earl again today, didn't you?"

"Well, yes, Clarence. It's not that I don't have faith in you. It's just that Earl is winning everything these days."

Over the next week and a half, Sande picks up a bevy of in-the-money finishes. He wins thirteen times while capturing the Youthful Stakes, Olympic Selling Stakes, Auburndale Handicap, Prospect Park Purse, Arizona Handicap, and the $6,000 Stuyvesant Handicap on Snob II. He also captures eleven second-place finishes including Mad Hatter in both the Excelsior Handicap and the Long Beach Handicap behind Sennings Park.

As Sande brings Edgar Allen Poe forward for the May 11 Olympic Selling Stakes, the horse is so full of running that Sande can't hold him back, and he canters the final two furlongs to the starting line. The early exercise does him no harm, and he wins the contest in the best time ever recorded for the stakes race. In the Arizona Handicap, Sande on Lord Brighton, breaks badly, coming out sixth in a field of seven. Lord Brighton quickly regains lost ground and leads for a brief period until Sande reins him back to fall in behind Muskallonge. Sande wears down Muskallonge on the stretch, and urges Lord Brighton to give more as Whisk challenges.

Earl and Marion Sande at their home in Saratoga Springs. Courtesy Sande Tomlinson Collection.

In the May 23 Excelsior Handicap, Sande on Mad Hatter makes a bid to defend his track record against Damask, Sennings Park, and Yellow Hand. Believing Mad Hatter up to the task, race fans bet heavily on him. Damask breaks first and sprints down the track with Sennings Park, Mad Hatter, and Yellow Hand trailing. Damask begins to drop off the pace entering the backstretch and Sennings Park takes over the lead. Sande and Mad Hatter get caught in a pocket and remain there, waiting for an opening. Fairbrother on Sennings Park gives his horse his head and widens the lead. Mad Hatter closes strongly but cannot catch Sennings Park.

Hildreth tells reporters, "In order to build up Rancocas Stable to ensure more winners, I keep a close eye on the upcoming crop of young horses. My close personal and professional friend, racehorse breeder John E. Madden, had a promising horse we purchased as a yearling. Zev carries a fine bloodline with a history of winning stakes races. Madden named the horse Zev after Harry Sinclair's counsel, Colonel J. W. Zeverly, and it's only fitting that the horse ride under the Rancocas colors. I predict you'll be seeing a lot of exciting racing from both Zev and Earl Sande in the upcoming year."

Twenty two-year-olds line up for the August 1 opening day maiden race at Saratoga. Comixa breaks cleanly and establishes a strong lead. Zev follows on the heels of Comixa and finishes driving hard but cannot close the gap. Four days later, Zev and Sande try again for a two-year-old maiden victory. The field starts slowly before Zev exhibits blazing speed in taking the lead and widening the gap. Sande eases up, and Zev wins handily. On August 11, Sande reins in Thunderclap and follows McAtee on Smoke Screen to the far turn. Swinging into the homestretch, Thunderclap turns on his speed and heads Smoke Screen for a second, before drawing clear for the Hudson Handicap victory.

Damon Runyon celebrates the victory and captures the nation's growing love affair with jockey Earl Sande by penning another poem.

> *Sloan, they tell me, could ride 'em;*
> *Maher, too, was a bird.*
> *Bullman a guy to guide 'em;*
> *Never much worse then third.*
> *Them was the old-time jockeys;*
> *Now when I want a win.*
> *Gimme a handy*
> *Guy like Sande*
> *Ridin' them hosses in!*
>
> *Fuller he was a pippin,*
> *Loftus one of the best;*

LADY MADCAP SMOKE SCREEN THUNDERCLAP
E. SANDE UP
SARATOGA AUG. 11 1922

**Earl Sande wins Hudson Handicap on Thunderclap at Saratoga in August 1922.
Courtesy Sande Tomlinson Collection.**

Many a time come rippin'
Down there ahead of the rest.
Shaw was a bear of a rider,
There with plenty of dome;
But gimme a handy
Guy like Sande
Drivin' them hosses home!

Spencer was sure a wonder,
And Miller was worth his hire.
Seldom he made a blunder
As he rode 'em down to the wire.
Them was the old-time jockeys;
Now when I want to win
Gimme a handy
Guy like Sande
Bootin' them hosses in!

For the August 15 Saranac Handicap, Hildreth saddles Sande on Kai-Sang and Laverne Fator on Little Chief in a field of eleven contenders. Fator takes Little Chief to the front with blinding speed and sets a torrid pace. Kai-Sang has trouble clearing the interference but makes a game attempt to catch the leader on the stretch turn. Little Chief sees the threat and moves away to secure the win. In the last race of the day, Sande powers Zev to withstand a challenge by Enchantment and preserve the win.

"The Thoroughbred Record" runs an August 26 cover photo of Earl Sande up on Zev. That same day, McAtee on Fly by Day establishes a fast pace in the Spinaway Stakes. Sande moves Edict up smartly upon entering the stretch, and under masterly riding, outfoxes McAtee for the win.

Damon Runyon responds with another Sande verse:

> McAtee knows them horses;
> Ensor's a judge of pace;
> Johnson kin ride the courses
> In any old kind o'race.
> All o' them guys are good ones,
> But, say, when I want to win;
> Gimme a handy
> Guy like Sande
> Bootin' a long shot in.

"Man, it's bad enough just losing a close race to Sande." McAtee complains. "First he sings his mount across the finish line in front of you, and then Runyon flashes it across the nation in his fancy poems."

Two days later, Zev and Sande compete in the Saratoga Albany Handicap. A rainy day and muddy track face the jockeys. Sam Hildreth and Earl Sande talk race strategy.

"What makes a good mud runner? I've been asked that question many times. I've never been able to answer it to my own satisfaction. I've seen all kinds run well on a slow track, long striders and short striders, big horses and small. Most of the get of Hastings, the line that sent Man o' War to the races, ran well in heavy going. The small hooves of the Hastings horses are supposed to furnish the explanation, maybe correctly. And yet I've seen horses with large hooves turn out to be the best kind of mud-larks. When you make up your mind that a certain kind of horse is better equipped than other types to run through the mire, and you're ready to put it all down in black and white for the benefit of future generations, along comes a representative of the type you indexed as inferior mud runners to upset your calculations. That said, Zev is a mudder. Still, don't let that give you a false sense of security about the mud-running ability of the other horses in today's race, Earl."

"Yes sir, Mr. Hildreth. I'll keep my eye on them."

Many owners scratch their entries in the day's events because of track conditions. Sande mounts Zev for the Albany Handicap, which tops the card for the day's race attractions with its $5,000 purse. Despite being burdened with the top impost of 126 pounds, Zev goes right after the early leaders and takes command of the race by the sixteenth pole. Sande stretches Zev's lead from two to four lengths and glides to a victory in the mud, ahead of the hapless McAtee on Vigil.

Sande closes out Saratoga racing with a third-place finish on Zev in the Hopeful Stakes and a second-place finish on Mad Hatter in the Saratoga Cup. Another second-place finish on Thunderclap in the Belmont Manhattan Handicap, behind Laverne Fator on Little Chief, follows.

Sande teams up with Kai-Sang to contest the September 9 Lawrence Realization against Clarence Kummer, on Harry Payne Whitney's Bunting, and Albert Johnson, on Rockminster. Hildreth considers scratching Kai-Sang because of an injury received when the horse struck himself during a workout at Saratoga earlier in the week. A record crowd of 20,000 cheers as Sande and Kai-Sang emerge from the paddock. Marion sits in a box with Mr. and Mrs. Sam Hildreth and adjacent to Mr. Sinclair's box.

Bunting and Rockminster bump out of the gate. Bunting gains the lead in a flash of speed. Rockminster recovers from the collision and passes Kai-Sang in the early going. Sande sits back and lets Bunting lead the pace. Just before the last turn, Rockminster moves up close to Bunting and laps upon him. On the homestretch, Sande urges Kai-Sang forward and passes both competitors before the final furlong pole. Kummer takes to the whip, while Sande continues to hand ride. Both horses pass in front of the judges charging hard and neck and neck. The race time comes in just slightly slower than the track record and world mark for the distance set by Man o' War two years previous. Sande and Kai-Sang receive a garland of roses to a great burst of applause. The victory adds $21,400 to Rancocas race winnings for the season.

"This is a good, honest fellow with everything that makes a fine racehorse. He may not be as big as some others, but he is all horse. He finished well despite concern over the injuries he received earlier," Sande tells reporters.

Proud of Earl's accomplishment, Marion breaks out in tears of joy.

Damon Runyon adds another bit of Sande poetry to history:

> *Kummer is quite a jockey,*
> *Maybe as good as the best.*
> *Johnson is not so rocky*
> *When you bring him down to the test.*
> *But say, when they carry my gravy;*
> *Say, when I want to win,*
> *Gimmie a handy*
> *Guy like Sande*
> *Bootin' them horses in.*

Sande and Zev set a fast early pace but tire at the end to forfeit the September 16 Belmont Futurity Stakes to Albert Johnson on Sally's Alley. Later in the day, Sande holds Mad Hatter under restraint in the early going, moves up steadily after the halfway mark, and whisks past Bit of White to take The Jockey Club Gold Cup. A week later, Sande drives three winners home, including the Potomac Handicap on Thunderclap, plus two other in-the-money mounts in five Aqueduct races. Sande earns the moniker "Wizard of the Saddle" when he earns another triple on October 24 with Empire City first-place finishes on Ten-Lec, Tufter, and Good Night. He closes out the season at Pimlico with wins on Rigel and Knobble and a second place finish on Dream of Allah.

Rancocas achieves another stellar racing year. Its winnings of $239,503 top all stables for the second consecutive year. In comparison, Commander Ross's stable only earns $151,483. Likewise, Sam Hildreth leads all trainers in money won, with $247,014, while Commander Ross's trainer, Henry McDaniel, ties with J. A. Parsons for most winning mounts with seventy-eight. Sande wins 32 percent of his races and places in the money an impressive 68 percent of the time. During the season, Sande captures five major stakes races on Grey Lag. He earns $253,431 for the year but trails Albert Johnson, who wins $345,054 in stakes but only 14 percent of his races. Mark Fator scores the most winning races with 188.

Top 1922 Jockey Standings							
Jockey	Mounts	1st	2nd	3rd	%	$Winnings	In Money %
Fator, M.	859	188	153	116	.22	$131,394	.532
Lang, C.	957	187	145	124	.20	231,293	.476
Wilson, T.	688	138	120	115	.20	74,660	.542
Owens, J.	849	123	113	127	.14	160,275	.427
Sande, E.	386	122	78	61	.32	253,431	.676

Top 1922 Jockey Standings by Percentage Wins (100 or more mounts)			
Jockey	Mounts	Won	Percent
Sande	386	122	.32
Eames, C.	434	101	.23
Fator, M	859	188	.22
Garner, M.	488	105	.22
Huntamer, J.	526	112	.21

As a two-year-old in 1922, Zev wins five consecutive races for Rancocas. He finishes second in the Belmont Futurity to Sally Alley, the money-winning two-year-old, and passes out after the race. Zev receives an injury in the Pimlico Futurity, and Hildreth retires him for the remainder of the 1922 racing season, looking ahead to 1923.

"Earl, how could you have invited the Sinclairs to our home? They live in a big mansion. What will they think of our little cottage?"

"Don't worry, Marion. Everything will be fine. The Sinclairs are regular folks. He started with nothing and still remembers what it is to struggle."

"Oh, Earl. I'm so nervous."

"Not as nervous as I was when we went to dinner together with your aunt and uncle."

Earl Sande and Sam Hildreth discuss racing strategy at Sande residence. Courtesy Ken Grayson Collection.

Chapter 9

Golden Age of Sports: The Race of the Century

"Sande is a great rider, probably the best rider on the American turf today. He is to horse racing what Dempsey is to boxing, what Ruth is to baseball," Runyon says.

"The New York Times" carries a photo of Earl Sande, dwarfed by Babe Ruth on one side and William Harrison (Jack) Dempsey on the other. The 1920s truly represent the "Golden Age of Sports." In addition to Dempsey, Ruth, and Sande, the decade includes such renowned and colorful sports figures as Gorgeous Georges Carpentier (boxing), Gaston Chevrolet (auto racing), Lou Gehrig (baseball), Red Grange (football), Tommy Hitchcock (polo), Bobby Jones (golf), Peter Manning (harness racing), John "Tug" McGraw (baseball), Paavo Nurmi (track), Charlie Paddock (the fastest human), Knute Rockne and The Four Horsemen (Notre Dame football), Gene Sarazan (golf), Tris Speaker (baseball), Bill Tilden (tennis), Gene Tunney (boxing), and Helen Wills (tennis).

Baseball fans follow Ruth as he hits fifty-four home runs in 1920, fifty-nine in 1921, and his long-standing record of sixty home runs in 1929. Over a fourteen-year period from 1918 to 1931, "The Babe" captures or ties the American League Home Run Championship twelve times while leading the New York Yankees to six American League Pennants and five World Series Championships.

Peerless Paavo Nurmi shatters Olympic records for the 1,500 meter, 5,000 meter, and 10,000 meter competitions and wins an unprecedented seven gold Olympic track medals. In 1923, Nurmi breaks the record for the mile run with a time of 4:10.4, a mark that stands for eight years.

Jack Dempsey's name on the card draws fans to boxing arenas across the country. In five Dempsey appearances, the gate proceeds exceed $1 million each, for a combined total of $8.5 million. Dempsey's ferocity makes mincemeat out of his opponents and he earns the moniker "The Manassa Mauler."

In the first radio-broadcast heavyweight title fight, Dempsey downs Georges Carpentier in the fourth round to retain his title. He dispatches six-foot-seven-inch Jess Willard in three rounds, despite being outweighed by nearly sixty pounds. After being driven out of the ring by Luis Firpo in the first round, Dempsey knocks him out cold in the second.

Dempsey also enjoys the social life. He marries again, this time to actress Estelle Taylor. He appears in a number of movies. Entertainment stars such as Charlie Chaplin, Tom Mix, Norma Talmadge, Bill Hart, and Florenz Ziegfeld assemble for his highly publicized World Heavyweight Championship bout with Gene Tunney. In a ten-round decision, Tunney out-thinks and out-boxes Dempsey to take over as champion of the world.

Red Grange tears up the gridiron during his first varsity year in 1923. "The Galloping Ghost" gains 1,260 yards and scores twelve Illinois touchdowns. Coach Bob Zuppke says of his gridiron star, "Red Grange is just about as easy a man to handle as I have ever known in my coaching years. When he climbed to stardom and became the most talked-of halfback in the United States, it never affected him. Conceit was foreign to his makeup. He is always modest, quiet and unassuming."

Within this atmosphere and era of athletic greats, Earl Sande captures the public's fancy as America's premier jockey. Runyon dubs him, "That Handy Guy named Sande bootin' those hosses in."

Laverne Fator gets the nod to ride Zev in the May 2 opening day Jamaica Paumonok Handicap. Rocket breaks running, with Zev and Dominique close behind. At the quarter, Zev takes the lead, and Dominique thunders a few lengths to the rear. Zev pulls ahead to an advantage of two and a half lengths but then tires. In the drive for the finish line, Dominque gains with every stride. At the wire, Zev outlasts Dominique by a neck.

Two days later, racing is marred by rough riding, resulting in jockey Thomas Nolan being sent to the St. Mary's Hospital with a brain concussion. The race stewards set down jockeys Arccardy and Taplin for five and six days, respectively.

"The New York Observer Herald" criticizes the recent flurry of incidents. "Rough tactics started early this racing season. Disregard of the racing rules by rogue jockeys must be dealt with severely. Stewards handed the violators a relatively light punishment in view of the serious results to a fellow-jockey, specially since he is a jockey of long experience and has in the past felt the heavy hand of discipline for similar indiscretions on the track."

Sande, on five-year-old Grey Lag, faces Clarence Kummer on Snob II in the May 5 Kings County Handicap. Grey Lag, looking as fit as ever, follows the pace set by Snob II through the backstretch. On the turn, Sande urges Grey Lag forward, and the horse closes the gap inch by inch until his nose edges out ahead of Snob II's. The two horses look eye to eye before Grey Lag pulls ahead and wins by two lengths. Sande closes out the day's racing with a win on Eaglet.

Two days later, Laverne Fator wins the $2,000 Garden City Selling Stakes, and Sande finishes first on Normana. The next afternoon, Laverne Fator lands second place on Better Luck and brings Bracadale to the winner's circle. However, the victory does not stand. Race stewards take the rough riding article to heart. They disqualify Bracadale and set down Fator as punishment for twice interfering with Margin.

"Too bad, Laverne. I know it's tough out there," Sande consoles his fellow jockey. "Nolan had an awfully close call last week. The stewards want to make a statement about rough riding."

"Sure, I don't mind that. But they need to apply the rules consistently. They can't let one jockey get all beat up in one race and ignore it and then set down another jockey in the next race to make it look like they're doing their job. I can ride as clean as the best of them but only if it's a level playing field. I don't like getting signaled out and penalized when the practice is rampant."

Rancocas owner Harry Sinclair requests the stewards to lift Laverne Fator's suspension in order for the jockey to pilot Zev in the Kentucky Derby. The stewards refuse. Sinclair threatens to appeal the decision. The appeal fails.

The May 10 Spring Handicap features a duel between Sande, on favorite Miss Starr, and Rice, on Cyclops. Sande's filly breaks first and sets the pace. Miss Starr defeats the challenge of Canaque but is not up to the task of holding off Cyclops, who finishes with a spurt. In other action the same day, Sande places first on Flying Cloud.

Thirty thousand fans turn out for the May 12 Pimlico Preakness. Zev, along with three other horses, shoulders the top weight of 120 pounds. Benny Marinelli and Vigil get away last in the field of thirteen and patiently work their way up through the crowd to take command after less than seven furlongs. Vigil holds off all comers and finishes one and a half lengths in front of General Thatcher to win $52,000. Sande on Zev poses no real threat in the race and finishes a disappointing next to last, ten lengths behind the leaders. "The New York Times" comments, "Zev quits after going six lengths. Zev's performance was a disappointing one, and careful study of the race brings to light no excuse for such a complete defeat."

Sande recovers by winning the Auburndale Handicap with Flannel Shirt, the maiden race for two-year olds with Sheridan, and placing second on Flying Cloud in the Lafayette. The following day, Sande warms up with a first-race victory on Dauntless and a second-place finish on How Fair, behind McAtee on Fly By Day, before he and Zev compete in the six-furlong Rainbow Handicap. Zev takes a commanding lead from the barrier, and the field never presents a challenge. Sande hand guides to the finish line, with Dominque trailing by a length and a half. At the end of the race, Sande takes Zev for an additional fast-paced mile workout. The win adds $3,250 to Rancocas's 1923 earnings.

Sinclair and Hildreth decide not to enter Zev in the Kentucky Derby. Sande argues long and hard with them to enter Zev in the Louisville contest, even if Fator can't ride him.

"The horse isn't ready. He performed poorly in the Preakness and is not in top shape to run."

"I know he's ready. He received a kick at the start of the Preakness and did not have the legs to run. He's healed now. Look at the stamina and speed he had in reserve after winning today's race. I took him the additional mile to prove he's in excellent condition and ready for the Derby challenge."

The owner and trainer finally concede, and Sinclair announces that Sande will ride Zev for the race at Churchill Downs. Sande readies Zev for his biggest challenge while still competing in the rest of the Jamaica racing season.

Sande scores two in-the-money finishes and then mounts Outline to compete in the May 16 Jamaica Rosedale Stakes for a $5,000 purse. The field of nine includes Eddie Kummer on Anna Marrone II and Mark Fator on Lady Diana. Nellie Morse breaks out front, with Anna Marrone II second, and Outline quick on her heels. Sande calmly remains in third until Anna Marrone II falters on the turn into the stretch. However, Nellie Morse keeps up a brutal pace and the lead. Stride by stride Outline closes the gap under the vigorous hand riding of Sande. As the two horses streak through the final sixteenth, the crowd sends up a roar. In the final dash to the wire, Sande takes to the whip and drives the Rancocas steed across the finish line, in front of Nellie Morse by barely a nose and in track record time for five furlongs. "The New York Times" headline reads, "Sande Puts Up Great Ride..Fairly Lifts Mount Across Finish Line to Beat Nellie Morse by a Nose."

The next day, Sande mounts Dot in the $6,000 Stuyvesant Handicap. Dot gets a clean break away from the barrier and maintains a comfortable lead until the final eighth. Then Sande gives Dot free rein to draw away and beat Moonraker by three lengths.

Reporters ask Sande, "Does Zev have a ghost of a chance in the Derby?"

"Let me explain it this way. Zev likes to be around other horses. When the exercise boys try to get him to run alone, he starts out and then balks after a short distance, refusing to run any further unless worked out with another horse for companionship. He also craves competition and gives his all to beat another horse. The other day, an exerciser took Zev out for a final breezer to keep him fit and trim for the Derby. After galloping a short distance, Zev heads for the rail and stops. At that moment, another horse whizzes by him. Zev pricks up his ears and accepts the challenge. He charges ahead and lets out for three-eighths of a mile at top speed, passing the other horse. Zev and I are both ready for the Derby. Place your bets, gentlemen."

Despite an article in "The New York American" on the day of the race listing Zev a 2 to1 favorite, Zev's disappointing run in the Preakness leaves him out of favor with racetrack bettors and race fans. Heavy betting rates Zev a 19 to 1 shot. The last horses to win with odds that long or longer were Donerail in 1913, a 91 to 1 long shot, and Exterminator in 1918 at 30 to 1. Unbeknownest to the public, Zev's injury in the Preakness caused his poor performance. Since healing, he won several races and trained well for the Derby.

"Marion, Zev is underrated. He has a lot to prove. I know Mr. Sinclair wanted Laverne riding today. I'm his second choice for this race, so I sit under the same cloud of uncertainty. The Kentucky Derby ranks as the top prize for jockeys. It's the mark we all shoot for in this game. I feel that we will both come through."

"I know you will, Earl. Uncle Sam and Mr. Sinclair may not believe in you and Zev, but I do. I'll be cheering you on."

In pre-race strategy meetings days before the event, Sande argues with Sinclair and Hildreth.

"We think you should hold rein on Zev in the early going. At the right moment, make your move to outrun the leaders," Hildreth says.

"Zev has quick speed and he breaks well from the barrier. Let me grab the lead and protect it. Nobody will be able to catch Zev if he establishes a good lead right from the start."

"You talked us into entering Zev in this race, Earl. We don't think he has much of a chance. If you have that much faith in him, I guess we'll have to leave it up to you on how to pace Zev."

"You won't be disappointed. Zev's ready to win this race and it's about time I came home with my first Kentucky Derby victory."

The largest field in Kentucky Derby history, twenty-one horses and riders, waits at the barrier for the forty-ninth Run for the Roses. The record-breaking crowd of 75,000 anticipates the start. The large mass of people include statesmen, sportsmen, captains of industry, politicians, and common folks. Young Pierre Lorillard, whose grandfather was the first American to win an English Derby, arrives by airship.

Harry Sinclair and Sam Hildreth do not attend the race. Hildreth's assistant, David Leary, performs the saddling honor on Zev. Sinclair decides to stay away from Louisville, stubbornly believing that Sande and Zev have no chance of winning. Faithful employee Sam Hildreth keeps him company. At the track, Jonas Mulford, a colored resident of Paris, Kentucky, places his small life savings on Zev after dreaming that the horse will win the Kentucky Derby. Track superintendent Tom Young, whose crew worked with great zeal to prepare the track, promises a perfect venue for the day's events.

The track bugler blows, the announcer shouts, "They're off," and Zev breaks fast from the tenth position, coming out of the barrier in fifth place.

Earl and Marion Sande enjoying a rare day off from racing. Courtesy Sande Tom-linson Collection.

Within the next few strides, Zev's great speed and Sande's superior hand riding take them to the front of the pack. Martingale pounds the turf close on Zev's tail throughout the race and gives Zev a run for the money down the stretch. The crowd goes crazy as Zev and Martingale streak toward the finish line. At the furlong pole, Martingale begins his biggest challenge and thunders toward Zev. It appears he is gaining strength, while Zev seems to weaken under the strain of the struggle.

Sande tells Zev, "I hate to do this, Kid," as he calls on the steed, this time with the whip. The horse responds with flaring nostrils, a stout heart, and a burst of speed. The Rancocas green and white crosses the finish line a length and a half ahead of Martingale. Preakness winner Vigil comes in third. Zev's victory adds $53,625 to Rancocas winnings and a $5,000 silverplate trophy from the Kentucky Jockey Club for Sinclair's trophy case. Jonas Mulford cashes in his $8,400 winnings and plans to purchase a house and take a vacation trip to Cincinnati. Sande's first Kentucky Derby victory enters the history books.

Kentucky Governor E. P. Morrow congratulates David Leary. "The struggle, the triumph, the glory and success of your great horse is complete. His place is safe for he is now a part of Kentucky's history. We have crowned him with cheers, decked him with flowers, enshrined him in our heart, his memory shall become a golden one and live long. We honor courage in man or woman, we express this love when we honor so signally the high heart of the thoroughbred. In the name of the Kentucky Jockey Club, and of every true lover of the horse and with the joyous assent and approval of this matchless audience, I present you this cup as a trophy of your victory, a victory that will thrill the continent and sound around the world."

Sportswriter Damon Runyon adds to his Earl Sande poetic praise with:

> *Fator's a first rate jockey,*
> *McAtee more than fare.*
> *Lang, he is young and cocky,*
> *And Kummer a horseman rare.*
> *But, say, when I want to win*
> *Gimme a handy*
> *Guy like Sande*
> *Bootin' them hosses in.*
>
> *Green an' white at the home stretch,*
> *Who do you think'll win?*

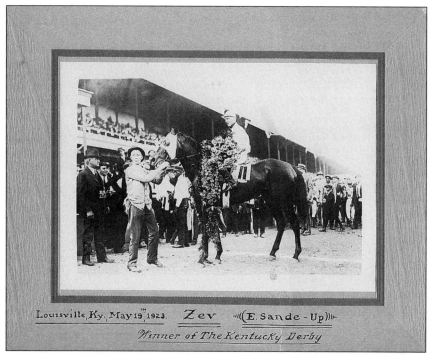

Louisville, Ky., May 19, 1923.   Zev   ·‹((E. Sande - Up))»·

Winner of The Kentucky Derby

Earl Sande on Zev wearing roses for winning the 1923 Kentucky Derby. Courtesy Sande Tomlinson Collection.

> *Who but a handy*
> *Guy like Sande*
> *Kickin' that baby in!*

After a week off, Sande returns to the track with a solid victory on Grey Lag in the May 24 Metropolitan Handicap. The 1923 Belmont Withers Stakes two days later features a contest between Sande on Zev, Clarence Kummer on Martingale, Coltiletti on Barbury Bush, and Dugan on Messenger, in a field of seven. Messenger breaks to the front of the pack, but Sande drives Zev to the fore within the first furlong, with Martingale at his heels. Sande keeps Zev comfortably in the first position and adds another length by the six-furlong pole. From there on, Sande and Zev enjoy an easy and clean trip, winning $18,000 for Rancocas. Sande tops out the day taking a $1,200 purse on Valor.

Sande scores a double with a victory on Fluvanna in the June 1 Floral Park Purse and Grey Lag in the $7,800 Suburban Handicap. Twenty-five thousand fans cheer Sande and Grey Lag as they trot back to the judges' stand after easily winning the historic Suburban Handicap, over Kummer on Snob II, and Laverne Fator on Mad Hatter.

Hildreth congratulates Sande, "Great riding Earl. You're really on a roll now."

Rancocas readies Zev for the $50,000 June 8 Belmont Stakes. Laverne Fator on Zev and Sande on Little Chief go through the paces in the final workout. A cold, brisk wind chills fans as they pile into the grandstand to witness the fifty-fifth running of the Belmont Stakes. Zev, with Sande up, breaks cleanly and within a dozen strides, hugs the rail. Martingale chases the leader but runs out of gas and falters. Then Chickvale takes up the challenge with a tremendous rush. Sande rides Zev out and wins by a length and a half. The crowd crowns Zev king of the three-year-olds with a solid round of applause and rousing cheers. Sande notches his second Belmont Stakes win on his belt.

"If it weren't for Zev getting hurt in the Preakness, I'd have ridden him to victory in the three toughest races on the American turf, Marion. Just like Johnny Loftus did on Sir Barton back in 1919, winning the Kentucky Derby, Preakness, and Belmont."

"It will come, Earl. I have faith in you."

Sande achieves another double, with wins on Humorette in the June 18 Aqueduct Canarsie Selling Stakes and Flying Cloud in the Olambala Handicap. Five days later, Rancocas scratches Knobble and Bud Lenner for the $4,000 Queens County Handicap. Instead, trainer Hildreth enters Sande on Zev for the competition.

Race fans give Sande and Zev a standing ovation as they parade up to the barrier. Sande pats Zev along side of his right cheek and tells him, "Looks like the fans want their money's worth today. Let's give them a run for their money."

Zev breaks fourth but quickly overcomes the three horses in front of him before a furlong passes. With powerful strides, Zev opens up a comfortable two-length lead.

Sande reins in Zev and says, "Take it easy, this one's in the bag. No sense expending too much energy."

The team coasts to victory but still wins with a time only a second slower than the track record. The crowd creates an uproar when Sande and Zev return to the stand. Zev earns the distinction as the first three-year-old winner of the Queens County Handicap since its 1902 debut. Sande completes his racing day by gaining the winner's circle again, this time on Maryland Bella.

"If the competition had put pressure on Zev, the brown colt would have easily shattered the record," Sande says.

"Zev needed a workout and we already worked the other horses in our stable to death." Hildreth explains. "He will have to give away a lot of weight in the Latonia Derby next Saturday and today was an opportunity to find out if he would be able to do so and perform well. He ran away with the Queens County Handicap today. That bodes well for the future."

Riding for other stables when Rancocas has no entries, Sande picks up more victories. Sande mounts Mrs. Payne Whitney's Untidy to capture the June 29 Aqueduct Gazelle Stakes with an easy two-length win over Sun Quest. Three races in a row fall to the Sande riding skill with victories on St. Allen, Frigate, and Tryster in front of a record-breaking Empire City crowd of 15,000 the first week of July.

Sportswriter Willie Fitzpatrick writes, "Not since the days of Tod Sloan have we had a jockey who can charm a racehorse like Earl Sande. Old fogies will remember that Tod could climb aboard a selling plater and make him beat stake horses. Sande possesses that same talent. Once he parks himself in the saddle, he seems to cast some sort of a spell over his mount and makes the dodo do things he has never done before. He talks to them and they obey. He kids them along and they fall for it. The wise Alecks said Tryster would lead for seven furlongs and then flop down for a nap. Instead of cracking, Sande let out a link and the colt increased his lead to a full length. This move won the race for him for he just had enough strength left to stick it out."

Sande rides St. James for George D. Widener and wins the $10,000 August 4 Saratoga United Stakes Hotel Stakes by two and a half lengths with blazing speed, and then takes Martingale's reins in a victory lap in the $3,500 Miller Stakes. Four days later, Sande wins the Sanford Memorial on Parasol and follows that the next day with a two-and-a- half-length victory, on Untidy over Sally's Alley in the Alabama Stakes.

The Jockey Club announces, "We've made final arrangements for the October 20 'Race of the Century.' It will feature an international match race of a mile and a half at Belmont Park. An American three-year-old will compete against Papyrus, the English winner of the Epsom Derby. Horses in the running to carry the American honors include Dunlin, Flagstaff, Martingale, My Own, and Zev."

Sande (third jockey from right) waiting to get weighed. Courtesy Sande Tomlinson Collection.

Making his bid for the opportunity to meet Papyrus, Zev, with Sande up, gives a solid win on September 1 and then takes on Untidy and Vigil in the September 8 Lawrence Realization. Coltiletti on Untidy breaks into the lead from the barrier, jumping out two lengths in front of Zev and Vigil. Rialto runs third place, and Sande keeps an eye on him through the backstretch. Straightened out, Sande raises his arm and lets go with the lash. By the time Zev and Untidy reach the furlong pole, the crowd is standing and cheering them on. Zev catches Untidy and sprints ahead to win by two and a half lengths. The race adds $24,410 to Rancocas winnings for the season.

"I didn't know if I would be able to catch Untidy, but Zev proved game and responded well to the lash."

Hildreth assures Sinclair, "We found out after the race that Zev cast a frog during the running of the Lawrence Realization. I have confidence that his foot will heal well and he'll be ready to run against Papyrus if The Jockey Club bestows that honor upon him."

While Zev heals, Sande mounts Sarazen for Mrs. W. K. Vanderbilt II's Fair Stable in the September 12 Belmont Champagne Stakes. As a game two-year-old, Sarazen beat the competition in every race.

Speaking of Sarazen at age two, breeder John E. Madden sneers, "It's time for me to sell out when you can breed a quarter horse to a plow mare and get a horse that can beat everything in America."

Sande gets the now three-year-old Sarazen away with a rush and takes a dominating lead. With the victory secure, Sande keeps the horse under restraint and wins the purse of $5,225 by two lengths over Aga Khan. In Doncaster, England, Papyrus loses to Tranquil in the St. Leger Stakes before a crowd of 150,000. Winners of the Epsom Derby typically fare badly at Doncaster, according to English turf condition.

The selection of the horse to represent American racing develops into a great controversy. Owners, race fans, and The Jockey Club heatedly debate the respective merits of My Own, Zev, and other possible entries. Belief that the American representative must be chosen at the Belmont National Sweepstakes is shattered when the selection committee agrees to take into account the results of the Lawrence Realization in which Zev competed. My Own, with Sande up, beat Untidy, guided by McAtee, in the National Trial Sweepstakes and Zev claimed the Lawrence Realization.

Under pressure, The Jockey Club tries to arrange a race between My Own and Zev. Hildreth agrees for Zev to meet My Own in a $50,000 race of a mile and an eighth, that being the distance he can run in his current condition. However, Admiral Grayson balks and demands a mile-and-a-half meeting, the length of the international match race. Negotiations break down and the elimination race between My Own and Zev never materializes.

Major August Belmont puts his oar in the water by stating, "There has been a great deal said about the Lawrence Realization and the Trial Sweepstakes. Untidy having run second in both and the condition of the track being practically the same, the comparison is all in favor of the performance in the Realization. Without a doubt, Zev should meet Papyrus."

The Jockey Club ends the controversy on October 5 by announcing the choice of Zev to represent American racing against Papyrus in the "Race of the Century." Admiral Cary T. Grayson's My Own serves as the first substitute, should Zev not be able to race.

So far in 1923, Zev won eight consecutive races, since losing his opening race in the Preakness, and earned more than $150,000 in purses for Rancocas. A victory against Papyrus would assure Zev of breaking Man o' War's money-winning mark.

Papyrus arrives from England and begins his workouts. Large crowds gather and witness Papyrus achieving fast times. In his final trials before the race, Papyrus unleashes great speed, equaling Man o' War's record. The racing world reacts, reducing the odds to even, from 3 to 1 in favor of Zev a week before the race.

England's leading jockey, Steve Donoghue, prepares for the big race. His background is similar to that of Zev's jockey, Earl Sande. Donoghue ran away from home at age thirteen and took apprenticeship with noted trainer John Porter. He lost his first race by a neck and won with his second mount. The older and more experienced Donoghue has been in the racing game since 1903 and counts many key races among his wins. Sande ranks as the premier rider on the American turf.

Jockey Club handicapper W. S. Vosburgh assesses Sande, "I've seen the best riders in action for more than fifty years. Sande is the best horseman seen in the United States in decades."

Oldtime jockey Bobby Odell ranks Sande. "Sande is different from most jockeys. If he can't ride square, he won't ride, that's all there is to it. He wins if he can, and if he sees a hole as big as your hat, he is going to try to go through it. He always holds his horse over before a race and if he doesn't like the way the horse is rubbed down, Sande rubs him down himself. He's best of all the jockeys."

W. C. Vreeland picks up the drumbeat for Sande, writing, "Earl Sande Like Caesar's Wife, Is Beyond Reproach, All Play Him, Not His mounts," and trying his own hand at Sande poetry:

> *Say, if you're blue*
> *And want to win*
> *Not lose, your*
> *Dough at the*
> *End of the day,*
> *Play...Sande*

More than 60,000 race fans converge upon Belmont Park, and an estimated $500,000 in gate receipts promises to create a new record in American racing annals. "The Oregon Statesman" headlines, "Zev goes to Post with odds of 6-5 Favoring Papyrus: Earl Sande of Salem, Premier American Jockey, will carry U. S. colors in International Race."

Leading up to the race, Zev develops a skin malady. It does not preclude his racing against Papyrus. In preparation for the race, Papyrus works out with Bar Gold and performs well.

Right after the third race of the day ends, fans pour out of the stands and make their way over to the paddock where Papyrus and Zev will be saddled and shown before the international race. As the royal equine visitor, Papyrus receives the larger paddock. Thousands of people crowd around the enclosure and admire Papyrus and his mate, Bar Gold, as they enter. His sleek, shiny, dark brown coat shows that the English horse is in prime condition. Soft felt boots protect his forelegs.

English trainer Basil Jarvis instructs the stable boy to lead Bar Gold and Papyrus around the paddock, giving the throng a chance to see the reigning English horse and challenger to Zev. Handlers remove the light blanket covering Papyrus and place the saddle on his back. Jockey Steve Donoghue arrives wearing primrose silks and talks last-minute race strategy with Jarvis. Donoghue mounts Papyrus and spurs the horse down the path to the track.

Steve Donoghue on Papyrus and Earl Sande on Zev ready for "The Race of the Century" at Belmont. Courtesy Keeneland-Cook.

Unlike the quiet crowd that admires Papyrus, partisan fans near Zev's paddock send up a rousing cheer for both Zev and favorite American jockey Earl Sande. In appreciation, Zev prances enthusiastically, giving the groom a bit of trouble controlling him. Pinkerton officers keep the crowd under control while handlers place Zev's saddle and blinkers. Sande receives final brief instructions from Hildreth before he mounts Zev for the "Race of the Century."

"Run right along with Zev if he goes to the front easily, but don't press him too hard if the Englishman wants to run his head off in the early stages."

Days of poor weather before the race do not deter fans or horses, as both Zev and Papyrus have reputations as mudders. Both gentlemen, Sande and Donoghue, agree not to steal the gate. If one or the other gets ahead, each promises to pull back to an even start. Zev takes an early lead on the soggy track, with Papyrus trailing closely for the first mile and a quarter. During the final quarter, Sande gives Zev his head and the colt responds with a terrific surge. Papyrus, apparently tired out, falls behind and loses by six lengths, even though Sande holds Zev under restraint. Rancocas wins $80,000, and $20,000 goes to Ben Irish, owner of Papyrus. The purse makes Zev the American leading money winner of all time. With ten solid victories, Zev earns in excess of $230,000 for Rancocas.

"I expected a hard fight all the way. I supposed that Papyrus was going to hang on until the last quarter and then open up. Zev was never better. He ran a great race and I am proud of him. I think he can beat any three-year-old in America over any kind of track," Hildreth says.

Papyrus's trainer, Basil Jarvis, responds with, "Zev is truly a wonder horse."

"I had the strategy of staying at close quarters to Zev if he passed me," losing jockey Donoghue explains. "This was my mistake. I should have gotten in front, if possible. Sande and Zev set a pace that was too much. I tried to move Papyrus up after we had gone half a mile, but he couldn't make it. Zev's flying hooves flung a hail of mud, and we had but to eat it. When we turned into the stretch, Papyrus gave everything. Zev moved faster and left us. Papyrus ran well enough. He did not have the speed to match Zev."

Sande comments, "I just let Zev have his head and sat pretty. In the stretch I asked for a little more and Zev gave it. We took it easy all the way. I was rather surprised we won so handily. Papyrus stuck right at our heels for a mile. I thought sure he was going to make us run some in the stretch.

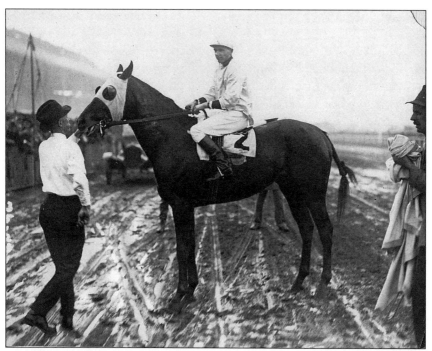

Earl Sande on Zev readying for "The Race of the Century" against Papyrus. Courtesy Ken Grayson Collection.

However, he couldn't stick when Zev started going. To say I'm tickled at winning would not begin to express my feelings. It was a wonderful victory. Zev raced beautifully under me."

"The Oregon Statesman" boasts, "It was Sande's generalship as much as Zev's greatness that brought victory to America. The little jockey who had piloted the Rancocas star to nearly all of his big triumphs outmaneuvered and out-thought his opponent."

Film producer Pathe covered the race with twenty cameras and releases the films in theaters across the country. The Irene Theatre in American Falls, shows the race in early November, with hometown boy Earl Sande on Zev. "American Falls Press" carries a photo of Zev pulling away from Papyrus in the stretch along with an article titled, "Earl Sande Wins Race of Career…Former American Falls Boy is the Idolized Jockey of America."

After Zev dispatches Papyrus back to England, race fans clamor for a match between My Own and Zev to settle the issue over which is the best American racehorse. The two horses are scheduled to meet in the $50,000

November 3 Latonia Championship. "The Idaho Statesman" headlines, "Boise Boy Will Be Jockey on My Own," and details how Laverne Fator will ride My Own and face American Falls jockey Earl Sande on Zev. Fator began racing at the Boise Fair Grounds after growing up in Hailey, Idaho, with his horse racing brothers. Before the race, trainers W. H. Brooks and W. P. Burch opt to have Clarence Kummer mount My Own instead of Laverne Fator.

While Sande readies for the Latonia Championship, he mounts Sarazen in an October 26 Laurel Special match race against Happy Thoughts with Schuttinger up. Sarazen immediately jumps to a comfortable lead before Sande reins him in. Sande repeatedly looks over his shoulder to assess any potential threat and let Schuttinger know who is in command of the race. Sarazen wins by two lengths.

After the race, Sande comments, "Speaking of happy thoughts, I settled an old score against Schuttinger because he outmaneuvered me when Eternal and Billy Kelly raced a few years back."

The next day, Sande spurs Big Blaze in the final strides of the race to edge out Legere on Modest and Marinelli on Aga Khan in the $5,000 Laurel Manor Handicap. Zev preps for the Latonia Championship by galloping to an easy victory, over Laverne Fator on Bracadale and Coltiletti on Tryster, in the October 31 Empire City Autumn Handicap. He wins by five lengths under restraint from Sande. After crossing the finish line, Sande takes Zev for an extra furlong to test his stamina.

American Falls telegraphs Sande: "We have named our upcoming rodeo, 'The Earl Sande Rodeo' in your honor."

"Nice to be remembered by the folks back out West."

As he prepares Zev for shipment to Latonia, Hildreth guarantees, "Nothing will keep Zev out of the race except a breakdown."

Other quality horses enter the Latonia Championship. The oddsmakers put Zev as a 3 to 5 favorite, followed by My Own, In Memoriam, Rialto, and Taylor Hay. Kentucky horsemen predict an upset by In Memoriam, throwing a monkey wrench into the hoped for outcome.

Hildreth tells Sinclair, "Zev is right and will show it. He shipped well from the East and will go to the post ready for a hard race. He can go the distance. He has been going along steadily, just as we wished, in all the work we mapped out for him."

My Own's owner, Admiral Grayson, contends, "My Own is in the best possible condition. This is the race we have waited for. I've always wanted him to go against Zev, and there will be no alibis if we are beaten. My Own's workout today convinced me that he is ready."

"The Salt Lake Tribune" carries an article indicating that Sande has the edge. "Earl Sande's intimate knowledge of the moods and whims and racing ability of My Own will serve as an advantage to Zev. There has been no instance in racing history in which a jockey so thoroughly knows the capabilities of his own mount and the chief rival of the mount, for Sande has a leg up on Admiral Grayson's My Own in six victories, and has handled Zev in ten of his feature contests. Sande, however, declines to predict the winner of the race."

Forty-five thousand race enthusiasts converge on Latonia for the much publicized one-and-three-quarter-mile battle between Zev and My Own. Zev owner Harry Sinclair, convinced that his horse and Sande will win the race, places $63,000 in bets in the track pari-mutual machines before the race.

In Memorium's jockey, Mack Garner, states, "If this ends up being a tight stretch battle, Mr. Sande will have to be satisfied with second money."

With the drop of the barrier, In Memorium shoots to the front within the first few strides. By the first quarter, the Rancocas colors of Sande draw into the lead. Under Sande's skillful riding, Zev pulls into the clear a mile and a half into the race, the distance in which Zev beat Papyrus not long ago. My Own trails Zev, with In Memorium close on his heels. Garner and In Memorium make their move and drive hard for the finish line, soaring past both My Own and Zev down the stretch. Tucked inside, In Memorium finishes the grueling race six lengths ahead of Zev, who beats My Own by eight lengths. The battle between Zev and My Own is over but pales with the defeat of both of them by In Memorium. With the "smart money" on either Zev or My Own, a $2 bet on In Memorium pays $23.60.

"I reached for my whip and went after Zev in the stretch, but he seemed to falter," Sande concedes. "In Memorium went by me as though we were tied. I have no alibis to offer. The best horse won."

Sinclair acknowledges, "Zev was beaten fairly. It was something of a shock to us, of course, for we had begun to believe that he was unbeatable, but there is no doubt that the best horse won the race."

For his riding skills exhibited on In Memorium and fulfilling his pre-race boast, Mack Garner receives a $10,000 bonus from owner Carl Wiedemann. In addition, Garner signs a $10,000 contract to ride for Peter Coyne in the 1924 season.

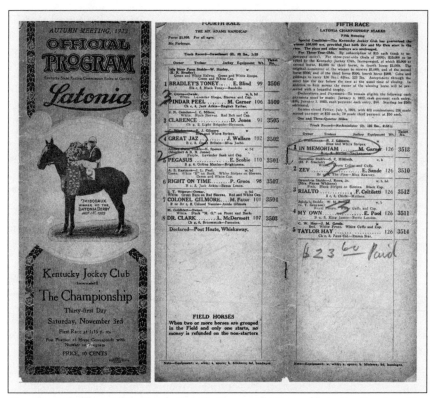

Zev versus In Memorium Match Race Program exterior and interior. Courtesy Dr. James Claypool.

Wiedemann says, "I challenge Rancocas for any amount of money for a match race between In Memorium and Zev. I gather the Rancocas stable is not particularly anxious for another run at our fine horse."

"Zev lost to In Memorium at Latonia in a clean-cut race. It doesn't convince me for a moment that In Memorium is a better horse than Zev. I figure it was just a poor race for Zev. It is not true, as Wiedemann charges, that we are afraid to race In Memoriam. I'm going to telegraph Kentucky racing official Colonel Winn right now that I am willing to race In Memorium for any sum from $25,000 to $100,000 a side, or higher if Wiedemann wishes, distance to be one mile or more," Hildreth tells reporters, before breaking off the interview and leaving the room.

A few days later, Wiedemann agrees to $10,000 a side, with another $10,000 offered by the racing association, for a race at a distance of a mile and a quarter to be run in Louisville. Meanwhile, Zev easily wins a nine-furlong Pimlico race against Homestretch and Tryster. Sande also pilots Top Sargeant to the winner's circle. Sande wins two in a row, with General Thatcher in the November 8 Reminescence Purse and Hephaistos in the Merchants' Handicap.

At Churchill Downs on November 17, the crowd grows loud with anticipation for the deciding race between Zev and In Memoriam. In the paddocks, Hildreth instructs Sande, "Lay behind with Zev until you hit the stretch and then let him go."

Zev breaks badly, and Garner on In Memorium takes the early lead and maintains it for the first six furlongs. Sande trails close behind, having Garner just where he wants him. Garner slacks off the pace to induce Sande to pass. The savvy Sande does not fall for the rouse, continuing to haunt In Memorium. Garner turns his head around several times to try to determine which way Sande will make his move. With a quarter mile remaining, Sande lets out a wrap and Zev shows great speed to the outside. He passes In Memorium, taking a two-length lead. Using the whip handily, Garner closes the gap, and at the wire both of the horses' noses bob wildly. Two of the judges give the nod to In Memorium, while the other three judges favor Zev. A slow motion camera shows the finish as inconclusive because of the angle. The win goes to Zev, the purse to Rancocas, and the riding honors to Sande.

"How do you like second money now, Garner?" Sande asks.

"The Groton Independent" front page headlines claims, "Sande Now Called World's Best Rider, Dakota Boy Gains Laurels by Masterful Riding of Zev." The article quotes turf rider Snapper Garrison, famous for his flashy "Garrison Finishes." "Son, whenever anyone asks you to name the greatest jockey in the world, don't hesitate. Just answer Earl Sande and you won't be far wrong. Not a flaw in his style. Gets his mount away from the post quicker and in better shape than any rider I ever saw. As fine a judge of pace as the turf has ever known, a great little thinker, game as a pebble and easy on his horse." Not to be outdone, the November 22, 1923, issue of "American Falls Press" carries an article citing, "Earl Sande, Falls Boy, Most Popular Jockey in America."

For 1923, Zev takes top money-winning honors for three-year-olds, with earnings of $272,008, surpassing Man o' War's 1920 record of $166,140. Zev wins twelve of his fourteen races while placing second once and out of the money once. Rancocas breaks all records for amounts won by an American stable in a single year with $438,849. Sam Hildreth takes top

Mack Garner and Earl Sande show they have no hard feelings. Courtesy Ken Grayson Collection.

honors for the largest amount of money won by a trainer with $392,124. Sande ranks as the nation's top jockey, with winnings of $569,394 for his employers, more than $224,000 greater than the highest ever earned previously by an American jockey in a single racing season. In comparison, the average American earns $1,393 per year, a dozen eggs cost 71 cents, a pound of butter cost 63 cents, and a loaf of bread cost 12 cents. During the year, Sande takes first in thirty-nine major stakes races, ten on Zev. He wins 28 percent of his mounts and places in the money 67 percent of the time. Another Idaho rider, Ivan Parke, captures the most first-place finishes, with 173, for earnings of $174,588. McAtee gathers second place in money won with $260,859.

Top 1923 Jockey Standings							
Jockey	Mounts	1st	2nd	3rd	%	$Winnings	In Money %
Parke, I	718	173	105	95	.24	$174,588	.519
Walls, P.	747	149	112	118	.20	208,400	.507
McAtee, L	489	123	83	79	.25	260,859	.582
Sande, E.	430	122	89	79	.28	569,394	.674
Wallace J.	877	112	110	139	.13	153,515	.411

Top 1923 Jockey Standings by Percentage Wins (100 or more mounts)			
Jockey	Mounts	Won	Percent
Sande, E.	430	122	.28
McAtee, L.	489	123	.25
Parke, I.	718	173	.24
Walls, P.	747	149	.20
McDermott, L.	616	111	.18
Horn, R.	740	106	.14
Wallace, J.	877	112	.13

One sportswriter of many praises the skills of Sande and Ivan Parke. "The remarkable career of Ivan Parke is a striking reminder of the great decline in horsemanship which has left its imprint on the quality of American racing. Parke is an exception and an exceptional jockey. Earl Sande had much the same sort of meteoric rise as Parke, but his horsemanship, with the passage of time, has taken on a brilliancy that renders his place secure in the history of American race riders. There have been few better horsemen than Sande in any era of American racing. To a natural aptitude for the profession, this young man, adds a greater degree of intelligence than is possessed by the average jockey. Sande's success has not been a matter of luck, for it takes merit to put him in a position where he is in demand for the best mounts. That a youth of his height should be able to ride at 115 pounds is remarkable, and calls for an amount of self-sacrifice that is not appreciated save by those who are familiar with the demands of the occupation."

"I've been thinking a lot about the future, Sam. As you know, I've been having trouble keeping my weight down and in good riding form. As a

Earl Sande escorted by police through crowd of admirers. Courtesy Sande Tomlinson Collection."

result, I've cut the number of mounts I accept. Maybe I should try riding in Europe where the allowed weights are higher."

"Nonsense, Earl," Hildreth counters. "You've put in some great riding this year, some of the best ever. With Zev coming back next year, and Mad Play and Bracadale coming along nicely, 1924 will be another memorable year for both Rancocas and Earl Sande."

Part 4

If A Guy Can't Ride, He's Not Living

Chapter 10

Tragedy at Saratoga

Hollywood beckons, and Sande appears in the 1924 release of *The Great White Way*, directed by E. Mason Hopper and starring Anita Stewart. The actress is supported by Tom Lewis, T. Roy Barnes, and Oscar Shaw. The story line centers on the prizefighting and newspaper worlds and includes glimpses of other well-known sports figures. Both Damon Runyon and Earl Sande appear in the picture. Vitagraph also starts production on a film titled *The Handy Guy*, featuring Earl Sande.

After filming, Earl and Marion visit the Sande family in Salem, Oregon. Reporters crowd around Earl and Marion, and bombard them with questions.

"What's it like being a famous movie star, Earl?"

"All I did was play myself. It wasn't hard."

"How about the upcoming racing season?"

"My trip West is one of pleasure. I would rather not talk shop. I had a strenuous season in the East, and a long time ago I promised my parents that I would come to Oregon for Christmas. I was delayed, however, and here I am almost two weeks late. Indoor training begins soon, and we will have to return to the stable before long."

Marion does talk a little shop. "There is nothing finer or more thrilling than a horse race. It is clean sport, and in these days of strict regulation, the best horse and best jockey usually win."

Scene from *The Handy Guy* featuring Earl Sande. Courtesy Sande Tomlinson Collection.

Asked to predict race action in the current year, Earl replies, "I believe that 1924 will be even more successful than this past season."

Controversy swirls around Rancocas owner Harry F. Sinclair at the opening of Jamaica racing. During its investigation of improprieties involving naval oil reserve leases on government-owned land in Wyoming, known as Teapot Dome, the United States Senate requests testimony from Sinclair and other representatives of Sinclair Consolidated Oil Company. After testifying five times, Sinclair refuses to appear a sixth time, contending that the Senate committee does not have the power to compel witnesses to testify and request personal papers and records.

Sweat beads on Sinclair's brow. His face turns red as he utters through clenched teeth, "I will reserve my evidence for the courts."

The United States government established the U. S. Naval Reserve near the Teapot Dome landmark of Wyoming in 1915. A June 1921 executive order from President Harding transfers the oil reserves from the Navy Department to the Department of Interior, under Secretary Albert B. Fall.

Sinclair organizes the Mammoth Oil Company in April 1922, the same month Secretary Fall leases the entire Teapot Dome reserves to the company. Under the terms of the agreement, the government will be paid royalties of 12 ½ to 50 percent. However, the royalties are payable only in oil certificates exchangeable for fuel oil and petroleum products at Mammoth Oil Company facilities.

During October1922, Sinclair's Mammoth Oil drills the largest well ever completed in Wyoming and the second largest in the country. Over the next year, the company invests $25 million in development of Teapot Dome. A year later, the U. S. Senate opens hearings to investigate improprieties associated with the Mammoth Oil Company leasing arrangement. Secretary Fall resigns his position "to pursue oil development opportunities overseas."

Charges of political immorality and rumors of payoffs and bribery abound in the press. The government files a March 1924 suit in Cheyenne to restrain Sinclair's Mammoth Oil from operating Teapot Dome. Sinclair not only faces court charges in Wyoming but is also under indictment by a Washington grand jury for refusing to answer questions, on advice of counsel, about his 1920 campaign donations.

"The Teapot Dome investigation has cost the government in excess of $32 million through April 16," Wyoming Senator Francis E. Warren, chairman of the committee on appropriations, reports.

Sinclair welcomes the beginning of the racing season as a diversion from Congressional committees, lawyers, and legal matters. However, the oil lease issue troubles him deeply and takes much of the enjoyment out of watching his horses race. Sinclair's off-the-racetrack troubles impact Rancocas stables as well. Unlike 1923, when Sande and Zev mastered the tracks and stakes races, 1924 brings a stable with no new superstar horse emerging to carry the Rancocas colors to victory time after time.

Zev shows great speed while training for the opening day April 29 Jamaica Paumonok Handicap. For six furlongs Zev turns in a pace of 1:11 4/5. In comparison, competitor St. James clocks at 1:12 3/5 for the same distance during his final workout.

Favorite Zev carries a heavy burden with the assigned weight of 130 pounds. The horses, led by Zev, receive a warm welcome from race fans. Little Celt and Dunlin break fast, and go ahead for a brief second before four-year-old Zev, with Sande up, takes command of first place. St. James, carrying only 112 pounds, finds his stride and wrestles the lead from Zev before a quarter of a mile passes under the horses' hooves. Soon daylight appears between the two horses and St. James cruises to a victory over Zev by two and a half lengths.

"Zev entered the race with better workout times, Marion. We should have won the race. The weight handicap makes it easier for untested and lower caliber horses to gain an advantage over mounts like Zev, who have already established a good track record."

"I don't understand the weighting system, Earl. Isn't the point to find out who is the best horse?"

"That's true in many races. But in handicap races, they try to level the playing field so that each horse has an equal chance of winning. It does not tell you who is the best horse. Often, an inappropriate assigned weight works to the disadvantage of the better horse."

"It seems unfair. I think it stinks."

"Those are the rules of the game. That's the challenge I accept when I take a mount. It's part of my job to overcome the assigned weight through race strategy, pacing, and horse savvy."

The next day, Sande mounts Tester for its three-year-old maiden race. The horse carries the top weight of 121 pounds through the muck, raw wind, and cold drizzle. Tester breaks well, and Sande backs him off to follow in the wake of the pace set by The Vintner. Down the stretch, Sande gives Tester his head, and the horse responds gamely, beating The Vintner by three-quarters of a length. Over the next two days, Sande gains the winner's circle on Pedagogue and Top Sergeant.

On May 3, Rancocas horses earn $8,000 with three first-place finishes and two second-place finishes. Laverne Fator wins the second race on Rancocas's Sheridan. In the Kings County Handicap, Zev totes 130 pounds and breaks fast, a neck behind Sunsini in the surge away from the barrier. By the time the field makes the paddock turn, Sande, on Zev, hugs the rail and clears traffic. Mad Play, with Fator up, gains ground and runs close in second position. Zev increases his lead to three lengths and then slacks off his pace, winning by a length and a half over Mad Play. Sande scores Rancocas's third win of the day by taking first on Sarzana, with Fator trailing on Superlette. The race crowd shows its appreciation for Sande's skillful riding with a rousing ovation.

Sande scores a May 5 triple, with first-place finishes on Aladdin, Honor, and Normal and a third-place finish on Wildrake. The next day, Sande mounts eight-year-old Mad Hatter, at odds of 10 to 1, to win a $1,000 purse over much younger horses. The crowd enthusiastically applauds the veteran horse and Sande as they enter the winner's circle.

"I've had some great races this week, Marion. I hope my good fortune carries over to the Preakness. I sure have not found the key to success in that classic race. I'm zero for three so far."

"You do so well in many other big races, Earl. I know you will win this one, too. Maybe this year will be the big breakthrough."

In the $54,000 Preakness, 12 to 1 Nellie Morse follows the pace until rounding the far turn, and then moves into the lead and finishes first. Laverne Fator, on Mad Play, comes in third, behind Transmute. Sande completes another frustrating Preakness far out of the money on Bracadale. After his poor performance in the Preakness, Sande sits out racing at Jamaica for the next week, in preparation for the Kentucky Derby.

Tulsa, Oklahoma-based and Cherokee-trained Black Gold shows both speed and weight-carrying ability while winning the May 13 Louisville Derby Trial Stakes by a convincing eight lengths. The western horse captures the public's attention. Based on his strength in the trial race, Black Gold gathers favorite status for the Golden Jubilee Kentucky Derby. Premier jockey Earl Sande originally gets the nod to ride Mad Play for the Derby competition on May 17, but ends up mounting Bracadale for Rancocas.

The Oklahoma wonder arrives in Louisville after winning twelve of his first fourteen starts, including the Louisiana Derby in New Orleans. Two Cherokees, Bill Fleetwood and Frank Touchstone, buy up tickets in the winter books at tremendous odds after Black Gold's New Orleans victory.

The field breaks in good alignment, with Transmute first surging ahead of the pack. He soon succumbs to Bracadale under Sande's urging. Bracadale increases his lead to three lengths after rounding the turn into the backstretch. Baffling and Chilhowee fight it out for second position. On the far turn, Black Gold makes his move, with Mooney riding hard. Turning for the drive home, Chilhowee shoots through on the rail and gains a brief lead, with Black Gold close on his tail. Bracadale falters and falls back. In the final drive to the finish line, Black Gold responds royally and wins by a short neck, earning the coveted Golden Jubilee winner's circle. Sande finishes fifth on Bracadale. Deafening applause for Black Gold lasts five minutes. Bill Fleetwood and Frank Touchstone cash in $250,000 in winnings and head to the Oklahoma oil fields to wildcat for their own black gold.

Controversy surrounds the final placements, as many observers claim that Bracadale finished third and not fifth as officially listed by the placing judges. One sportswriter calls the placement of Bracadale fifth "an inconceivable blunder." He contends the nearly identical colors of Rancocas Stable and the third-place finisher caused the confusion. "The Louisville Courier" agrees with the assessment that the placing judges made a mistake. However, the paper concludes it did not matter since Sande, on Bracadale, careened across the field, bumped into Black Gold, nearly knocking the horse to his knees, and should have been disqualified.

Sande and Bracadale regroup after taking some time off and enter the May 30 Belmont Withers Stakes. Sande stays off the pace set by Ladkin and Sun Pal. Eventually, Sun Pal races down Ladkin and takes the lead. A holiday crowd of 25,000 fans breaks into a cheer as Sande drives Bracadale close on Sun Pal's heels down the homestretch. With a surge, Bracadale takes over the lead and finishes in front of Sun Pal by two and a half lengths. Bracadale's win adds $19,000 to Rancocas earnings, and his stable companion, Sheridan, contributes another $750 with a third-place finish.

"Nice race, Bracadale, too bad you didn't give the same kind of performance in the Preakness and Derby."

Sande next mounts aging Mad Hatter, while Laverne Fator dons the Rancocas colors on Mad Play, to compete in the May 31 Suburban Handicap. Carrying a top weight of 125 pounds, Mad Hatter starts slowly and gradually inches his way up on the pack. Rialto and Mad Play burn themselves out, and Sande takes command at the head of the backstretch, keeping Little Celt a comfortable distance behind. The victory contributes $9,150 to Rancocas winnings and also makes Sande the first jockey in history to win two Suburban Handicaps in succession.

Sande follows up his victory on Mad Hatter with a next day maiden-race win on Pep to Peep at 12 to 1 odds. It's another case of Sande getting every pound out of his horse, and the crowd cheers his efforts.

Meanwhile, Harry Sinclair's oil problems are just beginning. Prior to the running of the $50,000 Belmont Stakes, the District of Columbia Supreme Court indicts Harry Sinclair, on June 5, for conspiracy in connection with lease improprieties on the Teapot Dome government oil lands in Wyoming. The following day, Sande scores a first-place finish on Thunderclap and two other in-the-money finishes.

While legal maneuverings proceed, a field of eleven gathers to compete in the June 7 Belmont Stakes. From the rail position, Sande breaks Mad

Play to the lead. At the turn, Sande reins in Mad Play and allows his stable-mate, Sheridan, with Laverne Fator up, to cut the pace. The two Rancocas horses maintain this position until the far turn when Sande urges Mad Play ahead to a two-length lead. Mr. Mutt charges toward the finish line, but cannot catch Mad Play.

"That's your third Belmont Stakes, Earl. How does it feel?"

"Like a million dollars, Marion. It's going to be a great year."

Five days later, the handicapper assigns Zev the top weight of 130 pounds for the June 14 Brooklyn Handicap. Mad Hatter draws a weight of 120 pounds. Prince of Umbria, carrying 107 pounds, sets the pace for most of the race, with Sande keeping Zev's nose at the leader's stirrups, and Dunlin only a head back. The three come swinging around the far turn and storm down the backstretch as close as three fleas on a dog. Realizing that he cannot shake off Zev, Prince of Umbria gives up the ghost and drops back. Callahan makes a move and Dunlin surges to the left, cutting off Enchantment and crowding Zev onto the rail. Hephaistos and Sunsini sneak through for first and second place, respectively. Zev takes fifth, Fator on Mad Play finishes far back in the pack, and Dunlin is disqualified for interfering with Zev.

"Marion, I thought we had a good chance today despite all the weight Zev gave up."

"I'm so thankful you didn't have a spill, Earl, when they pushed you to the rail."

Leading up to the June 21 Queens County Handicap, Sande wins the Lady Violet Handicap with Outline driving hard. Carrying a top weight of 127 pounds, Mad Hatter runs a tad short of the track record for the distance and takes the Queens County Handicap. The crowd reacts by giving Sande and Mad Hatter a reception fitting a big stakes champion. Sande scores another five wins between June 26 and July 6.

Zev ranks as one of the horses in contention to meet the French champion, Epinard, in the upcoming international match race. Other possible contenders include Baffling, Ladkin, Little Chief, My Own, Princess Doreen, and Rockminster.

After a first-place finish on Outline in the July 10 Bryn Mawr Purse, Sande mounts Majority in a $1,000 claiming purse race at Empire City. Around the first turn, Water Girl swerves against Majority, and both horses tumble to the turf. Sande narrowly escapes being killed in the crash. He picks himself up and makes his way over to Water Girl's jockey, seventeen-year-old George Cooper, who lies crumpled on the track. Sande calls the jockey's name, but he does not respond. Sande takes his jockey's cap and fans Cooper's face to no avail. The track ambulance arrives and transports Cooper to the hospital, where he is treated for serious injuries.

"I was so frightened when I saw your horse go down. Be careful out there, Earl," Marion warns.

"It's one of the dangers of the track, Marion. Cooper took a hard blow when Majority struck him, but he's going to be all right."

Mark Fator scores a double on July 15. First he wins on Bracadale, beating out Sande on Mad Hatter. Then he takes Honor to the wire, in front of Sande on Rival. Bracadale's win stands, however, race stewards suspend Fator for three days for crowding Bonaparte. Over the next two weeks, Sande picks up three more victories.

Racing begins at Saratoga Springs on August 4. Sande inks a double, with victories on Voltaic and Salacia. A day later, Sande and Thunderclap win the Pittsfield Claiming Handicap in a canter.

On August 6, 1924, Sande takes to the track and nods to Marion, who sits with Mrs. Vanderbilt. Sande's at the top of his racing form. He rounds the turn close to the rail in the first race, on James Butler's Spurt. Senor, with Benny Marinelli up, swerves toward the rail to take the lead. Senor bumps Gnome Girl, who slams into the fast-charging Spurt. Sande's horse stumbles and, one by one, Speckled Beauty, Semper, and Catheleen Ni Houlihan fall on top of the downed horse and Sande. Shocked cries from the stands pierce the air as the tangled mass of man and beast hits the turf. When the dust clears, the riders of the three horses who crashed into Spurt crawl out of the wreckage with minor scrapes. However, Sande lies unconscious with his leg crushed and mangled.

A wave of horror sweeps through the clubhouse as stablehands carry Sande's limp body to the track hospital in the secretary's building.

"No! No! It's Sande," exclaims Rear Admiral Cary T. Grayson, personal physician of the late President Woodrow Wilson and My Own owner. Grayson rushes to Sande's side from his private box and offers assistance. He quickly assesses the severity of Sande's injuries and orders, "Get an ambulance here immediately. This boy needs immediate medical attention."

Meanwhile, Mrs. Vanderbilt puts her arm around Marion to steady and comfort her. She assists the ashen-faced young wife to the track hospital. Admiral Grayson helps revive Earl. Seeing his wife, Earl whispers, "Don't worry about me. I'm only shaken up. Nothing serious."

Marion faints and is attended to by Mrs. Vanderbilt. An ambulance arrives and rushes Earl, Marion, and Sam Hildreth to the Saratoga Hospital. The Jockey Club's Joseph Widener telegraphs Dr. James Russell of the Roosevelt Hospital in New York City, "Come at once. Spare no expense. Sande seriously injured."

Widener next turns his attention to the jockeys. He berates them for rough riding. "Look at what your actions have caused. There goes the star of your ranks, a victim to the practice." He leaves the jockeys wiping tears from their eyes.

At the hospital, Marion and her friends await word of Earl's condition. Finally, the doctor emerges from the examining room with news.

Dr. D. C. Moriata explains the situation. "Earl has suffered two fractures of the left leg, one just below the hip and the other below the knee. In addition, one of his ribs is broken. He's still shaken up and needs his rest, but you can see him now. He's not in critical condition, but his injuries are very serious. You can be sure he will be given the best of care, Mrs. Sande."

Marion gently holds Earl's hand. Tears well up in her eyes. "Looks pretty bad, Earl. How do you feel?"

"Sore as all get out, honey," Earl says through clenched teeth.

He turns his head slightly toward Sam Hildreth and says with a soft laugh, "I think you trainers feed those horses too much, Sam. They sure weigh a bunch when they roll over you."

"The Doc says he doesn't know if you'll be able to ride again, Earl. You can always help out with the training or train on your own. I've taught you all I know, and you'd make a fine trainer," Hildreth says.

Earl first looks at Marion and then back to Hildreth. "If a guy can't ride, he's not living."

"That's enough talk about racing, Earl, you need your rest," Marion states in a firm voice. She pulls the sheets up to Earl's neck and gives him a kiss on the cheek.

The hospital visitors leave while Sande dozes off. Marion remains by his side all night. The next day she takes a room across the hall from Earl's to be close to him and have a place to rest and freshen up.

"American Falls Press" reports, "Sande, Famous Jockey Injured at Saratoga… trampled by four horses…unconscious when picked up." "The New York Times" headline reads, "Sande Badly Hurt, May Ride no More." "The Groton Independent" tells its readers, "Physicians say he'll never ride again.

Earl is a likeable sort of lad and he is well known by the younger men of Groton and community."

Speculation about Sande's riding career runs rampant. Rumors surface that the premier jockey already planned to retire after this season because he was having trouble maintaining weight to compete successfully. Fans argue whether or not the terrible accident will put an end to Sande's racing career.

The next day, Marion, Admiral Grayson, Dr. Moriarta, Dr. Russell, and Joseph Widener attend Sande's bedside during a news conference. Despite experiencing excruciating pain, Sande declares, "I'll fool them all. I'll ride again."

Racing industry visitors to the hospital include Saratoga Racing Association President Richard T. Wilson, Jr. and Treasurer George Bull, Harry Payne Whitney, Robert Gerry, Joseph Widener, and Mrs. Harry Sinclair. Telegrams from all over the country descend upon Saratoga Hospital with offers of condolences and hopes for a speedy recovery. Flowers sent by well-wishers and fans overflow Sande's hospital room and the hallway.

The doctors and nurses hold a more guarded belief about Sande's prospects of returning to racing. "The New York Times" says of Sande's promise to don his silks again, "That, however, is improbable with medical personnel calling Sande's condition, 'not so good.'"

Admiral Grayson explains the nature of Sande's injuries in non-technical terms. "There are two square fractures of the left leg, both clean breaks, one a little below the knee and the other about six inches higher. Above the upper fracture, Earl suffered a well-defined splintered condition on either side. Fortunately, no fracture of the knee or the hip joint occurred. Dr. Russell put Earl under ether and joined the fractured parts firmly together. We manipulated the intermittent portion into position and encased the whole leg in splints. We attached a weight of eighteen pounds to prevent shortening of the limb as it sets. If the treatment adopted last night is not productive, we will employ a treatment developed during the World War, and found successful in the most stubborn cases. As soon as Earl's condition improves to the point where he can be moved, we will transfer him to Roosevelt Hospital in New York, under the constant supervision of Dr. Russell."

Fellow Idaho jockeys Mark and Laverne Fator and Ivan Parke visit Sande in the hospital. They bring greetings from other jockeys, and news that the race stewards suspended Marinelli for his actions resulting in Sande's spill.

While Sande begins his long recovery, noted steeplechase jockey William Keating is thrown at Saratoga and his mount, Glen Reagh, rolls on top of him. One of the horse's hooves strikes Keating in the head. He is rushed to the hospital unconscious and in critical condition. After several days, Keating recovers consciousness and continues to improve. Marion offers her sympathy to Mrs. Keating.

Jockey Marinelli visits the hospital. "I'm sorry for the accident, Earl. I meant no harm. I was just rushing to get advantage on the track. I hope you have a speedy and complete recovery."

"Don't give it a second thought, Benny. You didn't do it on purpose. God has been good in sparing my life. As you know, others, like our friend Frankie Robinson, have not been so fortunate."

Marion greets the throngs of visitors and press who continue to visit the hospital. "Earl and I are overwhelmed by the avalanche of telegrams, cablegrams, and flowers. We are especially touched by the telegram sent by Papyrus's jockey, Steve Donoghue. I want to express my sincere appreciation for all the messages of sympathy that have come from friends and admirers of my husband. Earl also wishes to acknowledge the many acts of kindness he has received from members of The Jockey Club and the Saratoga Racing Association. He speaks confidently of a speedy recovery and a return to the saddle."

After several good days, Sande develops a temperature, and doctors report that additional X-rays show a broken left collarbone. Because of Sande's difficulties, hospital officials forbid visitors. Over the next few days, Sande's condition improves, and visitors are again permitted. However, his doctors announce that it is inadvisable to move Sande to New York or his home until he convalesces at least eight more weeks.

When Doc Pardee hears of Sande's accident, he comments, "That boy is music. He has wonderful hands, a fine mind, and sense of rhythm that makes him part of the horse. He's a past master in judging pace, and he knows how and when to use the whip. Mark my words, Earl Sande isn't down and out. He'll be back stronger than ever."

Will Rogers honors Sande by dedicating his August 17 column to him. Newspapers across the nation carry it.

> Out of the West came a skinny runt kid. He was born in the hills of South Dakota. On Sundays Cowpunchers and Ranchers would meet and have Cow Pony races. On account of being so small he was lifted up and a surcingle was strapped around

over his legs and around the horse. He was taken to the starting line on a straightaway and was "lapped and tapped." He had the nerve and seemed to have the head. So they cut the surcingle and he got so he could sit up there on one of those postage stamp things they call a Jockey's saddle. He kept riding around these little Country Shooting Gallery meets, and Merry-Go-Round Gatherings until he finally got good enough to go to a real race track at New Orleans. There he saw more Horses in one race than he had ever seen at one track before.

His first race he run 2nd. Then he said to himself "Why run second? Why not run first?" And he did. They began to notice that this kid really savied a horse. He spoke their language, Horses seemed to know when the kid was up, He carried a bat (Jockey's term for a whip) but he never seemed to use it. Other jocks would come down the stretch whipping a horse out when the best he could finish would be 4th or 5th. But not this kid. When he couldn't get in the money he never punished them. He hand rode them. He could get more out of a horse with his hands than another jock could get with the old battery up both sleeves.

He got to be recognized as one of the best, and he passed from one stable to another until he landed with the biggest, a real trainer and a real sportsman-owner. How many thousands of people in every line come to New York every year that want to make good, get ahead and be recognized! They come by the millions. How many, if anything happened to them, would get even a passing notice in the busy and overcrowded New York press. If some millionaire died, the best he could get would be a column, Then perhaps it wouldn't be read through by a dozen. But what blazoned across the front pages of every metropolitan daily a few days ago, in bigger headlines than a presidential nomination, bigger than the Prince of Wales will get on his arrival? In a race at Saratoga Springs, N. Y. a horse had fallen, and carried down with him a little skinny kid (that had slept in his youth not in a 5th Avenue mansion but in box stalls all over the country with horses, the horses he knew how to ride and the horses that loved to run their best for him).

Here was the headline: "Sande Is Hurt. He may never ride again." They don't have to give even his first name, few know it. They don't have to explain who he is. They don't have to tell which Rockefeller or Morgan it was. It was just Sande. There is only one. Our Sande! The boy who carried America's colors to victory over England's great Papyrus and its premier jockey, Steve Donoghue.

The ambulance rushes on the track and picks him up; it is followed by hundreds running afoot. The entire grandstand of people rush to the temporary hospital to see how Sande is, and hoping and praying that it's not serious. He revives only enough to tell his wife he is all right. Game kid that. Then he faints again, Mrs. Vanderbilt and the elite of society are assisting and doing all they can to help. A personal physician to a president of the United States is working over him. He could not have shown any more anxiety over the president than he did over this kid. When those thousands of pleasure seekers and excitement hunters rushed from the stands, and saw them lifting that lifeless looking form from that track ambulance there was not one that wouldn't have given an arm off their body if they had thought it would save his life and that goes for touts, and grooms, and swipes, as well as the public.

Some western people who don't know are always saying the Easterners have no heart, everything is for themselves and the dough. Say, don't tell me that! Geography don't change human nature, If you are right, people are for you whether it's in Africa or Siberia. A wire was sent by Mr. Widener, a millionaire racing official, to Dr. Russell, the great specialist of Roosevelt Hospital, N.Y. "Come at once. Spare no expense. SANDE is hurt." That's all Secretary Slemp could do if President Coolidge was hurt.

Mr. Sinclair withdrew all those horses from the remaining races. He would withdraw them for life if he knew it would restore this kid who worked for him, back to normal again.

Now what made this one hundred and ten pound half portion of physical manhood beloved by not only the racing public but by the masses who never bet a cent on a horse race in their lives? The same thing that will make a great man in any line—his absolute HONESTY. The racing public are very fickle and when they lose they are apt to lay blame on almost any quarter but, win or lose, they knew it was not Sande. To have insinuated to one of them, that he ever pulled a horse, would have been taking your life in your hands. What do you suppose he could have gotten out of some bunch of betting crooks to have pulled Zev in the big international race? Why, enough to retire on and never have to take another chance with his life by riding. He could have done it on the back stretch and no one would have ever known.

Ability is all right but if it is not backed up by honesty and public confidence you will never be a Sande. A man that don't love a horse, there is something the matter with him. If he has no sympathy for the man that does love horses than there is something worse the matter with him. The best a man can do is to arrive at the top in his chosen profession. I have always maintained that one profession is deserving of as much honor as another provided it is honorable.

Through some unknown process of reasoning we have certain things that are called arts, and to be connected with them raises you above your fellow man. Say, how do they get that way? A writer calls himself a literary man or an artist, There are thousands of them, and all, simply because they write, are termed artists. Is there a Sande among them? Caruso was great but he only had to show ability. He didn't have to demonstrate any honesty. Nobody tried to keep him from singing his best by bribery.

Now if you think the racing public and millions of well wishers are hoping for this kid's recovery, what about the horses? They knew him better than the humans did. Why, that horse would have broken his own neck rather than hurt Sande. Who is going to ride him in the next race and make him win and not whip him—not Sande. Who is going to sit on him just where he will be the easiest to carry? Not Sande. Who is going to lean over and whisper in his ear and tell him when to go his best? Not Sande. Who is going to carry a bat and not use it? Not Sande. Who is going to watch his hand on that starting barrier and have him headed the right way just when the starter springs it? Not Sande. No, the horses are the ones who are going to miss him.

If we could speak their language like he can, here are a few conversations that you will hear through the cracks in the box stalls: "Gee, I can't run, I don't seem to get any help. I wish Sande was back."

A three-year-old replies, "I wish there was something we could do. If they would just let us go up to the hospital and talk to him, he would savvy. I wish we had him here in a box stall. I would stand up the rest of my life and give him my bed. I would fix him some clean hay to lay on. He don't want those white caps and aprons running around. He wants to lay on a horse blanket, and have his busted leg wrapped up with bandages like he knows how to use on ours. I bet they ain't even got Absorbine up there. That kid would rather have a bran mash than all that goo they will feed him with up there."

The old stake horse 4 stalls down the line overhears and replies: "Sure, I bet they have one of them bone specialists. What that kid needs is a good vet."

The old selling plater butts in: "Sure, we could cheer him up if he was here. Them foreigners up there don't speak his tongue, That kid is part horse. Remember how he used to kid with us when he would be working us out at daylight when the rest of the star jocks was in the feathers. One morning I told him if he didn't quit waking me up so early in the morning I was going to buck him off. He got right back at me; he said, 'If you do I will get you left at the post your next race.' Gee, he sure did throw a scare into me. And, say, you couldn't loaf on that bird either. He knew when you was loafing and when you was try-ing, I threw up my tail one hot day to make him think I was all through. He gave me one cut with the bat and I dropped that tail and left there so fast I could have run over Man o' War. Gee, those were great days; do youse reckon Zev knows anything about it? I hope they don't tell him, it would break his heart. He sure did love that kid."

Harry F. Sinclair's personal car transports Earl Sande from Saratoga Hospital to Roosevelt Hospital in New York City on September 2, 1924, for further treatment and observation. His wife, Marion, and Dr. William White accompany him on the journey.

Sinclair states with great emphasis, "Nothing but the best treatment for my star jockey."

Clarence Kummer mounts Ladkins and Laverne Fator takes the reins on Zev in a race against the French champion, Epinard. Days later, Sande watches the race from his bed in Roosevelt Hospital, courtesy of a special private screening arranged by the "The New York American" sports department and International News Reels films.

Ladkins, with Kummer up, pushes past Epinard by a nose to claim the international race. Fator, on Zev, comes in fourth.

"Zev rode a good race, but I guess he missed Sande a bit," Fator explains.

Sande views the film and comments, "Oh boy, that was a race, wasn't it? It was like a trip to the track for me after weeks away. Everything was great."

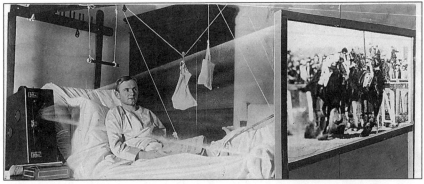

Earl Sande watching the International Match race with Epinard. Author's Collection.

After several more weeks in the hospital, Sande leaves the hospital on crutches, and settles down for recuperation at his father-in-law's Cambridge, Massachusetts, home. "The Blood-Horse" columnist Roamer writes, "Rumor has it that Earl Sande is convinced he has ridden his last race. There is a strong likelihood, when he is able to discard his crutches, he will weigh in the neighborhood of 140 lbs., and his ability to ever get down to riding weight is open to grave suspicion. Now that Tom Welsh has severed his connection with J. E. Widener's stable, some of the wise-acres insist that Sande will reappear on the scene next spring as Mr. Widener's trainer. Quite a compliment to Sande, albeit left-handed. Whether Sande has the ablility to succeed as a trainer is on the knees of the gods, but as Mr. Widen-

Clarence Kummer, winner of an International Race against Epinard. Courtesy Sande Tomlinson Collection.

er hasn't possessed a horse of real class since Naturalist retired, it is manifest Sande's new connection will be no bed of roses."

Earl returns with Marion to their home. He is briefly hospitalized in November because of a recurrence of kidney trouble resulting from the period of long inactivity.

"My wife has been at practically every race for the past few years, and has always been ready with a word of encouragement. With Marion's help I'm winning the fight for health and strength. I'll be back at the track next spring," Sande promises.

In December, Sande attends the New York City funeral of Major August Belmont. Afterward, reporters photograph him with a work horse, and in a long fur coat, holding his cane.

About the horse, Sande remarks, "Well, I sure like this guy. Good to be next to a horse again. I hope to be back on the track next year, where I belong."

Meanwhile, the State Board of Compensation convenes hearings to assign responsibility for Sande's medical expenses, incurred as a result of his

Earl Sande with New York work horse. Author's Collection.

accident while riding James Butler's Spurt at Saratoga. Board referee C. B. Wickham concludes that since Sande was not riding for Rancocas Stable at the time of the accident, Mr. Sinclair and his insurance company, Aetna, are not responsible. The hearing recesses until April, when the responsibility of James Butler and his insurance company will be determined.

Sande reacts to this news with disbelief. He seeks out Sam Hildreth. "Who runs Rancocas? Mr. Sinclair or the insurance companies? So much for 'nothing but the best treatment for my star jockey,' Sam. I guess it's a business and gets down to dollars and cents. If Mr. Sinclair won't do what's right, you can tell him to find another rider for next year."

With Sande's accident at Saratoga cutting his 1924 racing short, Ivan Parke leads all jockey categories, with 205 wins totaling $290,395. This marks the third year in a row that an Idaho-bred jockey tops the charts. Sarazen wins the most money for a three-year-old, with $95,640, a sharp drop from the $272,008 won by Zev a year earlier. Sam Hildreth still maintains the leading money-winning trainer spot, with $225,608. However, Harry Payne Whitney's stable takes top ranking, with $240,193 in win-

Earl Sande with cane on the road to recovery. Author's Collection.

nings, compared with $228,563 for Sinclair's Rancocas stables. Sande earns $131,125 for his employers, while winning 27 percent of his races and landing in the money 58 percent of the time.

Top 1924 Jockey Standings							
Jockey	Mounts	1st	2nd	3rd	%	$Winnings	In Money %
Parke, I.	844	205	175	121	.24	$290,395	.594
Wallace J.	898	165	126	126	.18	196,517	.464
Lang, L.	816	139	124	115	.17	163,645	.463
Maiben, J.	645	139	98	90	.22	285,030	.507
Walls, P.	745	135	134	104	.18	224,175	.501
Sande, E.	119	32	13	24	.27	131,125	.579

Top 1924 Jockey Standings by Percentage Wins (100 or more mounts)			
Jockey	Mounts	Won	Percent
Sande, E.	119	32	.27
Parke, I.	844	205	.24
Maiben, J	645	139	.22
McDermott, L.	635	123	.19
Paden, H	558	104	.19
Wallace J.	898	165	.18
Walls, P.	745	135	.18
Pernia, O.	631	116	.18

Damon Runyon captures the nation's sentiment with the following 1924 verse:

> *Maybe there'll be another,*
> *Heady an' game, an' true-*
> *Maybe they'll find his brother*
> *At drivin' them hosses through.*
> *Maybe-but, say, I doubt it.*
> *Never his like again-*
> *Never a handy*
> *Guy like Sande*
> *· Bootin' them babies in!*

Green an' white at the quarter-
Say, I can see him now,
Ratin' them just as he orter,
Workin' them up-an' how!
Green an' white at the home stretch-
Who do you think'll win?
Who but a handy
Guy like Sande
Kickin' that baby in!

Maybe we'll have another
Maybe in ninety years!
Maybe we'll find his brother
With his brains above his ears.

Maybe-I'll lay agin it-
A million bucks to a fin-
Never a handy
Guy like Sande
Bootin' them babies in!

Chapter 11

Comeback

"Plenty nice of you and Mrs. Pardee to put us up, Doc. The warm weather, good companionship, and being around a real western ranch will benefit my rehabilitation."

"Nonsense, Earl. That's what your friends are for. We'll have you throwin' that cane away and in the saddle again before you know it."

"It sure brings back a lot of great memories to be here in Prescott. I still remember that day Burr Scott and I rode into town on his old wagon, trailing those tired out race horses."

"Well, son, you've come a long way since then. Top rankin' in all of American horse racin' in 1921 and 1923. You probably would have made it again last year if it were not for your spill at Saratoga. I knew as soon as you took Tick Tack for a spin at the fairgrounds back in 1916 that you had it in you to be one of the great riders. Burr told me you had the special knack, and he darn sure was right. The folks around here are plenty proud that America's most famous jockey got his start at real racin' in Prescott."

"Thanks, Doc. You had a lot to do with my success. I'll never forget that."

"Understand you split with Rancocas."

"Had to, Doc. They wouldn't pay for my hospital bills as promised. I gave my all to them, and look how they treated me."

"It's a business, Earl. You get them insurance companies involved and

247

Earl Sande up on a horse again, with cow saddle. Courtesy Ken Grayson Collection.

what's right and what's done are two completely different things. You have to take care of yourself, Earl. Nobody else will do it for you. As for loyalty, just be true to yourself and those you love. That's all there is to it."

"Thanks for the advice, Doc. Looks like you folks have spruced up the fairgrounds since I was here last."

"Well, the work is never done improvin' things. It's not Churchill Downs or Belmont Park, but serves our purposes well. How about we start your return to the saddle western style? Your leg muscles are still out of shape from the accident and months of recuperatin'. As you know, when racin' you grip the horse with your thigh, knee, and calf, so these parts naturally receive the most strain. With your injuries, we need to keep the pressure off those areas until you are stronger and comfortable on a horse once again. Startin' rehabilitation with a cow saddle will help keep the strain off those areas until you heal up better, Earl."

"OK, you're the doctor."

"Well, let's say I'm puttin' my little bit of vet schoolin' to mighty good use for a change."

Earl and Marion return East in March. He files a New York racing application, which causes a stir when he does not list the stable for which he will be riding. The Jockey Club grants Sande his license. He appears in good spirits and lighter in weight than in recent years. In late March, Sande mounts the first thoroughbred since his accident at Saratoga in August and begins preparation for his return to the track.

On April 3, the District of Columbia Supreme Court dismisses the indictment against Sinclair in the Teapot Dome scandal on a technicality. However, Sinclair does not escape unscathed. A jury convicts him of contempt for refusing to answer questions and sentences him to seven months in jail and a $1,000 fine.

Earl poses in mid-April with his riding silks, boots, and caps. He explains his situation to newspaper reporters. "I promised you I would be back. I don't care to say any reason for Rancocas and me parting ways. I have nothing but the best of feelings toward Mr. Sinclair and Mr. Hildreth. I asked to be released from my contract, and that wish was granted. Now I'm looking toward the future. I've signed a first call contract with Joseph E. Widener for $25,000 and a percentage of the winnings. Other than that, I am entirely a free-lance rider. Mr. Widener was more than good to me when I was hurt at Saratoga. He stood by me throughout and now employs me. The accident is out of mind and won't affect how I ride or how effective I'll be on the track. I'm anxious to ride winners for Mr. Widener."

In the April 21 Havre de Grace opening day Newark Handicap, Sande trots Mrs. W. K. Vanderbilt II's Sarazen onto the track. Thunderous applause echoes from the grandstand, and Sande raises his cap to the crowd, which only causes more pandemonium and cheering. Marion waves her handkerchief from the stands. At the barrier, Sande waits for the long-anticipated first race after his accident.

The two track champions are no strangers. Sande rode Sarazen to victory when the red gelding made his debut in September 1923. They joined forces again five days later to win the Champagne Stakes. The team also won two other races, in late October 1923 and July 1924, before injuries sidelined Sande.

Sarazen answers the bugle call with a load of 129 pounds, and gives the major contender, Riddle's Big Blaze, a fourteen-pound advantage. Sarazen draws the post position on the inner rail, while Big Blaze starts from the outside position. Digit shows first, with Sarazen breaking nearly last. The Vintner takes the lead and sets a killing pace. Sande forgoes going wide and trails on the inside. On the stretch, Sande gives Sarazan his head and swings around The Vintner. Big Blaze moves up into second place and makes a run at Sarazen, to no avail. Sarazen wins the race in the record time of 1:11, breaking the mark set by Billy Kelly in 1919 and equaled by him in 1921. The riotous reaction of the crowd as track officials present a floral horseshoe to Sande proves the Sande of old is back in form. A tear streams down his face. In the grandstands, Marion weeps with joy.

"All I could think of as I shot past the finish post was that my wife and my mother would be greatly delighted. I'm embarrassed by all the applause, but grateful for the fans who have stood by me. When you sit on such a runner as Sarazen, you do not think of anything else but to win. I'm the proudest man in Maryland today."

Two days later, Sande suffers a gallstone attack and is rushed to the hospital. Marion comforts him back at home.

"Maybe you should wait for a while before you return to racing, Earl."

"No need to worry, Marion. The doctor says I'll be fine."

At the April 25 Board of Compensation hearing, the United States Fidelity and Guaranty Insurance Company attorney, William W. Dimmick, representing Butler admits that his client did indeed have an insurance policy in force.

Earl Sande looking over his riding gear in preparation for returning to racing. Author's Collection.

"My client's policy only covers employees engaged upon, or in connection with, the Butler farm at East View, New York. Since the accident occurred at Saratoga, the policy does not cover Sande's injuries."

Earl Sande and his mother after she sees him ride for the first time, on Sarazen. Courtesy Sande Tomlinson Collection.

Sande's attorney Frederick Kane counters, "Sande's riding was indeed 'in connection with' Butler's farm, and Butler's insurance company should cover Sande's expenses. My client has been harassed enough. Mr. Butler should be called to testify. His counsel states that he is in Florida and can not be reached. Last time he was elsewhere. You are afraid to produce him."

The matter remains unresolved. Referee Wickham indefinitely adjourns the hearing.

Earl exclaims with frustration, "This was the eighth hearing I've had to attend. Marion, send $6,000 to the hospital for payment. I'm not going to let my reputation get tarnished over the wrangling between insurance companies. Besides, all these hearings are distracting me from concentrating on racing."

That afternoon, a hearty ovation from 10,000 fans greets Sande as he mounts the scales at Belmont for the United Hunts Racing Association Meeting and his first New York race since his accident last August. Sande guides King O'Neill to an easy win in the Nassau Claiming Purse, but comes in sixth on Lanius out of a field of fourteen in the Initial Handicap, won by Gifford Cochran's 20 to 1 Flying Ebony by nosing out Laverne Fator on Superlette.

Sande moves along side Hastings aboard Flying Ebony on the way back to the stand. "That long shot Flying Ebony looked like a pretty fair horse today. Was this a fluke or does he have it in him to be a real contender?"

"He's got some good blood from The Finn and Princess Mary. You be the judge, Earl."

Jamaica's April 29 opening day begins with another rousing welcome for Sande as he takes Everglade Stable's Worthmore to the post. Noah jumps to an early lead while Worthmore remains behind the pack. Worthmore's chances appear dim. With a fury, Sande makes his move, breaks free of the crowd, and steadily gains on the leader. Shrieking fans jump to their feet as Noah and Worthmore barrel toward the finish line, with less than a hand's breadth between them. Sande gathers up Worthmore with loving hands, and the horse delivers a final thrust that puts them into the winner's circle by a nose. Enthusiastic fans send up a roar and shower Sande with flowers as Jamaica officials present Sande with a silver loving cup in honor of his riding career and return to racing.

Two days later, Pimlico fans heartily welcome Sande back with sustained applause and cheers. Sande and Sarazan easily capture the $25,000 Dixie Handicap purse and the crowd renews its ovation for Sande. Shortly thereafter, William Ziegler, Jr., takes second call on Sande's riding service for a reported $15,000, boosting Sande's salary to $40,000 plus a percentage of the Widener winnings and riding fees from other stables.

Sande celebrates with a May 5 win, aboard R. T. Wilson's Cannae in the Jamaica Montauk Claiming Stakes. Even more challenging, he mounts

Widener's Chatterer in the Pansy Purse to battle Rancocas's Barbary, ridden by Laverne Fator. Mr. Sinclair personally appears at the track to see his 6 to 5 favored horse and jockey compete.

Fator starts well and takes the lead early. Sande pulls Chatterer in behind the leaders and awaits a break in the traffic. Straightened out in the stretch, Sande makes his move with a hard drive. Chatterer catches Barbary in the last furlong and goes on to win by a length.

"Nice to see you again, Laverne. Give Hildreth and Mr. Sinclair my best."

"Couldn't lose to a nicer guy, Earl. As much as I would like to deliver your message, I think that job is better left to you."

Leading up to the May 8 Preakness, Sande takes Espino into the winner's circle for his first ride in Ziegler's purple silks. He also posts wins on Noon Fire and Adria.

In the sixteenth running of the Preakness, Maid at Arms breaks from the eleventh position and pulls sharply to the left, nearly pushing Sande, on Swope, over the rail. The disruption allows Clarence Kummer to take long-shot Coventry to the lead and an easy victory in the $52,700-purse race for Cochran.

A dejected Earl tells Marion, "Well, that's another disasterous Preakness in the Sande record book."

"Don't worry, Earl. Your Preakness victory will come. It will be all the sweeter because of your struggles to win it."

The same day Mark Fator and Benny Marinelli suffer injuries in a spill at Jamaica and Laverne Fator boots home five winners

"One more and I would have tied Earl for the world record," Laverne bemoans.

Widener does not enter a horse in the May 16, 1925, Kentucky Derby, and Ziegler's Our General, whom Sande was supposed to ride, trains poorly and is declared out of the race. Sande faces the prospect of not having a mount in the classic. Hungry for his second Kentucky Derby win, Sande offers Benny Breuning $2,000 to let him ride Quatrain and an additional $5,000 should Quatrain win. Negotiations fail. Herb Shimp, owner of the Chicago-based International Racing Stable, offers $5,000 to have Sande ride his colt, Mark Master. Flying Ebony remains the only other horse left without a rider. Owner Gifford Cochran had previously approached Clarence Kummer to ride Flying Ebony, but a contract riding engagement keeps Kummer in New York and prevents him from taking the reins. Ironically,

Sande admiring silver loving cup presented to him by Jamaica Race Track. Courtesy Ken Grayson Collection.

neither Commander Ross nor Sinclair's Rancocas Stable enters a horse in the fifty-first running of the Kentucky Derby.

"Mr. Shimp's offer is sure tempting, Marion, but I like to ride a winner and that horse doesn't have a ghost of a chance to win the Kentucky Derby. While Flying Ebony rates as a long shot, he does have a chance at the victory under the right circumstances."

For the first time in history, 6 million fans across the country listen to a radio broadcast of the Kentucky Derby, while 75,000 fans pack the stands and infield. Trainer William Duke saddles Sande on Flying Ebony for a long shot on the sloppy track at Churchill Downs. Those in the know give Flying Ebony little hope of contending in the field of twenty.

Duke advises, "Flying Ebony may be ordinary horse, however, he will be in there fighting to the finish. He won all three of his starts at this track and likes to run in the slop. I believe he will make a good account of himself. It's up to you, Earl, to make sure he is positioned to have a chance. Stay well up with the pace, and make your move at the top of the stretch."

"We'll see what kind of mudder he is."

Sande gets Flying Ebony away fourth, quickly takes to the front, and sets the pace for a spell. From the start, the race takes on the cast of a duel between Sande, wearing green silks with yellow hoops, on Flying Ebony, and Jake Heupel, riding Captain Hal. Heavy favorite Quatrain breaks slowly and never recovers, trailing far back on the track from the leaders.

Heupel takes Captain Hal to the lead and yells as he passes, "Goodbye, Sande, here goes the big black 'un!"

Captain's Hal showers mud on Sande and Flying Ebony as he heads down the track. Flying Ebony trails Captain Hal until the top of the stretch, when Sande calls on him. The horse gains with each stride, noses Captain Hal. The grandstands erupt with rousing shouts for Sande to bring Flying Ebony home.

"Go Sande. Go."

Sande turns toward Heupel and yells, "Let's see how your big black one likes the mud!"

In the final furlong, Flying Ebony draws away and finishes strong. Long-shot Flying Ebony earns the $52,950 purse and Derby gold cup for his owner and pays $8.30 on a $2 ticket. Fans cannot be restrained, and they pour onto the track to congratulate the public's jockey, Earl Sande.

"The best horse may not have won today, but the smartest horse did. I think he finally got tired at having mud flung at him," Sande says. "Heupel's mount seemed to have all the stuff they said he had and he went right after Flying Ebony and took the lead. I tested Flying Ebony's speed and found he had plenty in reserve. I eased my mount in the backstretch and took to following Captain Hal's pace, until we made our move in the homestretch. When I first took the mount on Flying Ebony, I knew he was a good horse and had a slight chance to win, but he proved better than I thought."

Back at Saratoga, Marion enjoys the evening with Marion Kummer. "Aren't you going to listen to the race to see if Earl wins, Marion?"

"Earl and I talked about it before he left. He thinks Quatrain is going to win and wishes he could have ridden him. He'll give his all, but I don't want to listen to his defeat. It's different when you there in person, you can see and feel what's going on. Radio is so impersonal. You don't get a sense of the action and see the horses make their moves."

Earl's chauffer arrives. "Doggone it, Mrs. Sande. Earl has gone and won the Kentucky Derby on that long shot, Flying Ebony. I had $10 on him, just out of loyalty, and it paid off big."

Marion Kummer hugs Marion Sande and the two talk about how thrilled Earl must feel. Back at the Kummers' home, Marion Kummer explains to Clarence, "I was very gracious and congratulated Marion on Earl's victory, but, at the same time, furious because Flying Ebony should have been your mount, Dear. It isn't fair that Earl wins the Kentucky Derby with your horse. All during dinner I was very happy for Earl and Marion, especially after all they went through last year, but I was very disappointed for you."

The next major racing sees Sande and Sarazen win the May 22 Belmont Metropolitan Handicap. In the June 13 Belmont Stakes, Albert Johnson, on American Flag, takes the lead from Sande, on Prince of Bourbon, rounding the far turn and wins in a canter. Over the next few weeks, Sande handily rides underrated Danby to a victory in the Hanover Handicap, breaks Edith Cavell well in the Astoria Stakes for a solid victory, guides maiden two-year-old My Eva to the winner's circle and takes another two-year-old maiden, Instructress, to the finish line first, all at Aqueduct. Sande mounts Danby for a win in the Hindoo Handicap.

"They're sure keeping you busy riding for all these different stables, Earl."

"I'm happy as a lark, Marion, as long as I'm riding horses. It's a great thrill to take some of these lesser known mounts to the post and match wits with other jockeys for an upset win."

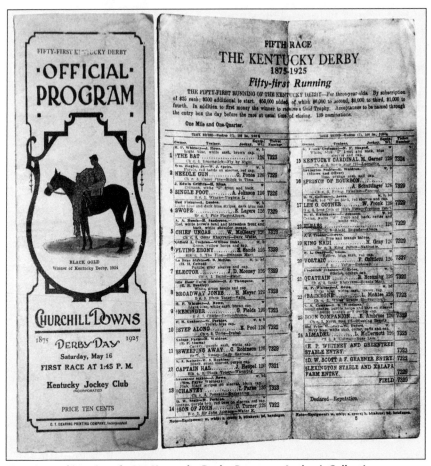

Exterior and interior of 1925 Kentucky Derby Program. Author's Collection.

"The fans don't care who you're riding, they just bet on you to win, Earl."

In Illinois, at Hawthorne, Sande takes Shuffle Along to the lead early and sets a brisk pace. Gibbons mounts a challenge but Sande races him into defeat, gaining the winner's circle in the July 11 August Belmont Memorial Handicap.

Another victory on Sarazen falls to Sande in the July 30 Empire City Fleetwing Handicap. The next day, Sande prepares for a return to Saratoga for the first time since his accident.

Marion asks, "Are you nervous today, Earl?"

"Sure there's a little apprehension. However, as the old saying goes, 'When you get throwed from a horse, the best thing is to get right back in the saddle again.' I'm trying to think of it as another glorious day on the Saratoga track."

A clubhouse reception welcomes Sande's long-awaited return to Saratoga. The band plays "Auld Lang Syne" while well-wishers welcome Sande back to Saratoga. He fails to win in his first outing and again on Sarazen six days later. His first 1925 win at Saratoga comes aboard Widener's Haste, in the August 8 Saratoga Special.

Sande and Laverne Fator match wits, with Sande gaining the winner's circle in fast time. He finishes out racing at Saratoga with a win upon Zephyretta in the August 20 Baldwin Purse, and aboard Haste in the $10,000 Grand Union Hotel Stakes the following afternoon.

"The pressure's off. Now it's time to get back to business," Sande tells Marion.

Moving to Belmont in September, Sande, on slow beginner Ruthenia, trails Black Maria round the far turn in the Tomboy Handicap. In sight of the finish line, Sande rouses Ruthenia to the lead and win for a $3,700 purse. He adds another $4,000 in winnings on Belair Stud's Aga Khan, in the Twin City Handicap, before going on to Aqueduct.

Sande's last win on Sarazen comes in the September 28 Arverne Handicap. Silver Fox breaks on top, with Sarazen close back. Carrying a hefty 130 pounds, Sarazen takes the track back in good time and settles in under restraint from Sande, while Extra Dry moves up into second. The win adds $3,375 to Mrs. Vanderbilt's purses and marks Sande's third straight trip to the winner's circle during the day's racing.

Sande rushes Nose Dive to the forefront with the lifting of the barrier in the last day of racing in the September 30 Aqueduct Stonybrook Claiming Stakes. He never looks back and wins the race easing up at the end.

Rancocas's Laverne Fator takes top jockey honors in 1925, with $305,775 in purses on eighty-one winning mounts. Sande completes the year ranking second in winnings, with $264,700, despite riding only 268 mounts in 1925 versus 430 in 1923. He wins 27 percent of his races, more than any other jockey, and finishes in the money 62 percent of the time. Riddle's stable takes top honors, with $199,143. Rancocas trails with $150,873.

Top 1925 Money Winning Leaders				
Jockey	Mounts	1st	%	$Winnings
Fator, L.	315	81	.26	$305,775
Sande, E.	268	72	.27	264,700
Maiben, J.	587	137	.23	264,200
Stutts, H.	720	149	.21	242,852
Barnes, E.	726	115	.16	198,765

Shuffle Along, with Sande up, winning August Belmont Memorial at Hawthorne, Illinois. Courtesy Sande Tomlinson Collection.

In January 1926, Sande and other well-known American turfmen attend a dinner for noted English trainers Fred Darling and Stanley Wooton. Other off-season activities of skeet shooting, quail hunting in South Carolina, and golfing give Sande time to relax after the demanding racing season. Spalding Sport Cards issues a set of American Jockeys including Johnny Maiben, Willie Munden, Earl Pool, Earl Sande, and Tod Sloan.

On March 25, Sande makes his first winter riding appearance since he broke into professional racing in New Orleans in 1918. Sande agrees to

Hawthorn
Derby Day
1925

J.W.Healy,   E.Sande   A.C.Bostwick

Trophy Presentation for August Belmont Memorial win at Hawthorne, Illinois. Courtesy Sande Tomlinson collection.

ride Princess Doreen in the Tijuana, Mexico, Cofforth Handicap, because of the suspension of Princess Doreen's jockey, Harry Strutts. Three days prior to the Cofforth Handicap, Sande accepts a mount in the sixth race. Serenader, carrying 115 pounds and giving sixteen pounds and twenty-one pounds to his closest contenders, rushes to the rail and keeps the rest of the horses at bay for a win by a length and a half. With the victory, Sande and Serenader set a track record for one mile and a sixteenth, with a time of 1:43 4/5. Three days later, Sande enters the $70,000 Cofforth Handicap on Princess Doreen. Dr. Clark shows in front, followed by Carlaris. Sande gets off in fourth place. Carlaris takes the lead and never relinquishes it, earning a seventh victory in ten starts. Sande finishes seventh.

Prior to the start of the New York racing season, The Jockey Club refuses to grant jockey licenses to Clarence Kummer and Mark Fator. Action was expected on Fator because of a rough riding incident the previous October. However, the action against Kummer comes as a surprise. The Jockey Club gives no explanation for its sanction against Kummer, who won more than $1 million in purses since 1918 and 21 percent of his 2,233 mounts, and in the process set two world records and four American records.

Earl tries to comfort Kummer. "It's not fair that The Jockey Club can set you down without giving any reason."

"Last year, after August Belmont died, I was left without a stable. When Log Cabin Stud took over many of Belmont's horses, I went with them. I had lots of differences with the owner, Averell Harriman, and we finally parted company under less than pleasant terms. Harriman has a lot of pull in racing circles, and I feel he is to blame for my license denial. It's another case of the big guy running over the rights and lives of the little guy."

"At least you're only denied racing in New York. It will be hard on your wife, but you can race out of state until you get reinstated here."

Jamaica racing opens on April 28, with Rancocas's Laverne Fator, on Silver Fox, winning the Paumonok Handicap. Sande starts the 1926 Jamaica season slowly, riding four losing mounts and placing only once in the money. Sande finally gets his first Jamaica win aboard Mino on April 30. The next day, he takes the Ridgewood Purse with ease on Oak Ridge's Cutitout. On May 3, Sande takes two out of five horses to the finish line first. He can't make weight the following afternoon, tipping the scales at 114 pounds.

"It's a real struggle, Marion. Dieting, sauna baths, and working out. All seems harder since the accident."

"Just do your best, Earl. I know you will get back in shape."

Sande establishes an early lead on Voltaic and captures a first-place win in the May 6 Olympic Claiming Stakes. Two days later, savvy Sande, riding Mino, steals a victory in the California Handicap from Little Asbestos.

Marion asks, "Are you sure you want to ride for Rancocas? It's a shame the way they treated you, Earl."

"A mount is a mount, Marion. I love to ride. It doesn't matter who owns the horse."

On May 10, Sande dons the Rancocas colors for the first time since before his injury. Sande lets Thurber set the pace, while he follows on Celidon. Thurber swings wide to frustrate Sande, but he catches the leader on the stretch and wins going away. Another win on Martha Martin gives Sande a double for the day. Closing out racing at Jamaica, Sande performs well enough on Sanford to win the Montana Handicap, but loses three races in a row to Laverne Fator. Sande fails to obtain a mount for the Kentucky Derby, which is won by Albert Johnson on Bubbling Over. Laverne Fator finishes a distant fifth on Pompey.

At Belmont's May 21 opening day, Sande mounts juvenile Osmand for the first time. He follows the pace set by Never Again. A furious battle

Earl Sande and mount after winning race in 1925. Courtesy Sande Tomlinson Collection.

ensues throughout the race, with Osmand emerging the winner by a nose in record time. Three days later, Sande takes Gifford Cochran's Sun Flag to the barrier and outclasses the Rancocas entry, Sabine, by ten lengths. On May 26, in the fifty-first running of the Withers Stakes, Haste, with Sande up, runs down the two pacemakers with searing speed and takes the lead. Well into the homestretch, Haste fades and gives ground to hard-charging Crusader and Espino. Sande rides Haste out to a slim victory over Crusader, who surely would have overtaken the leader in another furlong.

While at Belmont, Sande receives a silver cup from "The Turf Digest" for ranking as America's most popular jockey. Marion joins Earl for the ceremony and accepts a large bouquet of roses. On June 12, Crusader, Espino, and Haste rematch in the Belmont Stakes. Haste takes the early lead under the guidance of Sande. Crusader holds Espino off and moves ahead of Haste to take the win. Espino finishes second, driving hard; a tiring Haste comes in third.

Sande brings home victory in the June 16 Aqueduct Rockaway Claiming Stakes on Tester, despite a burden of 127 pounds. Other successes include capturing the Fairmont Derby on Haste and delivering a hard-riding finish on Prince of Bourbon in the Epinard Handicap. Twenty thousand Aqueduct race fans jam the grandstands for the running of the July 3 Dwyer Stakes. Chance Play jumps to an early lead. Crusader, with Sande up this time, trails back in the pack at the first turn. Laverne Fator spurs Dress Parade to the lead and sets a pace too fast for most of the other contenders. On the turn, Crusader kicks into overdrive and moves up, as others give up the chase. Chance Play retakes the lead from Dress Parade and works the fans into a frenzy. Still in the hunt, Crusader gains with every stride until both horses' heads bob along together. First Crusader's head pokes out in front and then Chance Play's. In the final strides to the finish line, Sande takes to the whip and lifts Crusader to victory by a nose, in track record time and only four-fifths of a second slower than Man o' War's mile-and-a-half record set at Belmont Park in 1920.

Sande and Crusader next team up at the Coney Island Racetrack in Ohio. A record crowd turns out to see America's premier jockey, Earl Sande, on Crusader, a son of Man o' War. In faultless fashion, Sande and Crusader bide their time behind Carlaris and Boot to Boot. After the eighth pole, Sande gives Crusader free rein, and the horse tears around the midwestern track and crosses the finish line first, mobbed by frenzied fans.

"I saved him as long as possible. I could have gone to Carlaris any time I wanted. Truth be told, Crusader never did run his fastest, and I let him out only for a short distance. He is one really great racehorse, and if a thoroughbred ever takes after his daddy, he does."

Sande's Tijuana mount back in March, Princess Doreen, performs better in the July 30 opening day Saratoga Handicap. The western mare takes measure of her eastern contenders and leaves them in the dust under the skillful riding of McTague. For his part, Sande mounts Osmand in another race and breaks the colt well. Candy Queen leads on the rail, with Osmand keeping pace on the outside. At the half mark, Sande urges Osmand to the lead. Thurber whips Candy Queen repeatedly, while Sande goes to the persuader only once, winning the Flash Stakes by three-quarters of a length.

On August 3, Sande scores a double on Corvette and Broadside. The next day, a too-confident Sande eases up on Dress Parade before the finish line in the Delaware Handicap and gets caught napping by Clarence Turner, on Single Foot, to lose by a nose. Sande redeems his pride by winning the Crown Point Purse on Kiev. Sande lands 8 to 1 Ruthenia a head in

Crusader with Sande up. Courtesy Keeneland-Cook.

front of favorite Corvette to win the Test Stakes three days later and then mounts another 8 to 1 horse, Flagstaff, in the Hudson Handicap, to beat favorite Gamble.

Sande and Osmand again appear on the racing card. Although Sande wears the Joseph E. Widener scarlet and white striped silks, he rides Chance Shot in the August 7 Saratoga Special. Albert Johnson takes Osmand's reins on Widener's other entry. Frank Coltiletti mounts favored Scapa Flow, winner of the United Stakes Hotel Stakes a week earlier.

Widener's trainer imparts race strategy to Johnson and Sande. "Albert, I want you to take Osmand to the front and set a torrid pace that will weaken Scapa Flow and give Earl the opportunity to release Chance Shot's stretch speed for the win."

The plan works exactly as laid out. Osmand drops off as the horses round the turn for the stretch. Scapa Flow pokes ahead briefly. Fans chant "Sande, Sande, Sande" as Chance Shot pushes Scapa Flow to the limit. He steadily pulls ahead, first by a nose, and then by a head and neck to win.

Sande tells Marion with some regret, "After my earlier wins with Osmand, I almost hated to beat that dear horse. It's his only loss this year."

Two days later, Sande encounters an uncharacteristic lousy day of riding. On favorite Corvette in the Salem Handicap, Sande misjudges the pace and finishes second by a head. He follows that up with a win on Royal Play but is disqualified for a foul. As Sande is called on the carpet to report to the race stewards, fans send out a chorus of boos. In his final race of the day, Sande finishes far back in the pack on Farm's Revolver.

After booting home Be Fair past the winning post first in the August 14 Congress Park Purse, Sande mounts Crusader the next day to compete in the Travers Stakes against Frank Coltiletti on Mars and Laverne Fator on Pompey. A record 25,000 fans crowd the grandstands. After the steeplechase competition, track president R. T. Wilson, Jr., opens the infield to prevent collapse of the grandstands.

Favored Crusader carries a handicap of 129 pounds. A poor start leaves Crusader standing at the post. Fator, on Pompey, flashes to the lead. Fans call for Sande and Crusader to take up the chase. The steed gives a valiant effort and makes up ground with every stride. Crusader catches Mars and pulls within two lengths of the tiring Pompey. Realizing that Crusader has expended too much in the process, Sande eases up on Crusader and finishes far in the ruck. Mars runs down Pompey and claims first place.

The August 21 crowd urges Sande on as he pushes 8 to 1 Kiev ahead of Pantella to win the $12,000 Grand Union Stakes by a slim margin. The thrilling victory marks the first of three Sande triumphs for the day. Three days later, Sande takes Crusader to the finish line first, with speed to spare, over second-place finisher Espino, to win the Huron Handicap.

Belmont's August 31 opening day breaks with a westerly wind and a nip in the air. The frigid weather, however, does nothing to cool down Sande's riding. He scores a double, first winning on Saleslady and then taking Bumpkin to the wire first in the Autumn Dash. The next day, Sande and Osmand challenge the field in the Nursery Handicap. Osmand shoulders a hefty weight of 127 pounds. Osmand gets away with a rush and leads throughout to win easily. Later, in the Brentwood Handicap, Sande mounts Dress Parade and gallops the horse to victory, for his second double in as many days.

Marion congratulates Earl, "Triples and doubles. You're really on a roll now, Dear."

"I feel like I'm back in the groove again, Marion."

On September 7, Sande conserves Altawood, who carries a load of 126 pounds. Sande goes to the outside to avoid interference and persistently

Coney Island, Ohio "Crusader" (E Sande. Up)
July 24th 1926.

Sande on Crusader after winning the Cincinnati Derby at Coney Island, Ohio. Courtesy Sande Tomlinson Collection.

gains ground on Sanford and Dazzler. Altawood passes Dazzler and surges to the fore in the final sixteenth, winning by half a length and driving. At Aqueduct Sande rates Saxon along in front of the field to win the September 21 Babylon Handicap.

Four days later at Havre de Grace, Crusader starts poorly and gets trapped in close corners going into the first turn. Down the backstretch, Sande works Crusader up on the outside. At the far turn, Sande gives Crusader his head, and the horse responds with a surge of speed, taking the lead and winning by a head in front of Display.

More than a week later, Osmand and Sande compete for the $15,000 Eastern Shore Handicap. In drizzling rain, Osmand and Sande battle Adios, with Laverne Fator up, for the lead. On the far turn, Sande swings wide to gain better position on Adios. Meanwhile, Jopagan sneaks through on the rail and threatens the two leaders. At the finish line, Osmand pokes his head in front of Adios and takes the purse.

On October 1, Sande mounts Man o' War daughter Taps in the Evergreen Handicap, on a muddy Havre de Grace track. Favored Prince of

Wales leads down the homestretch, after running by early leader Candy Kid. Sande lets Taps loose, and the filly finishes strong and eases her nose in front in the final strides. Sande repeats the exciting finish twice in the next week at Laurel to win the Cumberland Purse on Big Blaze and the Collington Handicap on Polly McWiggles. On October 13, Sande again mounts a whirlwind finish. This time he only comes in second, behind long-shot Golden Prince, who pays $386.20 on a $2 wager.

"I should have bet on Golden Prince today instead of on my prince," Marion says.

Finalizing racing at Laurel, Sande takes Poly to the wire first, delivers Prince of Wales to the horse's third and fourth wins in a row, earns a maiden race victory on Gormond, and guides maiden filly Fairness to the winner's circle.

Sande brings Crusader along and wins easily against Mars in the November 1 Pimlico Riggs Memorial. Twelve days later, Sande and Crusader finish out their 1926 racing together in the Pimlico Cup, coming in second behind Edith Cavell, but outpacing Princess Doreen.

Laverne Fator earns top jockey honors for 1926 by capturing both the highest winning percentage, at 28, and largest amount of purses won, with $361,435. Sande comes in with respectable numbers, with earnings of $307,605 and winning 24 percent of his mounts. He also finishes in the money 61 percent of the time. Harry Payne Whitney tops all stables, with $407,139, versus $111,840 for declining Rancocas. S. P. Harlan leads all trainers with $205,681. Crusader out-paces all three-year-olds, with purses of $166,033, the most won since 1923, when Zev captured $272,008.

Top 1926 Money Winning Leaders				
Jockey	Mounts	1st	%	$Winnings
Fator, L.	511	143	.28	$361,435
Maiben, J	485	115	.24	320,508
Sande, E.	298	72	.24	307,605
Dubois, D	713	134	.19	274,813
McAtee, L.	269	69	.26	273,055

"The American Racing Manual" compliments Sande's popularity with the race fans across the nation. "At the end of each year a new leader is proclaimed. But in the hearts and minds of the American racing public there is only one champion, the same one, year after year, at least has been the case for the past nine years. The acknowledged champion is none other than the peerless Earl Sande. The end of 1926 proved no exception in that respect, for the 'Old Master,' who never headed the jockey list of most wins in a given year, still reigns supreme as the best of our present day riders. Sande showed conclusively, during 1926, that he had lost none of the daring and uncanny skill that made him the real leader of his profession by topping the list of the stake winning jockeys, and completing the year with a percentage of .24. Sande has ridden over 800 winners in the past nine years and earned more than $2,000,000 in stakes and purses for the various owners for whom he rode. The greatest testimony to his skill is the percentage of .27 for nine years' riding."

Earl and Marion enjoy a quiet evening at home playing cards with their friends, Clarence and Marion Kummer. After the Kummers leave, Marion gives Earl a hug. "We have some wonderful friends, and your racing is going so well. I think 1927 will be our best year yet, Earl."

"As long as I'm still riding and have the best wife in the world."

Part 5

Test of Character

Chapter 12

Top Jockey Once Again
Tragedy Revisited

Earl and Marion, Mr. and Mrs. Sam Hildreth, and G. H. "Ham" Keene enjoy the off-season vacationing in Hot Springs, Arkansas, away from the cold northern winter. "Ham" develops racehorses for Joseph E. Widener, Sande's current employer, and jointly owns Kentucky's Keeneland Farm, with his brother.

"I hear you're getting Osmand primed for a run at the Kentucky Derby, Ham. How is training coming along?" Sande asks.

"Osmand looks pretty fine in winter workouts. He will be well-prepared if his progress continues on schedule," Keene says.

"He's certainly a strong horse and should be a good contender. Of course, Whitney's Whiskery ranks as the winter book favorite and will present a challenge. I sure would like to beat McAtee and earn my third Derby on Osmond."

Marion sits down next to Earl and sighs. "This is sure the life, Earl. We have time to relax and don't have to worry about the next day's races, except on which horse to place a bet."

"I agree. The spa's waters soothe my bones and aching muscles, and we haven't a care in the world."

Ham bids the couple good night and retires for the evening. An early morning knock at the Sandes' door brings Hildreth with disturbing news. "You won't believe this. Ham died unexpectedly in his sleep. The maid found his body. What a shock. He seemed perfectly healthy yesterday. We'll have to cut this vacation short. Just wouldn't seem right not to accompany Ham back to Lexington."

"We were just talking about how nice a vacation we were having with you and everyone. Now this. It's terrible. I feel so sorry for his family," Marion says.

Months later in Louisville, Sande and Osmand prepare for the Kentucky Derby. During an April 20 workout at Churchill Downs, Osmand attempts to catch Chance Shot but tires in the stretch, ending a length behind.

Sande whispers in the horse's ear. "You just do not seem to have it today, Osmand Baby."

A week later, the gelding exhibits blazing speed, ripping through the half mile slightly below the track record. News of Osmand's increasingly promising workouts improve his odds in early betting.

"That's more like it. You took off like a rocket. You're sure a great sprinter. Now we will see if we can get you to the finish line first."

An injury to Osmand's left forefoot causes Sande to postpone a few workouts to let the horse heal. On May 5, bandaged Osmand turns on decent speed despite a sloppy track.

Sande assures reporters, "We're on target for Osmand to compete."

In a warm-up race three days prior to the Derby, Sande mounts Osmand for a run at the Watterson Hotel Purse at Churchill Downs. The field of six breaks fast and Sande takes Osmand to the lead in a few strides. Jock, riding hard, forces the pace and keeps at Osmand's heels throughout, coming in second by a nose. Sande earns a double in two mounts, with another win on Chittagong in the seventh race.

"The Denver Post" recaps Osmand's chances in the fifty-third Run for the Roses. "In two public appearances this year, Osmand proved such a disappointment that turf followers completely turned away from him despite the fact that he has scored seven victories in ten starting efforts as a two-year-old and three-year-old. If it were not for the fact that Sande, the premier jockey of America, has the mount on Osmand, he would not be given a chance. But Sande knows more about horses than any boy of his generation and can do more with them. He is a wizard in the stirrups, and although Osmand is looked upon only as a sprinter, some people believe

Earl Sande and Hollywood actress Wanda Hawley admire Osmand in Louisville. Courtesy Ken Grayson Collection

that Sande can take him to the front in the derby. There is very little betting on Osmand, but a whole lot on Sande."

A field of eighteen hopefuls arrive in Louisville, however, owners scratch three horses before the contenders parade into Churchill Downs on May 14. Harry Payne Whitney's Whiskery still ranks as the pre-race favorite.

Whitney talks with reporters before the race. "Sure, Whiskery is the favorite, but I've had six favorites in the past thirteen Kentucky Derbys. The last time that my stable's colors flashed past the winning post first in this grand race occurred in 1915, when Regret took the honors. The only filly to ever win the Kentucky Derby. That was a real accomplishment, but it took place some time ago. It has been a long drought. As you know, Mr. Widener has a fine horse, Osmand, in this race, ridden by Sande. That alone should give any owner cause for concern."

"Osmand, Old Boy. How would you like to enter the winner's circle today? It would be my third trip and I highly recommend it," Sande says as the horses make their way to the post.

Fans mingle around the betting windows, trying to decide whether to place their money on favored Whiskery or on America's favorite jockey, Earl Sande. Mint juleps flow while men admire women in long sweeping skirts, who cast coquettish glances from beneath wide-brimmed, white hats.

Jock, on the rail, shows first, with Sande, on Osmand, and Scapa Flow close behind. Rounding the backstretch, Jock extends his lead to five lengths over Osmand, Rolled Stocking, and Scapa Flow. Whiskery, with McAtee up, trails the pack but stays within striking distance. On the far turn into the homestretch, Sande boots Osmand into gear and pulls alongside the striving Jock. At the final furlong pole, Osmand goes ahead of Jock and then increases his lead. Out of the dust of Osmand and Jock, Whiskery bolts forward. Within fifty yards of the finish line, Whiskery creeps up to within an inch of Osmand's nose. Fans jump to their feet as Osmand and Whiskery's hooves gobble up the remaining turf. With a sensational stretch drive, Whiskery wins by a nose and gives Linus McAtee his first Kentucky Derby victory.

Sande congratulates McAtee. "Welcome to the club, Linus. That's the best race I ever rode, and you beat me fair and square. I was only a furlong away from my fourth Derby Victory but that was the longest furlong I ever rode."

"Thanks, Earl. Now I'm only one Kentucky Derby victory behind you."

Chance Play opens his 1927 racing debut at the Belmont Toboggan Handicap on May 19. With Sande up, Chance Play breaks third, behind

Sarmaticus and Pompey. Sande hangs on them like a bulldog and finally wears Pompey out. He then turns his attention to Sarmaticus, gaining steadily. On the backstretch, he closes the gap and wins by a length and a half with speed in reserve.

Two days later, Sande rides Chance Shot in his three-year-old debut in the Freeport Handicap. Under a weight of 126 pounds, Chance Shot stays off the pace, set by Clearance, until the far turn. At that point, Chance Shot conquers Clearance and shoots around him to take the lead. Meanwhile, Medley cuts to the rail and gains precious ground. Carrying only 103 pounds, Medley skims over the track. Alert to the threat, Sande gives Chance Shot a couple of good swats and finishes his work with skillful hand riding. Chance Shot accepts the challenge and beats Medley to the wire.

Sande explains the close finish. "Chance Shot has a penchant for never doing more than he is compelled to do by his rider. He fell asleep in the stretch, and I had to wake him."

Sande and Osmand prepare for the May 30 Metropolitan Handicap, against a field including W. R. Coe's Black Maria, with Frank Coltiletti up. After the break, Sande passes Amberjack and keeps Black Maria at bay until the far turn. On the backstretch, Sande swings wide to carry the filly to the outside, but Coltiletti takes to the whip and bends to work with his hands and heels. His efforts pay off with a win, by a length, over Osmand.

Belmont Park's June 11 closing day features Sande in three races. Groucher, with Sande up, breaks well in the National Stallion Stakes and virtually decides the race in the first few strides, easily winning $22,710 for Harry Payne Whitney. In the Belmont Stakes, Sande takes Chance Shot to a good pace, rides under slight restraint, and then wins easily, earning $60,910 for Joseph E. Widener. In the final race, Sande rides his third winning mount of the day, taking Royal Play to the wire ahead of the pack.

"I never had any doubt of the outcome of the Belmont. Chance Shot broke well. I let him loaf along until the homestretch and then widened the gap for the victory. Sure is great to win my fourth Belmont. The triple today was a bonus."

Five days later at Aqueduct, Sande chooses his lanes carefully and drives two winners, Caporal II and Montanic, home first. His first 1927 ride on Crusader comes on June 18. Crusader is coming off a victory in the Suburban Handicap, with Laverne Fator up. Carrying a top weight of 132

Sande on Osmand at Belmont. Courtesy Keeneland-Cook.

pounds, Crusader breaks slowly and never poses a threat, placing out of the money.

During June, Sande appears in court to testify in a case involving flim-flam artist Sidney Marks. Working a variety of swindles, Marks first convinced friends to invest in his upcoming Broadway show, *Spices of 1927*, featuring Earl Sande. He then took his "investors" to Churchill Downs, where he told them that he had inside information on fixed races from a bookmaking friend. Marks's patsies pooled their money to bet on Canaan. The horse proceeded to win, paying $17.80 on a $2 bet. His "investors" jumped with jubilation when they calculated their winnings at almost $100,000. Marks explained that he would need a little time to collect the winnings. Police arrested him in New York after he failed to deliver the payoff. Investigation determined that Marks had warrants out for his arrest for similar swindles in the Bronx and Atlantic City, and for violating his parole from Sing Sing.

Sande joins former lightweight champion Benny Leonard, comedian Willie Collier, actress Olga Cook, and other well-known personalities to testify that Marks used their names without their knowledge. They also deny Marks's representations that he had business and personal relationships with them. Sande testifies that Marks did not engage his services to sing "Sid, Win for Me" in *Spices of 1927* and that he does not know the defendant. The jury convicts Marks of defrauding people out of $75,000 and returns him to Sing Sing for ten years.

Laverne Fator ribs Sande upon his return to the jockey room. "Heard you're headed for Broadway, Earl. Can I have your autograph?"

"That may be a bit premature. However, I am taking singing lessons from voice coach Estelle Wentworth, and Jack Dempsey promises to introduce me to Sherman Billingsley at the Stork Club. I understand Mr. Billingsley is very particular about whom he lets into his club. If you're real nice, I'll put in a good word for you."

On June 29, Gravita and Grange battle down the homestretch, only to have victory torn from their grasp when Sande takes Riddle's Astron to the outside and passes them in a flash, gathering up first-place money. Two days later, jockey Steve O'Donnell claims that Sande fouled him in the Peter Pan Purse when Polish bore over O'Donnell's mount, winning the race by less than a length. The race stewards determine the interference insufficient to warrant disqualification, and Sande's win stands.

In the July 2 Dwyer Stakes, Maiben, on Kentucky II, sets a deliberately slow pace. Flambino follows close behind, while Chance Shot, with Sande up, saves his energy. Chance Shot carries 126 pounds, versus 112 pounds for Flambino and 108 pounds for Kentucky II. Flambino drops back into third place. Straightened out in the stretch, Sande takes to the whip for the drive to the wire. The crowd cheers to no avail, as Chance Shot fails to close the gap and loses by two lengths. Ending racing at Aqueduct on July 6, Sande receives an ovation at the scales after winning two of his races with little effort.

Sande travels to ride Mrs. Harriman's Chance Play in the $25,000 July 9 Lincoln Handicap at Chicago's Lincoln Fields. He turns down a $1,000 fee, plus 10 percent of the purse, to ride Kentucky Cardinal because of his previous commitment to Mrs. Harriman. A crowd of 30,000 turns out for the event. Kentucky Cardinal takes an early lead, with Chance Play trailing in third place. By the first quarter, Chance Play moves to the forefront and increases the lead to three lengths by the wire.

Earl returns to Saratoga and shares in Marion's good news. "We're going to have a baby, Earl. I didn't tell you earlier because I didn't want you worrying."

"Hooray. If it's a boy, I'll teach him to ride like Burr Scott and Doc Pardee taught me."

Earl celebrates his impending fatherhood with a stunning victory in the August 1 opening day Saratoga Handicap. On a rain-soaked track, Mars launches a spectacular surge ahead of Black Maria and Frank Coltiletti, to win going away. Three days later, Sande wins on Stephanie and places second on Astron and Chance Shot.

"I miss having you in the stands, Marion, cheering me on, but it's more important for you and our baby to be home getting rest."

"I know it's best, Earl. Still, it's hard not seeing you race. In the past six years, I haven't missed many of your races."

"I'll tell you all about them when I come home every night. You just get your rest like the doctor ordered. You can see plenty of racing next year and the year after that. I plan to be in this racing game for a while yet. Remember, I still haven't won those three top races like Johnny Loftus did in 1919. I won't hang up my tack until I do, I promise."

On Aug 17, Sande and Osmand race to the finish line, lapped with three other horses. The crowd rises as one when the horses cross the wire in a blanket finish. A rousing cheer erupts as Osmand's number goes up first on the board and gives him the Saranac Handicap victory. Over the next ten days, Sande trims his racing schedule to spend more time with Marion, who is not feeling well. Because of Marion's condition, he refuses a mount in the $60,000 Hopeful Stakes, scheduled for September 3.

"It's just morning sickness, Earl. Go back to racing. I'll be fine."

"I'll take care of you, honey. Don't worry, everything will be all right."

By August 27, Marion runs a fever, and Earl continues to attend to her. He is at Marion's side when she dies on September 2, from a rupture of a tubular pregnancy.

The doctor comforts Earl. "There's nothing that could have been done, Mr. Sande. Once the pregnancy ruptured, we would have had to operate immediately, and there's no assurance that would have helped either. It's like a ruptured appendix, very serious and fatal if medical attention is not immediate. You have my sincere condolences."

Marion Kummer consoles a weeping Earl. "I don't know any other couple who was as devoted to each other as you two, Earl."

"Marion is gone. It doesn't seem possible. We were married six years and never had a cross word between us."

Marion's funeral takes place at Sacred Heart Church in Mount Auburn, Massachusetts. Floral tributes and condolence messages arrive from all over the world. The Vanderbilts, Riddles, Whitneys, Hildreths, Sinclairs, Fators, Kummers, Mrs. Harriman, and Joseph E. Widener represent the racing community. Marion is interred at St. Paul's Cemetery in Arlington, Massachusetts.

Marion Kummer visits Earl after he arrives back in Saratoga. "I know you're devastated right now, but you need to get back to racing. Marion would have wanted it that way. She's with you out there on the track. That's where you'll find her spirit, Earl."

"Maybe, you're right. It just seems so empty without Marion, though."

Two weeks after Marion's passing, Sande reappears at Belmont Park in Widener silks. Fellow jockeys and track friends greet him warmly in the paddock. The fans give Sande a respectful round of applause. During the day's racing, he drives Haste to a second-place finish, comes in out of the money on Rurik, and finishes the day with a win on Laddie.

Sande in Widener silks. Courtesy Sande Tomlinson Collection.

Sande looks to the stands where Marion would have sat, tips his cap and says, "That one's for you, Marion."

Sande, on Chance Play, and Ellis, on Bud Brown, battle wits for the September 17 Jockey Club Gold Cup. Chance Play sets the pace, and Bud Brown measures his every stride. Near the end of a mile, Ellis makes his move, and the two horses run head to head in the rush to the finish line. Ellis takes to the whip and pulls ahead a tad. He then bores in on Chance Play and forces Sande into close quarters on the rail. Bud Brown finishes first. Sande cries foul and the race stewards agree, disqualifying Bud Brown and giving Sande his fourth Jockey Club Gold Cup victory.

Ten days later, Sande sprints War Whoop to victory at Havre de Grace. He follows that up with an easy victory on Crusader in the Delaware Handicap the next day, and another win in a breeze, on Vespers, on October 1. Moving to Laurel for the October 5 Capital Handicap, Sande keeps Osmand under heavy restraint most of the going before giving him his head and winning easily. Two weeks later, Sande takes Crusader for a victory lap in the Cecil Handicap.

In the October 24 Somerset Handicap, Sande pulls Crusader up short because of interference from Ambrose on Mars. Even so, he spurs Crusader on to second place. After the race stewards disqualify Mars, Crusader takes top money.

Mars's trainer, Scott Harlan, vehemently complains to the race stewards. "Sande pulled one of his old tricks. He tries to get through a place that is impossible. Upon his arrival at the steward's stand, he claims he was fouled to cover up his blunder. Mars has a leg scar where Crusader struck him. Your disqualification is the most outrageous thing ever perpetrated on a racetrack. Ask any trainer who saw it what they think of the ruling, and they will agree with me."

The disqualification stands. Three days later, Sande wins on Mexcala and Fairness.

Harlan settles for a bit of revenge when Crusader finishes far out of the money in the October 29 Washington Handicap, while Mars finishes third.

Sande's old employer, Harry Ford Sinclair, makes news on November 4, when the court orders Sinclair's arrest for jury tampering.

"Looks like my old employer is having some tough times, too," Earl says.

The same day proves to be a critical point in Sande's racing career, as he competes in the $67,000 Pimlico Futurity. Racing down the backstretch, Sande, on Bateau, heads Reigh Count. Chick Lang holds Reigh Count close to the rail, while Bateau runs on the outside. Lang makes his move to go through, and Sande counters by driving close to the colt. The horses bump, and Lang has all he can do to keep the horse upright. Glade passes through for the victory, while Sande hard rides into second.

The race stewards interview the jockeys and disqualify Bateau. In addition, they rule the interference by Sande as deliberate, suspend him from the rest of the meeting, confiscate his riding badge, and expel him from the grounds. They turn his case over to the Maryland State Racing Commission for further action.

Well-regarded trainer Sunny Jim Fitzsimmons fumes. "The stewards made a mistake. I was standing infield and saw the whole thing. Sande tried to put over a riding trick, but Lang did the grabbing. Sande committed no foul!"

Within twenty hours, the Maryland Racing Commission convenes and upholds the sanction of the race stewards, suspending Sande from riding for the remainder of the Pimlico meeting. In addition, it strips him of his riding license, making it impossible for him to ride on any American track until the commission lifts the ban.

Sande tells reporters, "I have requested a formal investigation into my riding. I am not guilty of a foul. Lang grabbed my blouse when I tried to sneak by him. I want the opportunity to tell my side of the story and will produce three jockey witnesses who can confirm my version of the incident. I am sure it is a fair commission, and they will listen to the jockeys who were near the turn at the time of the incident. "

Joseph E. Widener, Sande's employer and president of The Jockey Club, joins in the chorus. "It's a shame that a jockey with the caliber and integrity of Sande is being railroaded."

Thousands of letters and phone calls in favor of Sande flood the commission's office. Angered by the uproar over Sande's suspension, Maryland Racing Commissioner James A. Latane declares, "Sande was not railroaded. Sande's action was witnessed by track judges and two members of the commission. We have granted Mr. Sande an informal hearing and will hear the evidence."

Another member of the commission, Jervis Spencer, Jr., maintains, "The hearing will have no impact on the action already taken. It may aid the commission in determining the length of Sande's expulsion, however. The stewards at Pimlico had no doubt that he deliberately fouled Lang. We saw no reason to call him before us because we had no doubt about his case. If Sande had asked to be heard before the commission, he would have been given that privilege."

"Seems like the commission had its mind made up before it even heard the evidence," Fitzsimmons says.

At the November 8 hearing, the commission listens to Sande's testimony. "It was Chick's purpose either to hold me back or pull himself up, I guess.

I know that he grabbed me and nearly pulled me from my saddle. Bateau rolled over and struck Reigh Count, sending him into the rail. It was all I could do to get back in the saddle again. That's the truth. It was Lang's fault."

Unmoved, chairman Latane states, "You came over to the inside and forced Lang and his horse into the fence. It is a wonder he and his horse were not killed. You not only jeopardized the life of Lang, but that of several other jockeys, not to speak of some very valuable horses. You spoiled one of our principal stakes."

Sande breaks in, "What about these boys here? You have not even listened to the jockeys who were in the race. Aren't you going to give them a chance, aren't you going to listen to the truth? I'm not so interested in having my jockey privileges restored as I am about having the guilty verdict removed from my record. I have pride in the work I have accomplished in racing and don't want my record blemished for something I have not done. I would never hurt anybody. I never have, and it makes me feel terrible to be accused of a malicious foul when I was merely scrambling back after being fouled myself."

After the three other jockeys verify Sande's story, Latane states, "They merely repeat what we have already heard. I think that is all." He rises and leaves the room.

Sande emerges from the hearing in tears. A crushed Sande tells reporters, "It's not fair. I didn't foul, and I don't want to be blamed for it. I only want a square deal, and they won't give me one."

Sportswriter John Kieran criticizes the hearings. "The Maryland Jockey Club called this lad to the stand, stripped him of his badge and took steps to bar him from riding at any track in the country. For what? Was it for 'pulling' a horse? No. Was it for cheating on the weight? No. Was it for association with crooked gamblers? No. It was for crowding a horse that was trying to get past him. That's the charge. In other words, he was trying too hard to win. Perhaps it was 'foul riding' as charged, and if it was 'foul riding,' the offending jockey should pay some penalty. Not even Sande should be allowed to violate the rules of the game. But, assuming that the crime was committed, does the punishment fit the crime? Was it fair to take a lad of Sande's courage, honesty, skill, and fame and publicly humiliate him so abjectly for the comparatively venial fault of trying too hard to win a race?"

In a letter to Maryland Racing Commission President Latane, Joseph E. Widener praises Sande and requests that the body lift the ban on the jockey by November 26. "It is only Sande's fine character and hurt feelings which prompted me to write you in this way. In my many years on the turf, I've known few, if any, jockeys who have proved such a credit to racing."

Latane responds with a written refusal, without convening a formal meeting of the commission. "We regard the present application as premature. Should Sande make application to us in 1928 for a license, we will give the matter most careful consideration."

"The Thoroughbred Record" strongly backs Sande. "It is unfortunate the Pimlico Futurity be the medium of a scandal involving the integrity of Earl Sande. He had built up by hard, skillful work in the saddle a reputation second to none. His name was a synonym for ability, courage, and honesty, and now to have the honor that surrounded his name stripped away at one fell swoop is difficult to comprehend."

Widener sends Sande overseas to investigate racing opportunities in Europe. Sande boards the White Star Liner Majestic on November 26 for his trip abroad. In England he reunites with Steve Donoghue, whom he beat in the great international match race between Zev and Papyrus. He also meets with numerous expatriate American jockeys but misses being in the States.

"What a year. Mr. Sinclair faces jail time. Commander Ross runs into financial difficulty and has to sell his horse racing operation to Mr. Harold Hatch. I lost my beloved Marion, and I'm banned from racing. What more could happen?"

Despite being barred from racing near the end of the season, Sande tops all money-winning jockeys, with purses of $277,877. He wins 27 percent of his mounts and lands in the money 56 percent of the time. The next closest jockey in winnings, Laverne Fator rode 224 more mounts than Sande. Harry Payne Whitney claims top stable honors, with earnings of $328,769. Sam Hildreth saddles the most winners, with seventy-two, while Sinclair's Rancocas Stable earns purses totaling $161,559.

Top 1927 Money Winning Leaders				
Jockey	Mounts	1st	%	$Winnings
Sande, E.	179	49	.27	$277,877
Fator, L.	403	112	.28	270,023
Bourassa, O.	593	120	.20	263,067
Maiben, J.	341	66	.19	247,715
Lang, C.	191	38	.20	244,546

"The American Racing Manual" praises Sande's 1927 performance. "Sande was the same brilliant star of old, as is attested to by the $277,877 he won in stakes and purses for the various owners for whom he rode. Earl Sande and Laverne Fator are undoubtedly the best of our present day riders."

Sande returns from Europe with Johnny Loftus in late January, aboard the Aquitania. Heavy seas make the trip very uncomfortable.

Sande comes down the gangplank with a sprightly step and tells dock-side reporters, "I've just finished the roughest ride of my life. I've scratched this boat from any further mounts. The first two days out nearly finished me, but now I feel fine and am anxious to get back in the harness again."

"Why didn't you ride in Europe?"

"I had a number of offers from prominent European owners to ride, but under the circumstances back in the States, I did not feel right accepting any mounts. The offers still stand, however, and if I cared to, I could do plenty of riding abroad. I did enjoy watching the steeplechasing and spent lots of time in France with my friend Frankie Keogh."

"Will you apply for reinstatement with Maryland?"

"I will meet soon with my employer, Mr. Widener, to discuss racing op-portunities. But first, I plan to visit my family in Salem, Oregon."

Upon his return from Oregon in early March, Sande enters New York's Roosevelt Hospital for a minor nose operation as a result of sinus trouble. The successful operation allows the jockey to breathe normally again.

The Maryland Racing Commission reinstates Sande during a special meeting on March 23. Sande begins training immediately at Belmont Park for the upcoming season.

"I got soft on my vacation overseas, but now I'm in tiptop shape. I look forward to a big racing season."

Sande forsakes riding in Maryland and opens the 1928 racing season at

Sande on board the Aquitania. Courtesy Sande Tomlinson Collection

Sande on Osmand with Mr. Joseph E. Widener, after victory in the 1928 Toboggan Handicap. Courtesy Ken Grayson Collection.

Aqueduct. He scores his first two victories of the year on Virmar, between April 25 and early May. At Jamaica on May 8, Sande and Virmar enter the winner's circle once again, after triumphing in the Rosedale Stakes. Poor showings on Grey Lag, Luccilite, and Ingrid lead up to the Kentucky Derby.

On the first day of the Belmont racing season on May 17, Sande mounts Osmand for the Toboggan Handicap. A misbehaving Scapa Flow delays the start at the post. When the field finally gets away, Scapa Flow jumps to the lead, with Osmand a few feet back, matching stride for stride. By the first furlong, Osmand exhibits exceptional speed and pulls ahead of Frank Coltiletti on Scapa Flow. Clarence Kummer, on Happy Argo, moves up to third place. Down the homestretch, Coltiletti takes to the whip, drawing Scapa Flow within striking distance of Osmand. Gaining inch by inch, Scapa Flow makes a final surge to the wire. The partisan crowd sighs relief as Osmand holds on for the victory. Sande also delivers Atlantis to the winner's circle in the sixth race.

Syl Peabody, owner of Martie Flynn, offers Sande a guarantee of $5,000, and one half of the $50,000 Kentucky Derby purse, if Sande wins. Sande mulls the offer over, but turns it down, opting to sit out the 1928 Kentucky Derby and ride at Belmont. Rumors fly that Sande does not wish to face favored Reigh Count and Chick Lang, after their last encounter resulted in Sande's suspension. While Sande finishes out of the money three times and captures second once on May 19, Chick Lang rides Reigh Count vigorously to win the Kentucky Derby. Martie Flynn finishes far out of the money.

Sande's next Belmont victory comes on May 25, aboard Scalawag. For the season so far, Laverne Fator leads all jockeys with twenty-one victories, while Sande ranks fourth with seven. In the Metropolitan Handicap, Sande makes the mistake of going wide around the turn on Chance Shot, while 12 to 1 Nimba cuts to the inside, saving much ground and winning the race.

After a series of out-of-the-money finishes and disappointing second-place finishes, Sande has a heart-to-heart talk with Mr. Widener. "I will fulfill my racing engagements the rest of this season and then retire. I can no longer take off the weight to get in riding trim. The constant weight loss is weakening me. It's not fair to your stable to have a jockey who's not at his best."

"I respect your decision, Earl. You've always given me all I asked, and I have no complaints. On the contrary, you have given my mounts some extraordinary rides."

Privately, he tells his mother, "Without Marion, it's no fun anymore."

The next day, Sande takes Bateau to the front from the barrier. Leading by four lengths, Bateau starts to lag under the weight of 121 pounds. Darkness, sensing vulnerability, launches an attack. Bateau rises to the challenge and wins by a length.

Sande's next major victories come in early July at Aqueduct. Sande, on Kiev, chases down a surprised Extreme to capture the July 3 Dominant Handicap. The next day, Sande mounts 5 to 1 Osmand for a run at the Carter Handicap purse. For the second day in a row, Sande makes the crowd breathless, with an exciting finish ahead of Byrd. At the end of the month, Sande celebrates Saratoga's opening day with perfect riding on Chance Shot to win the Saratoga Handicap going away. On August 5, Sande finishes second on Jack High in the United States Hotel Stakes, out of the money on Diavolo in the Miller Stakes (won by Chick Lang on Reigh Count), and first on Osmand in the American Legion Handicap.

Sande after winning a race on a muddy track. Courtesy Ken Grayson Collection.

Three weeks later, Sande delivers a poor fourth-place performance on Marine in the running of the Grand Union Hotel Stakes. The crowd remains silent as he rides past them after defeat. He then mounts Chance Shot for the Merchants and Citizens' Handicap. Edith Cavell starts fast and is trailed by Black Maria, Chance Shot, and Dangerous in the field of four. Fator closes the gap on Black Maria, while Sande follows suit. Into the homestretch, Black Maria leads, while Sande calls on Chance Shot. The horse shoots forward, steadily decreasing the distance. In the last fifty yards, Chance Shot looks Black Maria in the eye before putting on more speed and beating the other horse to the wire.

Sande again mounts Chance Shot for the September 8 Belmont Rampano Handicap. Running in the mud and conceding fourteen pounds to Sun Forward, Chance Shot sets the pace and maintains a good lead all of the way. He wins, under restraint from Sande.

September 15 is billed as Sande's last day on the track, and 40,000 Belmont race fans greet him with resounding applause. The band strikes up "Auld Lang Syne." He rides Osmand to victory in the Stalwart Handicap, finishes out of the money on Curate in the Futurity, and pilots Chance Shot to second place behind Reigh Count in The Jockey Club Gold Cup.

Sportswriter John Kieran reflects the feelings of race fans throughout the country. "The 'Flying Earl' slipped out of the saddle on Saturday after a career of twelve years or so on the turf, during most of which period he was the idol of the racegoers, the jockey for the crowd. They were Sande all the way. Thousands who didn't know a form chart from a weather report went to the track and played Sande across the board. The quiet lad with a sunny smile rode a larger percentage of winners than any of his rivals. He had good horses, of course. A good jockey deserved no less. With skill, courage, and honesty, he won fame and fortune. He rode to win. There was never any doubt about that, and it was one of the bright jewels of his crown. The crowd rooted for him. Horses ran for him. A great combination. He leaves a glorious record, and an empty saddle. It will be hard to fill."

Sande turns his attention to owning and training horses. He purchases Nassak from Rancocas for $35,000 and spends another $60,000 on horses from other stables.

Clarence Kummer ribs Sande. "I thought you were smarter than that, Earl. Owning horses is a losing proposition. You'd be better off hiring on as a trainer for another owner. "

"Well, we'll just have to see about that."

Jack Dempsey and Earl Sande watch intently on September 24, as Sande's 15 to 1 Chantry goes to the wire nose to nose with Everytime, while favorite Zest trails the pair by a length. Dempsey gives Sande a bear hug after the numbers board shows Chantry the winner. The Aqueduct crowd cheers

Earl Sande riding Jack Dempsey during a charity benefit. Courtesy Sande Tomlinson Collection.

the new owner's orchid silks with green collar and cuffs, as Chantry enters the Bellarose Claiming Stakes winner's circle.

Dempsey roars, "That's your first win as an owner and trainer, Earl. Who says you can't teach an old dog a new trick?"

Over the next two weeks, Sande's Nearby finishes second, and Spectre scores a victory for the new owner. Sande enters both Chantry and Spectre in the October 8 Jamaica Lynbrook Claiming Stakes, however, neither holds up in the competition, both succumbing to Stand By. On October 18, Sande suffers a personal and financial blow when a horse he purchased from John E. Madden dies from influenza. Three days later, Nearby places second in the Laurel Selima Stakes and pays $21.50 on a $2 wager.

Owner and trainer Earl Sande timing one of his horses during a workout. Courtesy Ken Grayson Collection.

Sande saddles Nassak to compete in his first race under the Sande colors, the Prince George's Handicap at Bowie. Nassak takes the lead out of the barrier and sets a fast pace. Sun Beau trails and mounts a late attack but cannot catch Nassak on the homestretch. The victory contributes nearly $9,000 to the Sande stable winnings and marks his first major win as an owner.

Sande tells Kummer, "Nassak looks like a champion. He finished today only four fifths of a second slower than the track record for a mile and a sixteenth. In one race, Nassak has earned back a fourth of the money I paid for him. I've been offered $60,000 for him but he's not for sale."

"I think you should take the $60,000 and run, Earl."

On November 21, Sande's Safety Pin finishes fifteen lengths behind the leader in a Bowie maiden race. His poor showing makes the horse a long shot in the next day's Fascination race. This time, Safety Pin breaks in good position and trails Fly Light for the first half. At the turn, he moves up and takes the lead, winning by three lengths and paying $44 for a $2 ticket.

Four days later, Sande's Nassak faces three horses he's already beaten -- Sun Beau, Misstep, and Distraction -- in the Bryan Memorial Handicap. Twenty thousand fans watch Nassak finish a distant third and, more importantly, suffer a leg breakdown.

Kummer offers Sande advice. "There's $60,000 down the drain, Earl. Your other horses aren't doing anything but eating hay and your bankroll. You have too soft a spot in your heart for these horses. You need to get rid of them, or they're going to break you."

"They're my life, Clarence. That would be like cutting off my right arm. Besides, I have a cushion in the stock market."

Sande also receives some friendly advice from Doc Pardee in a letter. "From what I read in the papers, you've had a string of tough luck with your horses. Maybe you should follow my example. After years of feedin' my old nags, I've finally hung up the reins on my own outfit, sold the livery in Prescott, and moved down to a ranch near Glendale. Believe it or not, I hired on as the stable master at the Arizona Biltmore on the outskirts of Phoenix. I still get to work with the horses. However, all the headaches belong to the head honchos. Some mighty big business and horse folks vacation here: the Wrigleys, Riddles, and Woodwards, to name a few. Come down for a visit in the off-season. Would love to see you again and chew the fat over old times."

"The American Racing Manual" notes Sande's retirement "the outstanding incident of the 1928 racing as far as jockeys were concerned. Sande has been the most premier jockey of the American turf for a number of years and leaves a profession that he enriched with notable feats of horsemanship, his glorious record of 942 winners out of 3,532 mounts and the remarkable percentage of .27 for eleven years, with $2,642,225 won on stakes

Doc Pardee chatting with a riding patron at the Arizona Biltmore Resort. Courtesy Arizona Biltmore Resort and Spa

and purses, setting the seal of his fame as one of the greatest jockeys of all times."

Top riding honors shift to McAtee, who wins 24 percent of his mounts and earns $301,295 in 1928. In comparison, Sande wins 20 percent of his mounts and purses, totaling $81,950 as a jockey, his weight problem and early retirement clearly impacting his competitiveness. Rancocas continues its decline, winning only thirty-five races for earnings of $84,238.

Faced with mounting stable losses, Sande requests special permission to ride his own mounts in 1929. This time the Maryland Racing Commission deals Sande a fair hand, altering the jockey rules to allow Sande and other owner/riders to ride their own mounts. He embarks on a rigid training schedule to get back within riding weight limits.

As an owner/trainer, Sande saddles Chantry, Spectre, and Maryland Luck for races at Bowie on April 5. Both Maryland Luck and Spectre bring home first-place finishes, while Chantry fails to place in the feature race. The next day, Sande scratches two of his horses because of muddy track conditions. However, he does enter Milady in the third race, carrying a weight of 109 pounds. Milady performs well and wins going away at the wire, paying $13.80 on a $2 wager.

Sande gets back in the saddle again at Havre de Grace on April 16. He mounts his own horse Hermitage. The horse takes command of the race early on the sloppy track. He pulls ahead by the first furlong and extends the lead for an easy four-length victory over Domineer. As a result of the change in jockey rules, the race marks the first time in Maryland history that a single person owned, trained, and rode a horse to victory.

"It was great to get back to the old saddle. It's only fitting that I takes up the reins again at 'The Graw,' for it brings back the golden days of the past years. I felt just like a kid getting ready for a vacation. What a thrill."

"The Cincinnati Enquirer" heralds Sande's return as a jockey. "They Never Come Back, Eh? Well, Earl Sande is One Who Did. Once more we saw the peerless rider come down the stretch to victory. Once more we witnessed a great reception tendered to the most popular jockey that ever strode a hoss."

Hermitage's impressive win in the Havre de Grace meeting ranks him as a heavy favorite, with Sande up, in the April 22 Beverwyck Purse. Hermitage breaks fast in the mud and establishes a front-running position through the first half of the race. In his first race of the season, 22 to 1 The Nut flashes past Hermitage. Two other horses follow The Nut, and Sande finishes a disappointing fourth.

At Pimlico on May 5, Hermitage leads into the homestretch before giving up ground and finishing third. In early May, Sande ships his string to Illinois after having his application for an Illinois permit as both a trainer and a jockey approved. None of his mounts perform well in the Illinois competition. He continues to nurse Nassak back to health in hopes of racing him later in the season. Rumors swirl that Sande will enter Hermitage in the 1929 Kentucky Derby.

Prior to the May 10 Preakness, Hermitage is listed with 30 to 1 odds, despite Sande's decision to ride the horse himself. Will Rogers arrives at the clubhouse to great commotion and applause. The Hollywood and vaudeville star takes a bow and waves his hat to admirers. Sande has never ridden a Preakness winner, and the jinx continues as Hermitage stops suddenly and finishes dead last, apparently injured.

After the race, Will Rogers says, "I bet on four horses, all to win, place and show. Blue Coat was tipped me by Governor Ritchie, who I think was working on commission. One was called The Nut. Well, birds of a feather must back each other. I bet on Earl Sande's Hermitage because Sande is a friend of mine. There was a horse called Soul of Honor from Oklahoma, there's real humor for you. I had all these tickets in my outside coat pocket and some Republican Senator or Congressman pinched 'em. I discovered it just as they got to the post, so my only hope was to pray for 'em all to lose, and they did. They all four ran last, so imagine that Republican scoundrel's embarrassment. The Lord is with us Democrats, but not often."

Henry Ford Sinclair enters prison to serve his seven-month sentence. He also pays over $2 million in taxes and penalties and returns oil properties with an estimated worth of $430 million to the U. S. government.

Hermitage's injury puts him out of contention for the Kentucky Derby, and Sande misses his second chance in two years to ride in the Run for the Roses. While nursing along Nassak and Hermitage, Sande enters Safety Pin in the May 24 Belmont Garden City Handicap. Sande's jockey, Eddie Benham, gets 20 to 1 Safety Pin off to a good start and maintains the lead into the homestretch. Folamile makes a bid, skinning the rail and saving ground, while Arcturus exhibits speed on the outside. The outcome remains in doubt until the wire, where Arcturus noses out Safety Pin for the victory. A week later, Safety Pin garners another second-place finish with a valiant homestretch effort.

Aqueduct officials set down leading jockey Laverne Fator for rough riding on June 18. They also remand his case over to The Jockey Club for further action. Within two weeks, The Jockey Club ends Fator's suspension.

Sande tells Fator, "Glad you got a little better treatment than I did."

"Seems like the race stewards and commissioners carry a grudge against the country's top jockeys. Wish you were racing more and taking the heat off me, Earl."

At Arlington Park in Chicago, Sande and Hermitage finish third in the July 3 Combat Purse, while Benham finishes out of the money on Hermitage on Independence Day. Sande's Safety Pin loses to Lady Broadcast by six lengths a day later in the Winnetka Purse. On July 6, in an ironic twist, Sande mounts Reigh Count for a ride down the track between the fifth and sixth races, to signal the champion horse's retirement from racing.

Sande whispers to Reigh Count, "No hard feelings, Old Boy. Now we're both put out to pasture."

By late August, Sande faces the futility of continuing to own racehorses. Unlike Maryland and Illinois, New York does not permit owner/trainers to ride their own horses. Rumors abound when Sande puts up seven of his horses for sale. In mid-September, Sande sells four more horses. However, Nassak is not on the auction block. Sande hopes to race the horse again.

Over months of rehabilitation, Sande keeps telling Nassak, "I came back. You can, too."

Nearby, whom Sande sold to George D. Widener, wins the September 21 Flying Fairy Handicap while ridden by Mack Garner. Four days later, Sam Hildreth dies, delivering another blow to Harry Sinclair's Rancocas Stable. Sande and Laverne Fator serve as honorary pallbearers.

"There goes a giant in the horseracing world, Laverne. It was an honor to be one of Sam's pallbearers."

"A lot of water has gone under the bridge since we sat up in Jobstown listening to Sam's tall tales. The world is sure changing."

Within a month, American lives changes forever on October 25, "Black Friday," the day the US stock market crashed. Sande's financial cushion disappears.

Laverne Fator tells Earl, "Everybody warned about the sharks at the racetrack. Nobody said anything about the crooks in big business and at the stock exchange."

"Nothing surprises me anymore. As Jack Dempsey says 'We have to roll with the punches.'"

On November 3, Mack Garner runs afoul of the race stewards during the running of the Pimlico Futurity. They suspend him for the balance of the meeting.

Sande catches Garner in the jockeys' room. "Congratulations on joining Fator and me in the elite suspension club."

During 1929, Sande rides ten mounts and finishes first once, a far cry from the performance numbers the nation's top jockey turned in for more than a decade.

Nassak never does return to race again. Sande rubs the horse behind his ears and whispers, "Guess we're good company for each other. A pair of broken-down racers."

Chapter 13

Road to the Triple Crown

"There stands the home of the next great American champion racehorse, Fitz." Belair Stud owner William Woodward points with his white cane down the wooded lane to the stone stable housing Gallant Fox. Woodward and his trainer, "Sunny Jim" Fitzsimmons, walk down the front steps of the 1700s mansion and survey Woodward's vast Bowie, Maryland, Belair Stud property.

Woodward boasts, "Belair ranks as one of America's oldest thorough-bred nurseries, and the oldest in Maryland. Many champions spent their early years here, going back centuries and beginning with the great stallion Othello. In the 1700s, Selima won a $10,000 inter-colonial race against mounts owned by Virginia turf giant William Byrd III and other prominent Virginia horsemen."

"It's a rich history, Mr. Woodward. I believe The Fox holds an excellent chance of adding to that legend this year. As a two-year-old, he finished out of the money only once.

"Yes, and in that race, the foolish horse let the others beat him out of the starting gate while he gazed at an aeroplane passing overhead."

"The most curious horse I've ever been around. He'll stop dead in his tracks to investigate a bird sitting on the rail. His in-the-money record of two wins, two places, and two shows masks his true potential. He finished strong in every race. A few furlongs more and victory beckoned. We will surprise a lot of folks if our winter work pays off and we get him in the right position to make his move earlier."

"This coming season's been seven years in the making. You came on board in 1923. On your advice, our syndicate bought Sir Gallahad III two years later. Marguerite bred and foaled Gallant Fox in 1927. Now, here we stand on the brink of making horse racing history. I can just feel it, Fitz."

"I sure didn't feel it in the spring of 1928, when we surveyed the group of yearlings. I harbored grave doubts about the chestnut, blaze-faced colt. The Fox's nostrils appeared too small. I thought it would be difficult for him to breathe in the heat of a race. I also found him the laziest horse in the stable. Unless we played tricks on him to get him to work, he just leaned against the stable wall and ate to his heart's content. What kept me interested in Gallant Fox is his 'evil eye.' It has so much white in it that it exhibits a wildness that is sure to scare the other horses into submission. That's why I cut away his blinkers enough to let this year's competitors feel the full brunt of his scrutiny and disdain."

"Yes, he wants to do things his own way and has contempt for those who challenge him. While I head West for a few months, you can correct his weak points and bolster his strong points. Reach me at the Arizona Biltmore when you're ready to hone our strategy as your workouts with Gallant Fox progress."

The two form an incongruous pair. A severe case of spinal arthritis contributes to Fitzsimmons's shortness and rounds his shoulders. Despite a business suit, vest, and bow tie, Fitzsimmons looks rumpled. In contrast, Woodward stands erect, despite his cane. His distinguished mustache and wire-rimmed glasses add sophistication to his appearance. A true Victorian, he dresses impeccably at all times.

William Woodward exudes success. A graduate of Harvard Law School, he managed Hanover Bank as president until its 1929 merger with Central Trust Company and then held the board chairman position. He serves as director of the Federal Reserve Bank of New York, president of the New York Clearing House, and director on the boards of several large American corporations. A longtime member of The Jockey Club, he assumes the board of stewards chairman position in 1930.

Fitzsimmons, a track veteran since the late 1880s, knows horse breeding and training backwards and forwards. Although a no-nonsense trainer, he always exhibits a happy-go-lucky attitude and earns the nickname, Sunny Jim from "New York World" sportswriter George Dailey.

Periodic telegrams to Arizona from Fitzsimmons keep Woodward informed on Gallant Fox's workouts and conditioning. "The Fox is filling out nicely and building up a fine set of racing muscles. After a lot of hard work, we've schooled him off daydreaming at the post, and he breaks well now. Three different riders had the reins on him last year. To get the most out of him, we need to be thinking about finding a steady jockey dedicated to riding The Fox. We need one with the skill and horse manners to convince him to run to his full potential."

Woodward enjoys the warm Phoenix winter and early morning horseback ride comradeship of Arizona Biltmore stable manager Doc Pardee. After unsaddling, Woodward admires Pardee's personal stable of horses.

"We'll need a good workout horse soon for The Fox, Doc. Any of your string up to the task?"

"Wrattler here represents the best of my lot. He'll make your horse work hard, keep him fit and competitive. He's yours for the askin'. You couldn't find a better fit for your horse."

"Thank you. I'll take you up on that, Doc."

"From what you've been tellin' me, this Gallant Fox comes with a fine pedigree. Is it owner's pride showin' through, or is this horse as good as you claim?"

"I'd be a fool to say there's no owner's pride. I believe we have a champion in the making. I've employed the best trainer in the business, working with The Fox since birth. From all of Fitz's reports, the horse is coming along on schedule. He's already the odds-on favorite in the winter books for the Kentucky Derby. Barring serious injury, we could win most big stakes races this year. I'd bet my reputation that he can win the three biggest American races — a feat not accomplished since Johnny Loftus rode Sir Barton to victory in the Kentucky Derby, Preakness, and Belmont in 1919."

"It sure doesn't hurt to have confidence in your trainer and horse. However, that's only half the combination needed to win big. Those three races come early in the racin' season, and most young three-year-old horses lack either the stamina or speed to compete effectively in all three races. On top of that, each race's unique characteristics regardin' track condition, weather, number of entries, and length add to the challenge. Even more dauntin', in the later races, you'll be competin' against fresh horses and jockeys who know your racin' strategy. It's a real grind to compete in those three races in that span of time, much less win all of them. In my opinion, it takes just the perfect partnership of horse and jockey to win that triple challenge."

Earl Sande after working Osmand in preparation for 1930 racing season. Courtesy Ken Grayson Collection.

"I know Fitz will bring The Fox to the season a potential championship horse, up to any challenge. You're correct, Doc, about finding the best jockey. That's the big remaining question that separates us from an unprecedented racing season."

"I think I can help you there, too."

"Do you know of a new boy not connected to other major stables?"

"Not exactly, but I know the right jockey. One who represents a clear match with The Fox and is available. None other than Earl Sande."

"A great jockey in his day, one of the best, but injuries and weight problems took their toll. He only won one race last year, despite riding to pay off debts incurred by his stable. Besides, he's retired."

"I know the kid can be coaxed into racin' again this year. He's already helpin' Widener, workin' out Osmand at Belmont. It wouldn't take him long to get back into ridin' trim. You couldn't ask for a better horseman and one who knows horses in and out. If anyone can urge Gallant Fox to give his best, Sande's your man. I guarantee it."

"I'll talk to Fitz about this when I get back to Belair next week. Thanks for the advice, Doc."

"Glad to help out. A great horse deserves a great jockey."

At Belmont in early April, Sande dismounts and tells reporters, "Osmand's in the best shape I've ever seen him. We've been working out every morning for the past few weeks, and he wants to run. Mr. Widener's jockey and Osmand should win quite a few races this year."

"How about you, Earl? You going to ride for Widener? How come you haven't applied for your Jockey Club license?"

"Just haven't decided yet if I want to race this year. Mr. Widener's leaving the decision up to me. That's all, boys."

Woodward arrives back at Belair and watches Fitzsimmons put Gallant Fox through the paces. That evening, they sit on either side of Woodward's desk and conference about potential jockeys to ride Gallant Fox in his three-year-old debut.

Fitzsimmons pats his vest pocket. "I've written down my first choices in my work diary. It's a pretty short list. Clarence Kummer announced his intention of launching a comeback this year. His riding talent and experience qualify him as a possibility. Along with Laverne Fator and Earl Sande, Kummer ranks among the best jockeys this past decade. Speaking of Sande, he renewed his Maryland license and is riding at Havre de Grace this week."

"I've done some homework on jockeys also. Sande finished far back in the pack in his first 1930 comeback race and did not land in the money until three days later. How does that figure into your thinking, Fitz?"

"Doesn't bother me a bit. Sande rose to the top of jockey ranks with cleverness, skill, alertness, and quick thinking. Those traits mark the great jockeys, and he still possesses them. If he stays disciplined, doesn't overdo his training, and stays around 114 pounds, he can get back to his top form. Right now he's riding mules. Give him a real horse and you'll see what he can still accomplish on the track."

"Your short list matches mine, Fitz. Kummer and Sande. Prompted by Doc Pardee back in Arizona, I'd give my nod to Sande. His smoothness in the saddle and great hand riding finishes are what we need to win. I'd rather trust in his great ability, while not perhaps up to his best form, than a jockey of lesser talent and experience."

Fitzsimmons pulls out his work diary and plops it down for Woodward to see. Woodward reads, written in big red letters, "Earl Sande, Gallant Fox jockey."

Woodward rises and says, "That settles it then. I'll telegraph Sande at Havre de Grace tonight."

Fitzsimmons tears a page out of the back of his diary and hands it to Woodward. "Here's the hotel where Sande can be reached."

Woodward telegraphs Sande: "Earl, I would like to talk to you about riding Gallant Fox for Belair Stud this year. I can be in Havre de Grace tomorrow. Please advise."

Sande reads the telegraph and thinks, "Must be pretty important if Mr. Woodward wants to come to Havre de Grace right away."

He telegraphs back: "No need for that. Racing winds up here for me tomorrow and I will be at Jamaica next week. We can talk then. Best regards."

Woodward and Sande meet to iron out the details. Woodward offers a season contract with the usual riding fees.

"My horse can outrun anything on the track today. If tested, he can meet the challenge several times to defeat his opponents."

"It's not that I don't believe you, Mr. Woodward. Let's just say it's in both of our interests if we take it slow. My riding may not be up to par. I don't want to put you in the position of being obligated to ride me when there are better performing jockeys available. On the other hand, if I ride Gallant Fox well, I want a piece of the action. I took a good look at The Fox and watched his workouts today. Like you, I believe your horse will win a lot of races this year. For now, let's agree to a one-race deal. Doc Pardee tells me you're a man of your word. That's good enough for me. A handshake will seal the deal. "

Earl offers his hand to Woodward, who seizes it and shakes it firmly. "Fair enough, Earl. Fitz will take care of your needs and help you prep The Fox for his debut in the Jamaica Woods Memorial."

Gallant Fox works out against Doc Pardee's Wrattler. Sande prepares for his first New York mount in a year and a half. He complains to "Sunny Jim," "The Fox gallops away from the competition. When he realizes he has a good lead, he stops to look around, figuring his work is done."

"You need to pace him. Let him know you require more of him. By the time we finish training, you and The Fox will be closer than Burns and Allen."

Sande talks strategy with Gallant Fox during workouts and as he brushes the horse down the night before the April 26 Woods Memorial. Earl's stomach turns when he mounts Gallant Fox in the paddock. He bends low in the saddle and whispers in the horse's right ear. "This is it, Pardner. We both have a lot to prove. Let's not let our boss and fans down."

A cheer rises from the grandstands as Sande and Gallant Fox enter the track. Sande doffs his riding cap to the crowd. Woodward pours himself a gin and tonic and brushes his white pants as he sits in his box to watch the race. His shoulders tighten in anticipation.

Crack Brigade breaks to the front early. When Sande gallops Gallant Fox to move on the leaders, the other jockeys close ranks and prevent him from breaking through. Woodward clenches his drink. Turning the corner into the backstretch, Gallant Fox runs fourth behind Crack Brigade, Desert Light, and Spinach, respectively. At the far turn, Sande drops Gallant Fox back to clear traffic. Woodward's jaw locks. In an instant, Gallant Fox emerges from the pocket and swings to the outside.

He attempts to sweep past Desert Light and Spinach. Spinach gives up the ghost, but Desert Light, with Mack Garner swinging his whip, goes wide to try to take Gallant Fox out of the running. Woodward sucks in a sharp breath and spills his drink.

An aroused Gallant Fox accepts the challenge, leaving Garner eating dust. Sande turns his attention to Crack Brigade and gains ground with every stride. At the quarter pole, Woodward jumps to his feet and cheers Gallant Fox to the lead. He wins drawing away.

Jockey Garner analyzes the outcome for reporters. "I knew Gallant Fox as the horse to beat. I tried to box Sande in with Desert Light and help from Spinach. Unfortunately for me, Sande thinks a quarter of a mile down the track and didn't fall for my strategy. When that failed, I swung wide to take him out of the picture. When I bore out, Gallant Fox shot past Desert Light in a flash. I knew then it was over."

Sande downplays Garner's remarks and credits the win to Gallant Fox. "As long as there's a horse in front of The Fox, you can ride him backwards and he will use his competitive spirit to find a way to win."

With Gallant Fox's first 1930 win in the books, Woodward and Sande talk terms. Woodward offers a flat $10,000 for the season, plus the regular riding fees.

"I have a lot of faith in your horse, Mr. Woodward. I propose riding for 10 percent of the purses won this season. If I ride Gallant Fox to victory, I make money. If I fail, well, I'm willing to make that gamble. I intend to win every race with The Fox this year."

"It's a deal, Earl. It's only fair that we both prosper if you and Gallant Fox perform as expected."

"The big test will come next week. I have yet to break the Preakness jinx. In my long career, it's the only major stakes race I never conquered. It

The Preakness

Sande on Gallant Fox winning the 1930 Preakness. Courtesy Doc Pardee Library, Phoenix, Arizona.

comes early this year, before the Kentucky Derby for the first time in a long while. Maybe that's enough to change my luck."

"At least we will know soon."

At 9 to 5, Gallant Fox enters as the heaviest favorite to go to the Preakness pole. An unusually warm May 9 brings out 40,000 fans to see Gallant Fox, ridden by America's favorite jockey. Throngs of people swarm the paddock area to catch a glimpse of the pair before the race. Responding to the saddling bell, Sande mounts The Fox and leads the parade to the new starting gate system. The bugle call sounds, and fans send up thundering applause and loud cheers. Sande tips his cap in appreciation.

At the barrier, Sande tells Gallant Fox, "This is number two, Pardner. You're not superstitious are you?"

Gallant Fox gets off to a decent start from his inside position. With a flash, Tetrarchal charges from the outside, followed by Crack Brigade, and cuts off Gallant Fox. By the first turn, Sande trails six lengths behind the leaders, locked in close quarters.

Woodward looks through his binoculars and says, "It doesn't look good."

Sande backs Gallant Fox off and takes to the outside on the backstretch, losing more precious ground. Gallant Fox shakes his head in frustration.

Woodward now places the binoculars in his lap and drops his head. "It's hopeless. Damn Preakness curse."

With fifteen lengths to close and eight other horses in front of him, Sande tells Gallant Fox, "It's a matter of heart. Let's get at it." Hands and heels go to work, and Gallant Fox takes off like a meteor. He passes the also-rans and catches up to both leaders, Tetrarchal and Crack Brigade. Realizing his fate, Tetrarchal drops from contention, leaving Gallant Fox and Crack Brigade to swing around the far turn battling for the lead.

Upon hearing wild cheering, Woodward lifts his head and raises the binoculars to his face in time to see Ellis lay the whip on Crack Brigade's hide time after time. The horse responds and heads Gallant Fox.

Within one hundred yards of the finish line, Sande lets out a single snap of the whip and sings in Gallant Fox's ear, "We can do it, Pardner, we can do it."

Gallant Fox pricks his ears and digs his hooves into the ground with increasing speed and longer strides. He stares down Crack Brigade before leaving him three-quarters of a length behind at the finish line.

The frenzied crowd chants, "Sande! Sande! Sande!" as the sweat-streaked, dirt-covered jockey and Gallant Fox return to the scales.

Maryland Governor Albert C. Ritchies presents William Woodward with the Woodlawn Vase, the coveted turf trophy dating back to 1860. Final betting drops Gallant Fox's odds to even money, and Woodward earns $51,925. Sande's Preakness share totals $5,192, more than half of the flat fee offered to him to ride Gallant Fox for the entire season.

Reporters converge on Sande and he relives the race. "We were in a lot of trouble going into the first turn. I had my doubts for a while. The Fox erased them from my mind. I never experienced a horse close ground like he did in that run up the backstretch. I wasn't a bit worried after The Fox's display of electrifying speed. He sure put an end to my eleven-year Preakness jinx. See you at the Kentucky Derby, boys."

Sunny Jim adds with pride, "Once The Fox maneuvered out of the box, I knew I had saddled a winner."

After Sande's exciting come-from-behind Preakness victory, sportswriter Vernon Van Ness describes Sande as "The Greatest Jockey Since Immortal Tod Sloan. In the heart is courage, in the hands is strength, in the head is the brain. Every jockey must have some share of each of these to be at all successful. Combining all three of them in the greatest measure, he becomes great. That is why there are so few great jockeys, why there is only one Earl Sande."

Earl Sande with Doc Pardee's Wrattler and Gallant Fox preparing for 1930 Kentucky Derby. Courtesy Sande Tomlinson Collection.

Woodward ships Gallant Fox to Louisville in a private railcar, accompanied by his trial horse, Wrattler. Sande works him out while reporters gather at the track.

"The locals find Gallant Fox a bit light in the quarters, where a route horse typically carries plenty of beef. Do you think he can stand up to the pressure, Earl?"

"Gallant Fox looks fit. He's a great horse. Take a good look at him, boys. He's a big, colt with powerful shoulders and hindquarters. Barring any accidents, I predict Gallant Fox the Kentucky Derby winner, despite what the locals think."

"We know you broke your Preakness jinx last week. However, no Preakness winner ever followed that up with a Kentucky Derby victory. Sir Barton won both in 1919, but the Derby ran first that year. Can you break two jinxes in a row?"

"History is made one race at a time. Come back on Saturday and find out."

"If you're successful, it will be your third Kentucky Derby victory in eight years. You'll be tied with the great colored jockey, Isaac Murphy, the only rider to ever win three Kentucky Derbys, with his victories in 1884, 1890, and 1891."

"Pretty good company, I'd say."

"How about the weather, Earl? You'll be going up against some pretty good mudders in Tannery and Uncle Luther. Word around the track says Gallant Fox has no liking for bad going and fails to respond to you in the mud."

"Don't let track gossip cloud your thinking. My doubts about The Fox over a heavy and muddy course are gone. I am convinced that he can run on any kind of track and I have no worry about the outcome Saturday. We don't worry about the weather because The Fox is ready to gallop, rain or shine."

"How about that fancy starting box contraption, Earl? Will that give you any trouble?"

"You can't stop progress. It will level the playing field and give everyone a fair chance to get away cleanly."

Three days of rain create a sloppy track. Woodward sits as a guest in Joseph E. Widener's box. Other guests include Lord Derby and Senator Camden.

1930 Kentucky Derby program. Courtesy Ken Grayson Collection.

Lord Derby asks, "What chance do you give your horse today, Mr. Woodward?   Gallant Fox has never run a race in the mud and comes across as a temperamental horse. What's to prevent him from telling Sande he'll have nothing to do with the gooey stuff?"

Gallant Fox, with Sande up, takes the lead in the 1930 Kentucky Derby. Courtesy Ken Grayson Collection.

Earl Sande and Gallant Fox win the 1930 Kentucky Derby by two lengths. Courtesy Doc Pardee Library, Phoneix, Arizona.

"Mud or no mud, I think nobody will beat Gallant Fox today unless they are of Man o' War stature."

"You hold your horse in pretty high regard," Senator Camden says.

"I think you will find that high regard justified by the end of the afternoon, Senator."

Fifteen horses answer the call to the post. A clear favorite, Gallant Fox's odds drop to 6 to 5 in heavy betting. The press picks up on the national attention given to Gallant Fox and anoints him "The Fox of Belair." As the last strains of "My Old Kentucky Home" fade away, Sande guides the horse into the seventh starting gate opening.

Gallant Fox breaks well and comes out in fifth place. As in the last two races, Sande remains in close quarters during the first three furlongs. Knowing that the going along the rail proves heavy in the mud, he chooses an outside path to close on Alcibiades, who shows the way by two lengths. Sixty thousand drenched fans cheer, "Come on, Sande!" Straightening out on the backstretch, Gallant Fox takes command and moves in front of the field.

Woodward turns to Lord Derby and says, "It's over. Sande's got the race won now. And Senator, I believe you understand the high regard Gallant Fox holds on the track."

From that point on, Sande holds Gallant Fox in restraint. Gallant Knight works his way up through the field but provides only a minor challenge before Gallant Fox wins by two lengths, with plenty in reserve.

Fans swarm out of the grandstands and mob Sande and Gallant Fox. Sande's face wrinkles with smiles. The Fox stands majestically as race officials lift the floral horseshoe over his head in the rain, then he nods with approval to the crowd. William Woodward strides across the field and grasps Sande's hand.

"Congratulations on your third Kentucky Derby victory, Earl. Now on to the Belmont."

Woodward poses with Sande and Gallant Fox for the photographers and says to the dripping press reporters, "You saw history in the making here today. Sande ties Isaac Murphy with three Kentucky Derby victories, and The Fox won both the Kentucky Derby and Preakness. While Sir Barton achieved that feat in 1919, The Fox accomplished it with full weight up. Sir Barton carried a maiden allowance in the Derby."

Lord Derby makes his way through the crowd and presents a gold trophy to William Woodward and Earl Sande in a drizzling rain. "I was pleased to

Earl Sande moving across muddy ground through throngs of people after winning the 1930 Kentucky Derby. Courtesy Ken Grayson Collection.

see a good horse win. Furthermore, I would like to see a good horse like yours, Mr. Woodward, increase its reputation. I congratulate you, I congratulate your jockey, and last, but not least, I congratulate your horse. I hereby dub your jockey the Earl of Sande."

Harry Sinclair chomps on a cigar in his box and tells everyone within earshot, "That's my boy, Earl Sande. He rode my horse, Zev, to victory in the 1923 Kentucky Derby. He and Zev set many records and I'd be the first one to congratulate Sande and Gallant Fox should they succeed in breaking some of them."

As Sande receives accolades from well-wishers, Damon Runyon works in the Churchill Downs press box. The victory adds $50,715 to Woodward earnings and puts another $5,072 into Sande's pocket.

A cigarette dangles from his lips as the keys on his typewriter flash another Sande verse around the world.

Say, have they turned the pages
Back to the past once more?

Back to the racin' ages
An' a Derby out of the yore?
Say, don't tell me I'm daffy,
Ain't that the same 'ol grin?
Why it's that handy
Guy named Sande,
Bootin' a winner in!

Say, don't tell me I'm batty!
Say, don't tell me I'm blind!
Look at that seat so natty!
Look how he drives from behind!
Gone is the white of the Ranco,
An' the white band under his chin,
Still he's that handy
Guy named Sande
Bootin' a winner in!

Maybe he ain't no chicken,
Maybe he's getting' along,
But the 'ol heart's still a-tickin'
An' the old bean's goin' strong.
Roll back the year! Yea, roll 'em!
Say, but I'm young agin,
Watchin that handy
Guy named Sande,
Bootin' a winner in!

With the Preakness and Derby wins, Gallant Fox rises to celebrity status, while Sande reigns supreme as America's favorite jockey. Fans flock to see Sande and The Fox work out in preparation for the third great race of 1930, the Belmont Stakes.

Sande rides Petee Wrack for J. R. Macomber in the May 30 Suburban Handicap. Also a foal of Marguerite, Petee Wrack trails Distraction, The Nut, and Curate. Halfway down the backstretch, Petee Wrack stretches out, and Sande goes to the front. Around the far turn, just about every horse makes a move to unseat Pettee Wrack from the lead. Sorties closes down the middle. Distraction rushes up on the outside. The Nut slashes to the rail. Curate catches Petee Wrack on the homestretch. Sande withstands all challenges, Petee Wrack wins driving. The victory claims a new Sande record: the first jockey to win three Suburban Handicaps. His wins aboard Grey Lag in 1923 and Mad Hatter in 1924 also set a record, as the only time a jockey won two Suburban Handicaps in succession.

Press coverage leading up to the Belmont poses the contest as a match race between Gallant Fox and Harry Payne Whitney's Whichone, the 1929 champion juvenile. Headlines proclaim "The Greatest Dual Since Sande Beat Papyrus on Zev." Whichone wins his initial 1930 race and then follows that up with a commanding victory in the Withers Stakes. Both horses train well for the racing duel. On June 3, Fitzsimmons clocks Gallant Fox at Belmont at 1:50 flat for a mile and an eighth, a tad above the world record. Despite Gallant Fox's show of blazing speed, oddsmakers give Whichone the edge at 4 to 5, with Gallant Fox at 6 to 5.

Johnny Loftus visits Sande in the jockey club several days before the running of the Belmont. "While it's nice to be the only jockey to have won the three great American races in a single year, Earl, if someone comes along to match that achievement, I hope it's you. Good luck."

"Thanks, Johnny. After I won the Preakness, I felt nothing can stop me now. It's my turn after all these years."

Before the Belmont, on the evening of June 5, Sande rides in an automobile driven by jockey Edward Barnes. After dinner out, the two head for home to retire early.

"You have two of the three big ones in the history books, Earl. Are you nervous?"

"Nothing to be worried about, Gallant Fox does all the work. I just have to give him a chance to run."

A tire bursts on a car driven by Harry Gross and he loses control, causing a three-car collision. The car in which Sande is riding flips over and throws its occupants out. An ambulance arrives and transports Miss Reifer, an occupant of the third car, Harry Gross, Edward Barnes, and Earl Sande to the Jamaica Hospital. Doctors treat Miss Reifer for injuries to her face, body, and right leg; Gross for a fractured nose and facial cuts; Barnes for minor injuries; and Sande for lacerations to his nose, cheeks, and hands.

"My first thought was that I would not be able to race on Saturday," Sande tells Woodward.

"Those black eyes and cuts look pretty serious, Earl. Are you sure you are up to riding?"

"My hands tape up fine but the cuts under the eyes are the worst. They sting when I smile or grimace. I'm a bit sore from the rollover, but nothing will keep me from winning this race."

Sande mounts Gallant Fox and takes him for his final pre-Belmont workout. Both horse and rider perform with precision.

Fitzsimmons turns to Woodward and says, "It looks like Sande and The Fox are ready to take care of business."

A massive traffic jam and torrents of rain fail to prevent crowds of people from surrounding the stall area to catch a glimpse of super-horse Gallant Fox with bruised and bandaged Earl Sande in the saddle. Because of the pouring rain, saddling takes place in the stalls instead of the paddocks. Only four horses answer the call to the post: Gallant Fox, Whichone, Questionnaire, and Swinfield.

Just before Sande heads onto track, Fitzsimmons grabs the reins and advises him, "You know what to do, Earl. We've been over it a million times. From his demeanor today, Gallant Fox is itching to run. Whatever you do, don't let mud get thrown in The Fox's face. He won't like that."

"I don't want to get any mud in my face either, Mr. Fitzsimmons."

At the rise of the barrier, Gallant Fox breaks to the front with a flurry of strides. At the quarter, Sande rates his horse along like the master rider he is. Through the half and into the far turn, Gallant Fox keeps the field at a safe distance.

Woodward sits on the edge of his seat. He reaches into his pocket and pulls out a horseshoe and says, "Being ahead is even more agonizing then following the leaders. Come on, Sande. Keep the other horses at bay."

On the homestretch, Workman lays his whip on Whichone and makes his challenge. Whichone closes within a length of the leader.

Fitzsimmons leans forward and yells, "Give him the evil eye and show him who owns this track."

Gallant Fox plays with the contender for a few strides, flashes his blaze eye toward Whichone, and then runs the legs off the contender. He wins by three lengths, going away and with plenty of speed in reserve. Despite the heavy running in the rain-soaked track, Gallant Fox gallops to a new record for the mile-and-a-half race. Questionnaire finishes another four lengths back, and Swinfield comes in last, fifteen lengths behind Gallant Fox.

Sande explains his strategy. "I was worried about getting mud in my face and having my cuts reopened, so we went to the lead early. After that, all I had to do was let The Fox run."

The victory adds $60,040 to Woodward's 1930 winnings and boosts Sande's take by another $6,004. Gallant Fox's earnings total more than

Earl Sande on Gallant Fox winning 1930 Belmont Stakes in a breeze and completing the Triple Crown. Courtesy Doc Pardee Library, Phoenix, Arizona.

$200,000 and put him in the league of top money earners with Man o' War, Zev, Sarazen, and Crusader, all of whom Sande rode.

Woodward reaches Sande and thrusts the horseshoe in his hand. "Here's a gift from Doc Pardee for winning the Triple."

They stand together as the Belmont Trophy is brought forward. Woodward's prediction to Fitzsimmons about Gallant Fox comes true. Cameras flash and capture the trophy presentation. Woodward says, "With this decisive win, The Fox is the unquestionable three-year-old champion, and Sande, with his fifth Belmont win, ranks as the best jockey of all time."

Woodward leads Sande back over to Gallant Fox. He beams with pride and says, "Ladies and gentlemen, I present to you Earl Sande and Gallant Fox, Triple Crown winners."

Up in the pressbox, Damon Runyon leans back and says, "Boys, you've just witnessed history in the making."

Runyon turns to the fledgling reporter next to him. "Son, it's time you learned how to make poetic history. The typewriter's all yours. Give it a shot."

> *Loftus wearing the black and gold,*
> *Made his horses's muscles ripple.*
> *With moves both strong and bold,*
> *Set the standard with the Triple.*
> *Say can anyone match that feat?*

Earl Sande on Gallant Fox. Author's Collection.

Many tried without success.
Say, what we need
Is a Handy Guy
Bootin them hosses in!

Fator, oft times, called a hero,
Entered the Derby, Preakness, and Belmont Stakes.
Rode hard but scored a zero,
Getting the mounts but not the breaks.
Say can anyone match that feat?
Many tried without success.
Say, what we need
Is a Handy Guy
Bootin' them babies in!

Kummer, Ensor and McAtee,
All sought racing's Holy Grail.

Earl Sande and Woodward exhibit Belmont Trophy won in 1930 on Gallant Fox. Courtesy Sande Tomlinson Collection.

Laid out their Triple strategy,
Only to see their efforts fail.
Say, can anyone match that feat?
Many tried without success.
Say, it's true,
The Handy Guy named Sande
Bringin' that Triple in.

Epilogue

Earl Sande aboard Gallant Fox won nine of ten 1930 races. After the Belmont, they also captured the Dwyer Stakes by a length and a half, Arlington Classic by a nose over Gallant Night, Saratoga Cup by a length and a half, Lawrence Realization inching out Questionnaire, and Jockey Club Gold Cup with ease. The team's only loss took place in the August 16 Travers. Beaten by 100 to 1 shot Jim Dandy, they ran the race in the stickiest Saratoga mud seen in many years.

Gallant Fox retired to stud with 1930 earnings of $308,275, beating the record set by Zev in 1923. The Fox's lifetime winnings of $340,665 also set a world record. Sande rode forty-three mounts in 1930, taking 11 of them to the winner's circle, placing second nine times, and third four times. He earned $327,375 for the season, his best year since 1923 when he and Zev shattered records. Sande's 1923 Earnings record stood for an astounding twenty years. That same year, the average American earned $1,494. In the midst of the Great Depression, butter cost 44 cents per pound, a loaf of bread 9 cents, and a dozen eggs 41 cents.

Sande was grief-stricken when his friend and fellow jockey, Clarence Kummer died of pneumonia in December 1930 while attempting to lose weight for a riding comeback. Over his career, Kummer won 18.8 percent of his races and jockeyed some of the country's best race horses, including Man o' War.

321

Sande did not race in 1931. He provided NBC radio commentary on the Kentucky Derby. "The American Racing Manual" lamented Sande's retirement, "The name of the 'peerless' Earl Sande, the outstanding American jockey of the past decade, is missing from the jockey list of 1931."

Sande married Clarence Kummer's widow, Marion, on February 18, 1932. They honeymoon in Miami, where he announced his intention to return to riding. He placed third in his first comeback race on April 16 at Jamaica. He scored his first 1932 victory ten days later on Old Master.

On May 7, Sande rode his final Kentucky Derby, placing fifth on Over Time. At the end of July, Sande mounted James Butler's Apprentice in a test against William Woodward's mount Pardee, named after Sande's old friend and mentor. Entering the race, Sande had already piloted Apprentice to two victories. Ironically, the race was so close, the judges declared the Yonkers Handicap a dead heat. For the year, Sande earned first place honors thirteen times, placed second sixteen times and third eleven times. He earned $22,282 in purses for his owners. Despite receiving offers to ride in France and Australia, Sande retired from riding to train horses for paper manufacturing magnate Colonel Maxwell Howard.

Sande saddled his first victorious horse for Howard, St. Hubert, on July 12, 1933, at Empire City and scored another three victories in the next five days. Over the next four years Sande turned in a respectible showing as a trainer but failed to develop a major horse for Howard. During the off-season he attended various sports and charitable functions. With other athletic figures such as Gene Tunney, Tommy Hitchcock, and Tug McGraw; Sande appeared at a sports dinner benefit for the needy.

He made his professional singing debut at the Stork Club in March 1935. As "Collier's" reported, "His voice reached every corner of the night club and his personality reached out to, and gripped everyone who was there. You watched him, and as you watched you could not help but think of the Sande you once knew – the Sande of iron hands and steel nerves, the Sande who was born with a clock in his head so that he always knew just how fast his horse was going, the Sande who – the rose-tinted walls of the night club receeded, the voice of Sande faded away and you felt a breeze on your forehead and you caught the odor of fresh hay..."

Laverne Fator, in a fit of delirium, fell out of a second story Jamaica Hospital window and suffered serious injuries on May 16, 1936. The next day, Earl and Marion Sande comforted Mrs. Fator as Laverne died.

Earl Sande and second wife, Marion. Courtesy Sande Tomlinson Collection.

In early January, Sande purchased Fencing and Sceneshifter for Howard. Fencing won by a head driving hard in a March 5, 1937, race at Hialeah Park in Miami. Sande moved Howard's string of twelve horses to Churchill Downs and Douglas Park for Kentucky racing. He saddled both Fencing and Sceneshifter for the 1937 Kentucky Derby. Fencing gave up the ghost

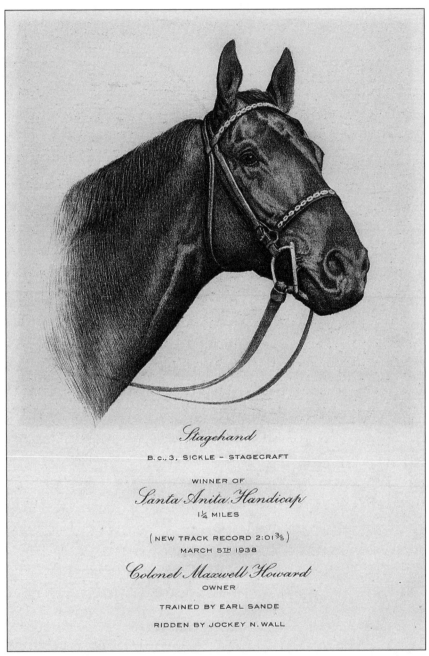

Stagehand

B. c., 3, SICKLE – STAGECRAFT

WINNER OF

Santa Anita Handicap

1¼ MILES

(NEW TRACK RECORD 2:01⅗)

MARCH 5ᵀᴴ 1938

Colonel Maxwell Howard

OWNER

TRAINED BY EARL SANDE

RIDDEN BY JOCKEY N. WALL

Santa Anita Ball progam to celebrate Santa Anita Handicap win. Courtesy Sande Tomlinson Collection.

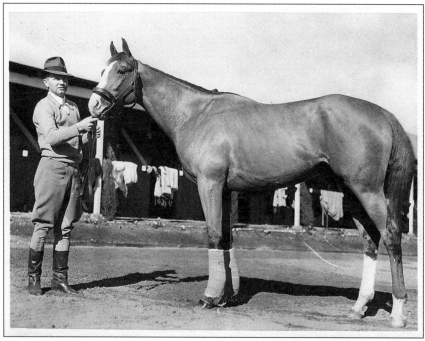

Trainer Earl Sande and The Chief. Courtesy Ken Grayson Collection.

early and quit while Sceneshifter got caught in traffic, losing much ground on the final turn. Sceneshifter came on at the end for fifth place finish. Sceneshifter placed second in the Belmont Stakes. Sande purchased The Chief in late 1937 for Howard.

Sande discussed the Howard stable's top horses. "Sceneshifter is a great horse with a big heart but he hasn't been able to win a big stakes race. Our two-year-old Stagehand may prove to be a solid horse as well as The Chief."

The highlight of Sande's training career came in 1938. In a hard driving finish, Stagehand beat Dauber in the $60,275 February 22 Santa Anita Derby, paying $13.20. Two weeks later, Stagehand took on the highly-regarded and 19 to 10 favorite Seabiscuit in the $137,000 March 5 Santa Anita Handicap. Popular racetrack wisdom declared, "It Can't Be Done." No three-year-old alive could beat Seabiscuit claimed the clockers, trainers, backstretch reporters, and handicappers. Everybody but Sande. Coming from behind, Stagehand raced wide and beat Seabiscuit to the wire in a photo finish, establishing a track record for a mile and a quarter. No three-

Trainer Earl Sande and Stagehand. Courtesy Ken Grayson Collection.

year-old had ever won the Santa Anita Derby and Santa Anita Handicap. The defeat marked the second year in a row Seabiscuit lost the Santa Anita Handicap by a nose.

Sande stated, "Stagehand's in great condition, he's won more than $133,000 in twelve days, and we're headed to the Kentucky Derby. I believe we may win that contest."

Leading up to the Derby, The Chief won the Daniel Boone Purse and turned in a track record performance while beating Stagehand in the Derby Trial Stakes at Churchill Downs. Two days later Sande scratched Stagehand due to an illness and entered The Chief in the Kentucky Derby. The Chief finished a distant fifth and fell ill after the race. Both horses recovered for the June 18 Dwyer Stakes, which The Chief won while Stagehand took third money. Stagehand rebounded to tie a track record in the July 9 Empire City Handicap.

Sande ended 1938 as the top money-winning trainer with earnings of $226,495 and the only person to have led both the jockey and training

Trainer Earl Sande and owner Colonel Maxwell Howard. Courtesy Sande Tomlinson Collection.

ranks. Maxwell Howard took the honors among owners and Stagehand upstaged all three-year-old horses with winnings of $189,710. The New York Turf Writers Association also honored Sande for his training accomplishments at a banquet.

The Jockeys' Community Fund and Guild hosted Sande at a testimonial dinner following the 1941 Preakness for his "fairness and sportsmanship" and as the jockey who contributed the most to his profession. Actors Robert Young and Don Ameche personally congratulated Sande at the dinner. Throughout the forties, Sande appeared at many charity and bond sale events with Jack Dempsey, Red Grange, and Babe Ruth. In the early 1940s, Sande saddled The Chief, Credentials, Foe o' Woe, Party Buster, Mad Anthony, Boiling On, and Tedious Miss.

Zev died in July 1943, and Earl suffered the loss of several more good friends the following year. Otho B. Scott died on March 7, 1944, in Menlo Park, California, where Burr had retired near family and a racetrack. Colonel Maxwell Howard died in late 1944 and left Sande $10,000 and directed that his stable and equipment be sold with up to 20 percent of the proceeds to be paid to Sande for disposing of them. Several months later, English jockey Steve Donoghue died. He won six Epsom Derbies and lost the 1923 international match race on Papyrus to Sande aboard Zev.

Hearing of Donoghue's death, Sande said "I am sorry. Steve was a real sportsman all the way."

Sande continued training and owning some mounts into the late forties. He achieved some success with Stage Fire, First Stage, Prop Girl, Staging, Stage Kid, Copper Boy, Big Stage, and Surf Rider. Marion filed for divorce in 1946 but the two remained friends for life.

In mid-November 1947, jockey Buddy Ensor's body was found in a Queens Cemetery. Under treatment at Queens Central Hospital for pneumonia, Ensor wandered away from the facility. The low point of Sande's training career began in April 1948 with the announcement by the Thoroughbred Racing Protective Bureau that it was investigating allegations of the doping of one of Sande's horses after a routine saliva test revealed traces of morphine.

Sande commented, "I wish they would get this straightened out soon. It isn't doing my name any good with all these rumors circulating."

He also wrote to Doc Pardee, "You know I would never do anything like this to any horse. I can't believe these charges."

On May 1, Eddie Arcaro booted home Citation for his fourth Kentucky Derby victory, surpassing Sande and Isaac Murphy's record. Two days later, federal narcotics agents arrested Sande for allegedly doping Big Stage. Normally handled within the state racing commission, the move by the federal agents was unprecedented. Conviction of the charge could have resulted in a two year to five year sentence. The Jockey Club immediately handed Sande a sixty day suspension, disqualified Big Stage's April 21 win, and redistributed the $4,000 purse. It also suspended Sande's foreman and groom for thirty days.

Sande testified that he had ordered his foreman to give Big Stage an extract of caffeine during a workout four days before the race. Federal agents testified that the saliva test showed a trace of morphine. After hearing all testimony, the federal grand jury refused to indict Sande on charges of illegal possession of narcotics and charges were dropped.

Stewards of The Jockey Club admitted that it was possible Sande inadvertently used the same bridle on race day, causing the failed saliva test. However, Marshall Cassidy, assistant secretary of The Jockey Club stated, "Sande was set down for violation of a rule of racing. The suspension will stick."

Sande responded, "I had the caffeine extract applied to the strap in workouts to prevent the horse's tongue from going over the bit. I don't know what happened. I never gave a horse dope in my life."

Veterinarian Doc Hinshaw has served for many years for the Arizona Racing Commission and the racing industry investigating drug use in horse racing. He says, "The saliva tests used back in Sande's days were unreliable and not used anymore. Sande's version of using a caffeine extract during training rings true. Trainers often used extracts on tongue-ties during workouts to prevent the horse from getting his tongue over the bit and to help the horse breathe easier."

With suspension ended, Sande's Stage Kid won at Aqueduct on July 12 and again two weeks later but the downtime proved fatal. A coughing epidemic struck Sande's horses, forcing him to sell most of his stable. Stagehand and Sceneshifter sold at auction in late 1948. By the end of the year, Sande's stable of twenty mounts dwindled down first to five horses and then two two-year-olds. Sporadic victories from 1949 to 1952 fail to stem the downslide of Sande's fortunes.

Faced with high debts in 1953, at age fifty-four, Sande dusted off his tack and returned to the track once more. He already refused a track steward job at $100 a day because he considered it a charity offering. Two months of dieting on fish brought his weight down from 138 to 113 pounds.

In an ironic twist, he mounted Honest Bread at Belmont for his comeback attempt. Honest Bread started once in winter racing and finished out of the money. He had been injured but trained well. Race fans rewarded the

Earl Sande with treasured memories of key races during his storied racing career. Courtesy Ken Grayson Collection.

balding, gritty jockey with thunderous applause which grew louder as he mounted his horse and entered the track. Sande refused to wear goggles because he never wore them all the years he was racing and didn't see any

Earl Sande on scales for 1953 comeback attempt. Courtesy Ken Grayson Collection.

reason to change tradition. Sande broke the gelding on top and led into the stretch where the horse faded, placing third.

In the jockey room after the race, he sang "Back in the Saddle Again." He said of his return to racing, "I had a good ride."

Fellow jockey Nick Wall said, "Frankly, they didn't think you'd go a quarter of a mile. You rode a damned good race."

At Jamaica on October 14, Sande mounted Honest Bread in the third race and finished second by a nose. He then took the reins of Miss Weesie in the seventh race. Miss Weesie broke slow from the barrier, and then Sande maneuvered his mount up through the pack. In the stretch run, Sande moved Miss Weesie ahead of Piedmont Lass and challenged favorite Will Be There, ridden by Eddie Arcaro. The fans broke into pandemonium as Sande beat Arcaro to the wire by half a length, gaining his first 1953 comeback victory.

Newspapers across the country once again flashed Damon Runyon's verse:

> *Maybe there'll be another,*
> *Heady and game and true*
> *Maybe we'll find his brother*
> *At driving them horses through.*
> *Maybe—but, say, I doubt it,*
> *Never his like again.*

Sande retired for good as a winner. In its yearly report, The New York State Racing Commission referred to Sande's victory, "This was New York racing's finest hour in 1953."

Two years later, Sande entered the Racing Hall of Fame with its inaugural inductees. The class included such racing immortals as Isaac Murphy, Tod Sloan, Laverne Fator, Edward Garrison, Daniel Maher, George Odom, Nash Turner, George Woolf, James McLaughlin, and Fred Taral. The horse inductees all raced in the 1800s. Of the five trainers inducted, Sam Hildreth joined Sande in the Hall of Fame that first year.

Also in 1955, Pimlico established a Jockey's Hall of Fame and inducted Eddie Arcaro, Earl Sande, and George Woolf. Sande was later inducted into the Fair Grounds Race Course Hall of Fame in New Orleans, Arizona Hall of Fame, and South Dakota Sports Hall of Fame.

After being inducted into the Racing Hall of Fame, Sande said, "It's an honor to be inducted with the top US jockeys, trainers, and horses. But the best thing about racing was all the fine people I met along the way."

Many of Sande's mounts made it into the Hall of Fame in 1957 with Gallant Fox, Gray Lag, Man o' War, Sarazen, and Sir Barton receiving the honors. James Fitzsimmons made the roster in 1958 and Zev joined the group in 1983.

Sande died in Oregon at age sixty-nine on August 21, 1968. Buried in Salem, Oregon's Belcrest Memorial Park, he rests next to his parents and sisters, Eva and Helen.

C. W. "Doc" Pardee retired as stable manager of the Arizona Biltmore and Resort to his ranch near Glendale, Arizona, where he worked with forty thoroughbred horses. In 1958 he helped form the Race Horse Breeders of Arizona, and it named him the first president. He was elected to the Arizona Horseman's Hall of Fame in 1965. The Pardee Library at Paradise Park in Phoenix holds his large racing collection. He died in July 1975 at age ninety.

Commander J. K. L. Ross filed for bankruptcy in 1928. Two years later, a court awarded $1 million to Ross and his creditors, voiding a trust set up for the former Mrs. Ross. In April 1931, Ross married Iris Delisser, the daughter of a wealthy Jamaica planter. He and his new wife settled in the British West Indies. Eight months later, the Appellate Court reversed the lower court and awarded the former Mrs. Ross the $1 million trust fund. He died on July 25, 1951, at age 75, after a long illness. Per his request, burial took place at sea within sight of his Montego Bay residence.

Sir Barton raced thirty-one times and finished first thirteen times. Commander Ross sold the 1919 Triple Crown winner in 1921 for $100,000. Sir Barton failed at stud and was unceremoniously sold to the government as a US Army Remount stallion in Nebraska. Wyoming rancher J. R. Hylton bought Sir Barton from the government and the horse died on his ranch on October 30, 1937. His remains lie buried beneath a life-size statue of the Triple Crown winner in Washington Park, Douglas, Wyoming.

Grey Lag sired 19 foals and then became sterile. Returned to racing, Grey Lag won his two starts at age nine and a year later won one of four starts before retiring again. After his owner died, Grey Lag was sold as part of the estate. At age thirteen, the new owner shipped Grey Lag to race in Canada. In four starts, he never came closer than third, earning $40 in 1931. Sinclair repurchased the horse and let him spend the rest of his days at Rancocas.

Harry Ford Sinclair sold a large portion of his horses in 1930. From 1921 through 1929, his Rancocas mounts won 599 races and earned $1,894,786. Sinclair's Zev took over the money-winning honors from Man o' War in 1923 and held the top spot until Sande and Gallant Fox eclipsed the re-

The empty Earl Sande saddle. Photo by Mary Buckingham Maturi. Taken by permission of Earl Sande niece Kaye Smith.

cord in 1930. In August 1931 one of Sinclair's horses was found poisoned at Saratoga. Sinclair sold his remaining horses several weeks later and the

Rancocas Farm in 1944. He resigned from Sinclair in 1949 and died on November 10, 1956, at age 80.

Gallant Fox retired to stud after 1930. He sired Omaha, the 1935 Triple Crown winner, making Gallant Fox the only Triple Crown winner to sire another. In 1937, "Horse and Horseman Magazine" named Gallant Fox The Horse of the Decade. He died on November 13, 1954.

Alfred Damon Runyon earned his spurs as a cub reporter on "The Denver Post" and later its, rival, "The Rocky Mountain News." He covered Pancho Villa's border raids for William Randolph Hearst and found Villa watching horses races in Juarez.

Runyon's distinctive writing style and ability to capture the vernacular and earthly characters of the sporting and underworld endeared him to readers of "The New York American." A collection of his short stories, *Guys and Dolls*, made Broadway and motion pictures box office success. Other Runyon stories that made it to the big screen included *Little Miss Marker, Sorrowful Jones, Forty Pounds of Trouble, A Slight Case of Murder, The Big Street*, and *It Ain't Hay*. A lifetime of smoking Turkish Ovals led to throat cancer and his death on December 10, 1946.

Appendices

America's Triple Crown Winners

Year	Jockey	Horse	Owner
1919	Loftus, Johnny	Sir Barton	J. K. L. Ross
1930	Sande, Earl	Gallant Fox	Belair Stud
1935	Saunders, William	Omaha	Belair Stud
1937	Kurtsinger, Charles	War Admiral	Samuel D. Riddle
1941	Arcaro, Eddie	Whirlaway	Calumet Farm
1943	Longden, Johnny	Count Fleet	Mrs. John D. Hertz
1946	Mehrtens, Warren	Assault	King Ranch
1948	Arcaro, Eddie	Citation	Calumet Farm
1973	Turcotte, Ron	Secretariat	Meadow Stable
1977	Cruget, Jean	Seattle Slew	Karen L. Taylor
1978	Cauthen, Steve	Affirmed	Harbor View Farm

Earl Sande's Lifetime Statistics

Year	Mounts	First	Second	Third	%Wins	% in Money	$Won
1918	707	158	122	80	22.3	50.9	$138,872
1919	346	80	67	58	23.1	59.2	126,042
1920	355	102	80	56	28.7	67.0	228,231
1921	340	112	69	59	32.9	70.6	263,043
1922	386	122	78	61	31.6	67.6	253,431
1923	430	122	89	79	28.4	67.4	569,394
1924	119	32	13	24	26.9	58.0	131,125
1925	268	72	54	40	26.9	61.9	264,700
1926	298	72	66	45	24.2	61.4	307,605
1927	179	49	33	19	27.4	56.4	277,877
1928	104	21	20	10	20.2	49.0	81,950
1929	10	1	0	5	10.0	60.0	1,683
1930	43	11	9	4	25.6	55.8	327,375
1932	78	13	16	11	16.7	51.3	22,282
1953	10	1	1	1	10.0	30.0	4,500
Lifetime Percentage of Winning Mounts				26.4 %			
Lifetime Percentage of in-the-money Wins				60.9 %			

Sande's lifetime percentage of winning mounts ranks third among Racing Hall of Fame jockeys and his remarkable percentage of in-the-money finishes also ranks near the top.

One of the leading authorities on the history of the turf, Tom Gilcoyne, commented, "Few jockeys were as good as Sande and certainly nobody was ever better."

National Museum of Racing
Comparative Hall of Fame Statistics
(Selective 1900-Present, Retired Jockeys)

Jockey	Lifetime Winning %	Career
McKinney, Rigan	39.2	1929-1939
Bostich, George	28.4	1927-1949
Sande, Earl* (1)	26.4	1918-1953
Shilling, Carroll	25.2	1904-1912
Miller, Walt (1)	25.2	1904-1909
Gomez, Arelino	24.0	1944-1981
Loftus, Johnny*	23.7	1909-1919
Parke, Ivan	23.4	1923-1925
Ycaza, Manuel	22.4	1956-1984
Shoemaker, William	21.9	1949-1990
Fator, Laverne (1)	21.7	1919-1933
Ensor, Lavelle "Buddy"	21.1	1918-1945
Hawley, Sandy	21.0	1968-1998
Workman, Ron	20.0	1926-1940
Arcaro, Eddie*	19.8	1931-1961
Hartack, William	19.8	1953-1974
Butwell, Jim	19.7	1907-1928
Cauthen, Steve*	19.1	1976-1993
Woolf, George (1)	19.1	1928-1946
Kummer, Clarence	18.8	1916-1928
Longden, Johnny*	18.6	1927-1966
Cordero, Jr.; Angel	18.3	1960-1992
Stevens, Gary	18.0	1979-1999
Ussery, Robert	17.5	1951-1974
Krome, Julie	17.0	1981-1999
Velasquez, Jorge	17.0	1963-1997
Garner, Mack	16.6	1914-1936
McAtee, J. Linus	16.2	1914-1932
Johnson, Albert	15.7	1917-1929
Turcotte, Ron*	14.9	1961-1978
Kurtsinger, Charles*	12.8	1924-1939

* Triple Crown Winners
(1) First Inductee Class of 1955

Major Races Won by Earl Sande

5 Belmont Stakes
3 Kentucky Derbys
1 Preakness
5 Jockey Club Gold Cups (called the
  Jockey Club Cup in early runnings)
4 Withers Stakes
3 Lawrence Realizations
3 Suburban Handicaps
3 Dwyer Stakes

Triple Crown Races

Belmont Stakes
1921 Grey Lag
1923 Zev
1924 Mad Play
1927 Chance Shot
1930 Gallant Fox

Kentucky Derby
1923 Zev
1925 Flying Ebony
1930 Gallant Fox

Preakness
1930 Gallant Fox

Major Race Wins by Year

1918
Catonsville Handicap on Salestra
Columbus Handicap on Billy Kelly
Dixie Handicap on Cudgel
Eastern Shore on Billy Kelly
Eclipse Handicap on Billy Kelly
Grab Bag Handicap on Billy Kelly
Liberty Handicap on Cudgel
Melrose Stakes on Dorcas
Roland Park Handicap on Smart
  Money

Sanford Stakes on Billy Kelly
Schenectady Handicap on Cudgel
Stafford Handicap on Motor Cop
Valuation Stakes on Major Parke
Wakefield Handicap on Chasseur
Waterloo Purse on Milkmaid

1919
Arlington Purse on Boniface
Black-Eyed Susan Stakes on Billy Kelly
Bouquet Handicap on Milkmaid
Capital Handicap on Billy Kelly
Eastern Shore on Billy Kelly
Harford Handicap on Billy Kelly
Havre de Grace Highweight Handicap
  on Billy Kelly
Hip Hip Hooray Handicap on Billy
  Kelly
Kenner Stakes on Milkmaid
Merchants & Citizens' Handicap on
  Cudgel
Philadelphia Handicap on Billy Kelly
Pimlico Oaks on Milkmaid
Plattsburg Handicap on Assume

1920
Ardsley Handicap on Dry Moon
Bowie Handcap on Mad Hatter
Catonsville Handicap on Carpet
  Sweeper
Cincinnati Trophy on Star Voter
Clark Handicap on Boniface
Delaware Handicap on Boniface
Downs Creek Handicap on Boniface
Excelsior Handicap on Boniface
Fall Highweight Handicap on Lion d'or
Grab Bag Handicap on Osmand
Harford Handicap on Billy Kelly
Hillside Handicap on Krewer
Ladies Handicap on Milkmaid

Linstead Handicap on Lord Brighton
Maginn Memorial Handicap on
  Boniface
Melbourne Handicap on Boniface
Merchants & Citizens' Handicap on Sir
  Barton
Miller Stakes on Man o' War
Mount Kisco Stakes on Donnacona
Pikeville Handicap on King Herod
Pimlico Spring Handicap on Boniface
Salem Handicap on Milkmaid
Saratoga Handicap on Sir Barton
Westchester Handicap on Mad Hatter

1921

Africander Handicap on Thunderclap
Arverne Handicap on Dunboyne
Bellair Handicap on Elected II
Belmont Stakes on Grey Lag
Bowie Handicap on Boniface
Bronxville Handicap on Purchase
Carlton Stakes on Knobble
Cedarhurst Handicap on Georgie
Clover Stakes on Budana
Continental Handicap on Thunderclap
Cosmopolitan Handicap on Mad
  Hatter
Couching Club American Oaks on
  Flambette
Devonshire International on Grey Lag
Domino Handicap on Sennings Park
Dwyer Stakes on Grey Lag
East View Stakes on Kai-Sang
Freeport Handicap on Grey Lag
Great Neck Handicap on Donnaconna
Hudson Handicap on Thunderclap
Jockey Club Gold Cup on Mad Hatter
Keene Memorial on William A
Knickerbocker Handicap on Grey Lag
Lake George Handicap on Sennings
  Park
Metropolitan Handicap on Mad Hatter

Mount Kisco Stakes on Grey Lag
Pimlico Fall Special Serial Weight #2
  on Knobble
Rainbow Handicap on Dominique
Rockaway Stakes on Valor
Stafford Handicap on Knobble
Watervilet Handicap on Thunderclap

1922

Albany Handicap on Zev
Astoria Stakes on Suweep
Champlain Handicap on Mad Hatter
Jockey Club Gold Cup on Mad Hatter
Kings County Handicap on Mad
  Hatter
Lawrence Realization Stakes on Kai-
  Sang
Pierrepont Handicap on Mad Hatter
Potomac Handicap on Thunderclap
Spinaway Stakes on Edict
Stuyvesant Handicap on Snob II
Youthful Stakes on Bud Lerner

1923

Alabama Stakes on Untidy
Autumn Championship on Zev
Bayview Handicap on Knobble
Belmont Stakes on Zev
Bowie Handicap on My Dear
Brooklyn Handicap on Little Chief
Canarsie Selling Stakes on Humorette
Champagne Stakes on Sarazen
Edgemere Handicap on Little Chief
Empire City Handicap on Tryster
Fall Highweight Handicap on Fair
  Phantom
Fashion Stakes on Nellie Morse
Gazelle Stakes on Untidy
Interborough Handicap on Knobble
International Match Race vs Papyrus
  on Zev
Kenner Stakes on Martingale

Kentucky Derby on Zev
Kings County Handicap on Grey Lag
Laurel Special on Sarazen
Lawrence Realization on Zev
Manhattan Handicap on Little Chief
Manor Handicap on Big Blaze
Metropolitan Handicap on Grey Lag
Miller Stakes on Martingale
National Trial Sweepstakes on My
   Own
Pimlico Fall Serial Weight-for-Age
   Race No. 3 on Zev
Queens County Handicap on Zev
Rainbow Handicap on Zev
Rosedale Stakes on Outline
Sanford Stakes on Parasol
Saratoga Cup on My Own
Saratoga Sales Stakes on Salacia
Saratoga Special on St. James
Stuyvesant Handicap on Dot
Suburban Handicap on Grey Lag
Toboggan Handicap on Mad Hatter
United States Hotel Stakes on St. James
Withers Stakes on Zev
Zev/In Memoriam Match Race on Zev

1924

Belmont Stakes on Mad Play
Carter Handicap on Sarazen
Kings County Handicap on Zev
Queens County Handicap on Mad
   Hatter
Saratoga Sales Stakes on Voltaic
Suburban Handicap on Mad Hatter
Tremont Stakes on Young Martin
Withers Stakes on Bracadale

1925

Astoria Stakes on Edith Cavell
Arverne Handicap on Sarazen
Dixie Handicap on Sarazen
Fleetwing Handicap on Sarazen

Grand Union Hotel Stakes on Haste
Great American Stakes on Navigator
Hanover Handicap on Danby
Hindoo Handicap on Danby
Jockey Club Gold Cup on Altawood
Kentucky Derby on Flying Ebony
Latonia Championship Stakes on Naldi
Metropolitan Handicap on Sarazen
Newark Handicap on Sarazen
Paumonok Handicap on Worthmore
Saratoga Special on Haste
Tomboy Handicap on Ruthenia
Twin City Handicap on Aga Khan

1926

Babylon Handicap on Saxon
Brentwood Handicap on Dress Parade
California Handicap on Mino
Collington Handicap on Polly
   McWiggles
Dwyer Stakes on Crusader
Eastern Shore Stakes on Osmand
Evergreen Handicap on Taps
Epinard Handicap on Prince of
   Bourbon
Flash Stakes on Osmond
Grab Bag Handicap on Osmond
Grand Union Hotel Stakes on Kiev
Havre de Grace Cup Handicap on
   Crusader
Huron Handicap on Crusader
Montana Handicap on Sanford
National Stakes on Osmond
National Stallion Stakes on Chance
   Shot
Nursery Handicap on Osmand
Potomac Handicap on Chance Play
Riggs Memorial Handicap on
   Crusader
Saratoga Special on Chance Shot
Test Stakes on Ruthenia
Withers Stakes on Haste

1927

Belmont Stakes on Chance Shot
Capital Handicap on Osmand
Cecil Handicap on Crusader
Delaware Handicap on Crusader
Freeport Handicap on Chance Shot
Grab Bag Handicap on Nassak
Jerome Handicap on Osmand
Jockey Club Gold Cup on Chance Play
Laurel Stakes on Osmand
Lincoln Handicap on Chance Play
Merchants & Citizens' Handicap on
  Chance Play
National Stallion Stakes on Groucher
Saranac Handicap on Osmand
Saratoga Handicap on Mars
Somerset Handicap on Crusader
Tobaggan Handicap on Chance Play
Tremont Stakes on Diavolo
Withers Stakes on Chance Shot

1928

American Legion Handicap on
  Osmand

Carter Handicap on Osmand
Coaching Club American Oaks on
  Bateau
Dominant Handicap on Kiev
Merchants & Citizens' Handicap on
  Chance Shot
Rampano Handicap on Chance Shot
Rosedale Stakes on Virmar
Saratoga Handicap on Chance Shot
Stalwart Handicap on Osmand
Toboggan Handicap on Osmand

1930

Arlington Classic Stakes on Gallant
  Fox
Belmont Stakes on Gallant Fox
Dwyer Stakes on Gallant Fox
Jockey Club Gold Cup on Gallant Fox
Kentucky Derby on Gallant Fox
Lawrence Realization on Gallant Fox
Preakness on Gallant Fox
Saratoga Cup on Gallant Fox
Suburban Handicap on Petee-Wrack
Wood Memorial Stakes on Gallant Fox

Earl Sande/Laverne Fator Comparison

Over the years, a number of articles appeared comparing the relative riding skills of Laverne Fator and Earl Sande. Once and for all, I would like to put this issue to rest. While Fator was certainly an excellent rider, an objective comparison of the following statistics shows that Sande outranked his fellow Idaho jockey, especially in the big races.

Fator never finished higher than fifth in his four Kentucky Derby outings, Sande won three and came in second twice in eight trips. Fator never finished higher than third in three Preakness attempts, Sande won one out of eight. Fator went zero for four in the Belmont, Sande won five.

In 1923, Sande won thirty-nine stakes races, Fator won thirteen. During Fator's best year, 1926, he rode 143 winners for purses totaling $361,336 (an average of $2,527 per race). That same year, Sande rode 72 mounts and won $307,605 (an average of $4,272 per race.) Overall, Sande won a higher percentage of races, bigger races, and more money despite riding more than 1,200 fewer mounts.

	Fator	Sande
Leading money jockey	1925, 1926	1921, 1923, 1927
Triple Crown Winner	-----	1930
Kentucky Derby Victories	0	3
Preakness Victories	0	1
Belmont Victories	0	5
Mounts	4,948	3,673
Winning Mounts	1,075	968
% of Winning Mounts	21.7	26.4
% In-the-Money Mounts	56.0	60.9
Top Money Winning Year	$361,336 (1926)	$569,394 (1923)
Total Lifetime Winnings	$2,408,720	$2,998,110

Racing Glossary and Jargon

Across the board: A bet on a horse to win, place and show.

Allowance race: A race in which a basic weight allowance for age and sex of a horse is varied by added weight penalties for past successes. The weights are adjusted to try to give each horse an equal chance of winning.

Also ran: A horse that does not finish in the top three spots.

Backstretch: The straightaway on the far side of the racetrack.

Bandage: Strips of cloth wound around the lower part of a horse's leg for support or protection against injury.

Barrier: The starting gate.

Bat: A jockey's whip.

Blanket finish: The end of a race when the horses finish so close together they could be covered by a blanket.

Breezing: Working a horse a short distance under restraint.

Bugboy: An apprentice jockey. Denoted due to the asterisk or "bug" next to the jockey's name indicating that jockey carries an apprentice allowance weight.

Cast a frog: Injure a foot.

Cayuse: An Indian pony.

Chart: A comprehensive account of a race showing the position of each horse at various stages of the race.

Claiming race: A race in which any horse can be purchased or "claimed" for the amount for which the horse is entered.

Clerk of the course: The racing official who is in charge of the course and meeting arrangements.

Clerk of the scale: The racing official who controls weighing out and weighing in.

Clocker: One who times the speed of a horse.

Clubhouse turn: The turn to the right of the grandstand.

Dead heat: A race in which two or more horses tie for first place and divide the purse between them.

Driving: A horse running under extreme pressure.

Eighth Pole: The pole one-eighth of a mile before the finish line.

Exercise boy: One who exercises the horse in the morning. A job often taken by aspiring jockeys.

Far turn: The turn off the backstretch.

Fast track: One that is totally dried out. Footing is even.

Field: The entire group of starters in a race.

Flank: The side or thigh of a horse.

Front-runner: A horse who usually leads, or tries to lead, the field as far as he can.

Furlong: One eighth of a mile.

Garrison finish: A late rush resulting in a narrow margin of victory, named after Edward "Snapper" Garrison, who perfected the finish at the turn of the century.

Gate: Starting mechanism.

Gelding: A castrated male horse.

Get: Offspring of a horse.

Girth: A strap encircling a horse's body to secure a saddle on its back.

Good track: A track that is between fast and muddy. Footing is firm, but moisture remains in the strip.

Groom: A horse caretaker, responsible for horse's appearance, bandaging, and taking the horse to and from the paddock.

Handicap race: A race in which the weights are adjusted to try to give horses an equal chance of winning.

Handicapper: The race official who arranges or assigns weights for handicap races.

Head of the stretch: The beginning of the straight run home.

Heavy track: A track that is muddy and drying out, but not good. Footing is sticky.

He pulled up bad: A horse that became lame.

He refused his last race: A horse that won't break from the starting gate.

Hock: The joint of the hind leg. Corresponds to the human ankle.

Homestretch: The straightaway leading to the finish line.

Hot walker: A stable hand who leads a horse to cool him down after a race or workout.

In the money: A horse that finishes first, second, or third.

Judge: The person or persons who witness the finish and declare the result.

Length: The length of a horse from nose to tail, about nine feet.

Maiden: A horse that has not won a race.

Maiden race: A race for horses that have never won.

Muddy track: A track that has water soaked into the base. Footing is deep and slow.

On the nose: Betting a horse only to win.

Open race: A race in which every horse carries the same weight.

Paddock: The area where the horses are saddled and viewed prior to a race.

Place: A second-place finish.

Plater: A horse that runs in claiming races.

Post: The starting point for a race.

Post position: A horse's position in the starting gate from the inner rail outward.

Purse: A race in which the owners do not contribute to the prize. The money distributed to owners.

Rabbit: Horse that sets the pace.

Rubber: Stable employee who rubs down the horses.

Scratch: To withdraw a horse from a race.

Set down: Suspend a jockey from racing.

Show: A third-place finish.

Silks: The jacket and cap worn by a jockey.

Sloppy track: A track that has water saturating the cushion but not yet soaked into the base. Footing is splashy but even.

Stakes race: Originally, a race in which the owners put up "stakes." Today, the track adds money to these stakes.

Stayer: A horse that runs well for long distances.

Stewards: Track officials responsible for enforcing the rules.

Stick: A jockey's whip.

Stifle: The joint next above the hock and near the flank in the hind leg. Corresponds to the human knee.

Stretch call: Position of horses at the eighth pole.

Stud: A stallion used for breeding.

Surcingle: A girth that binds a saddle to the horse.

Swipe: One who rubs down horses.

Tack: The saddle and other equipment worn by a horse during exercise or racing.

Tout: One who gives tips on racehorses for an expected compensation.

Under wraps: A horse running under restraint.

Valet: An employee who takes care of a jockey's equipment.

We haltered him: We won him in a claiming race.

Weighing-in: After a race, the riders of the first four horses are   weight.

Weighing-out: Jockeys must be weighed before each race. The trainer is responsible for his horse carrying the right weight, which includes jockey, hood, blinkers, saddle and other equipment.

Weight-for-age race: A race in which younger horses receive the benefit of a lighter weight.

Win: A first-place finish.

Wire: The finish line.

Bibliography

Books

Biracree, Tom and Wendy Insinger. *The Complete Book of Thoroughbred Horse Racing*. Garden City, NY: Dolphin Books, 1982.

Blumenthal, Ralph. *Stork Club: America's Most Famous Nightspot and the Lost World of Café Society*. Boston: Little, Brown, 2000.

Bradley, Hugh. *Such Was Saratoga*. New York: Doubleday, Doran & Co., 1940.

Breslin, Jimmy. *Sunny Jim*. Garden City, NY: Doubleday, 1962.

Bryant, Beverly and Jean Williams. *Portraits in Roses*. New York: McGraw-Hill, 1984.

Buchanan, Lamont. *The Kentucky Derby Story*. New York: E. P. Dutton, 1953.

Champions of American Sport. New York: Harry N. Abrams, 1981.

Clark, Patrick. *Sports Firsts*. New York: Facts on File, 1981.

Claypool, James C. *The Tradition Continues: The Story of Old Latonia, Latonia, and Turfway Racecourses*. Fort Mitchell, KY: T. I. Hayes Publishing, 1997.

Connelly, W. L. *The Oil Business As I Saw It: Half a Century with Sinclair*. Norman, OK: University of Oklahoma Press, 1954.

Danzig, Allison and Peter Brandwein, editors. *Sports' Golden Age: A Close-Up of the Fabulous Twenties*. New York: Harper, 1948.

Donoghue, Steve. *Donoghue, Up!* London: Collins Publishers, 1938.

Garraty, John A. and Mark C. Carnes. *American National Biography*. Oxford: Oxford University Press, 1999.

Groton Centennial History. Aberdeen, SD: North Plains Press, 1981.

Hervey, John. *American Race Horses*. New York: The Sagamore Press, 1938.

Hewitt, Abram S. *The Great Breeders and Their Methods*. Lexington, KY: Thoroughbred Publishers, Inc., 1983.

Hildreth, Samuel C. and James R. Crowell. The Spell of the Turf. Philadelphia: Lippincott, 1926.

Hotaling, Edward. *They're Off! Horse Racing at Saratoga*. Syracuse, NY: Syracuse University Press, 1995.

Jay, Peter A., editor. *Havre de Grace: An Informal History*. Havre de Grace, MD: Sparrowhead Press, 1994.

Living Legacies: Railroad Stations of Brown County, South Dakota. Aberdeen, SD: Aberdeen/Brown County Landmark Commission, 2002.

Markoe, Arnie, editor. *The Scribner Encyclopedia of American Lives, Sports Figures*. New York: Scribners, 2002.

Newman, Neil. *Famous Horses of the American Turf, Volume I*. New York: The Derrydale Press, 1931.

_____. *Famous Horses of the American Turf, Volume III*. New York: The Derrydale Press, 1933.

Noggle, Burl. *Teapot Dome: Oil and Politics in the 1920s*. Westport, CT: Greenwood Press, 1980.

Pachter, Marc. *Champions of American Sport*. New York: Harry N. Abrams, 1981.

Parmer, Charles B. *For Gold and Glory*. New York: Carrick and Evans, 1939.

Roberts, Randy. *Jack Dempsey: The Manassa Mauler*. Baton Rouge, LA: Louisiana State University Press, 1979.

Robertson, William H. P. *The History of Thoroughbred Racing in America*. New York: Bonanza Books, 1964.

Ross, J. K. M. *Boots and Saddles*. New York: E. P. Dutton, 1956.

Stoneridge, M. A. *Great Horses of Our Time*. New York: Doubleday, 1972.

Stratton, David Hodges. *Albert B. Fall and the Teapot Dome Affair*. Ann Arbor, MI: University Microfilms International. 1984.

_____. *Tempest over Teapot Dome*. Norman, OK: University of Oklahoma Press, 1998.

Thoroughbred Racing and Breeding. Baltimore, MD: Thoroughbred Racing Association of the United States, Inc., 1945.

Truitt, Evelyn Mack. *Who Was Who on Screen*. New York: R. R. Bowker, 1983.

Woodward, William. *Gallant Fox, A Memoir*. New York: Derrydale Press, 1931.

Magazines and Journals

American Heritage
American Racing Manual
Arizona Thoroughbred
The Backstretch
The Blood-Horse
The Bloodstock Breeder's Review
Collier's
Derby Magazine
Exhibitors' Trade Review
Harford Historical Bulletin
Horse and Horseman
Horse World USA
Horseman's Journal
Kentucky Derby Diamond Jubilee
Life
Literary Digest
The Maryland Horse
National Turf Digest
Newsweek
Popular Mechanics
Real West
Saturday Evening Post
South Dakota Magazine
Spur
The Thoroughbred of California
The Thoroughbred of Canada
Time
Turf and Sport Digest
Yav Magazine

Newspapers

American Falls Press
Arizona Republic
Baltimore Sun
Boston Daily Advertiser
Boston Evening Transcript
Boston Globe
Boston Herald
Capital Journal (Salem, Oregon)
Cincinnati Enquirer
Claremore Progress (Claremore, Oklahoma)
Cleveland Plain Dealer
Denver Post
Detroit Free Press
Groton Independent
Harford Democrat

Horse Times
Idaho Statesman
Kentucky Post
Lexington Leader
Los Angeles Herald-Examiner
Louisville Courier-Journal
New Orleans Times-Picayune
New York Times
Oregon Daily Journal
Oregonian
Prescott Journal-Miner
Racing Form
The Record (Havre de Grace, Maryland)
Salt Lake Tribune
The Thoroughbred Record

Index

353

Chapter 14

Trailing Earl

The double meaning of this chapter's title, *Trailing Earl,* aptly marks the eightieth anniversary of Earl Sande and Gallant Fox capturing the second American Triple Crown. For decades, other jockeys trailed Earl on the track as he broke records, captured major stakes races and earned his place in American thoroughbred history as arguably the top jockey of all time.

Consider the following Sande accomplishments:

World record six consecutive victories in one day—lifetime 26.4% winning mounts, #3 of all Hall of Fame jockeys—lifetime 60.9% in-the-money mounts, #1 of all Hall of Fame jockeys—Sande owned the Belmont with 5 victories in 10 years—Racing Hall of Fame Inaugural Class Inductee—winner of the 1923 International Match Race aboard Zev vs. Papyrus —winner of 39 stakes races in 1923, a record that stood for 30 years—guided Zev in 1923 to beat Man o' War's 1920 money-winning record—top money-winning jockey 1921, 1923 and 1927—one of the greatest sports comebacks of all time—only person to earn both top money-winning jockey and top money-winning trainer status—trained Stagehand, who beat Seabiscuit in the 1938 Santa Anita Handicap—3 Kentucky Derby Victories—5 Jockey Club Gold Cups—4 Withers Stakes—3 Lawrence Realizations—3 Dwyer Stakes.

Sande's achievements are all the more remarkable when you consider racing has not crowned a Triple Crown Winner in over 30 years, since Steve Cauthen aboard Affirmed. Recent racing history relegates Funny Cide with Jose Santos, Smarty Jones with Stewart Elliott, Afleet Alex with Jeremy Rose, Big Brown with Kent Desormeaux and Calvin Borel on multiple mounts to the ranks of Triple Crown near misses.

We trailed Earl as we traveled to racetracks in 22 states and Canada and the London Book Fair to tell his story and make new generations of race fans aware of his unique place in thoroughbred racing. To be sure, some of the highlights include an hour long live interview on Earl with Kentucky Public Radio on top of Churchill Downs during Derby Week, a live HRTV interview with *Race Day America* co-hosts Carolyn Conley and Scott Hazleton, a national AP story on Sande's accomplishments, and national radio coverage on Fox Sports Syndicated *The Drive* and *Good Day USA.*

However, equally fun were the stops at county fair racing venues such as Tillamook, Oregon and a pre-meet barbeque with horse owners and stable crews at the Western Montana Fair. Check out the *Triple Crown Winner: The Earl Sande Saga* website at www.triplecrownwinnerearl sande.com to see where we visited and future Trailing Earl events.

Authors Rick and Mary Maturi on top of Churchill Downs after Kentucky Public Radio interview.

We enjoyed the above activities telling Earl's story and most important of all, meeting fine folks along the way. We echo Earl's sentiment, "the people who cross our path make the journey worthwhile." We thank all who shared racing stories and their love for horses and racing. Several of the first people we met were Stacy and Steve Swenson, owners of the *Groton Independent* in Groton, South Dakota when we started our journey to search out Earl's roots. Stacy shares her enthusiasm and personal journey trailing Earl.

It's amazing how one phone call can alter your life. I still remember the day I answered the phone at the *Groton Independent* office, only to find Richard Maturi on the other end. So began my journey back into another time, another place, with Earl Sande in the lead. Having the chance to witness a book as it makes its journey from a thought in an author's mind to sitting on my bookshelf was a rare treat. The research took on a personal hue as I met Earl's relatives. Their eyes danced as they shared family treasures about Earl, a postcard, a photo or a story. I was able to see past the list of accomplishments, the history of Earl's wins and losses. He grew more personal, more real for me. Looking out at the South Dakota landscape where Earl lived brings him to life. Earl always felt a fondness for this state of his birth and talked about South Dakota whenever he could. He had quite a following in this rural area of hard working settlers and farmers. Each week the Groton newspaper passed along news of his races, his life.

I was given the opportunity to help re-visit the life and times of Earl Sande; jockey, trainer, husband, son, brother, uncle and singer. I was proud to share the research Richard Maturi uncovered in his travels with the people who could once again call Earl their native son. Meeting the Sande family relatives, who had always kept Earl's story close to their heart, proved to me the strength of Earl's appeal. The years did not dampen his success, his life stood enriched by the passage of time.

I cherish the friendship forged with Richard and Mary Maturi. They are wonderful people who have done Earl justice, caring for his life story as friends. Their trips to South Dakota were filled with laughter as we chased down leads about Earl's life. At times we knew Earl was helping our search, leading us, guiding us, just as he had done on the back of a horse in a big race.

The day my husband, Steve, and I met Earl's nephew, Sande Tomlinson, at Earl's grave was emotional. I remember my eyes tearing as I crouched down beside his headstone. I laid a red Kentucky rose beside his name, etched in the stone. It was proof of my association with a man known to me only on paper or through words. Whatever hesitation still inside me disappeared as I ran my fingers across his birth and life dates. Earl's life had ended, but his story, his kind spirit, his talent all race on with no finish line in sight. As the ghosts of horses past race the wind, one will always carry a too tall, skinny kid, born in South Dakota, named Earl.

—Stacy Swenson

Both Stacy and Steve proved instrumental in the South Dakota Legislature honoring Earl and his accomplishments with its issuance of a Commemoration which reads in part, "Now, therefore, be it Commemorated, by the Eightieth Legislature of the State of South Dakota, that Earl Sande, a native South Dakotan, who gained prominence as a

Stacy Swenson, Rick Maturi and Mary Maturi at Brown County Fair Races. Courtesy Stacy Swenson.

Stacy Swenson and Sande nephew, Sande Tomlinson, at Earl Sande gravesite. Courtesy Stacy Swenson.

jockey in the 1920s, the Golden Age of Sports, is arguably the best all-time jockey America has yet produced."

We are also indebted to Brett and Debbie Crompton of the *Power County Press* in American Falls, Idaho, who helped uncover the Sande family's life in Idaho and spearheaded the effort that led to the Idaho Legislature Proclamation on Sande's life and achievements. Idaho House Proclamation No. 3 reads in part, "Now, therefore, be it Proclaimed by the members of the House of Representatives, that we recognize and commend a native Idahoan who gained national prominence as a jockey in the 1920s during the Golden Age of thoroughbred racing, who won the 1930 Triple Crown on Gallant Fox...and who ranks as the top jockey of all time and Idaho's contribution to thoroughbred racing."

Brett reports, "The legend of Earl Sande remains alive and well in American Falls, Idaho. Newcomers may not know his story but recently Idaho Commerce Department Director Roger Madsen spoke of Earl Sande in his comments to the American Falls Chamber of Commerce. In addition, I ran across an account that said, 'When a racing man wants money he goes to New York or Chicago. When he wants a horse, he journeys into Kentucky. But for a rider, he turns to Idaho.'"

We also need to mention other great friendships formed due to our quest of Earl Sande. Ninety-plus year-old Josephine Scott Werner provid-

South Dakota Legislature

HOUSE COMMEMORATION NO. 1019

Introduced by: Representatives Elliott, Dennert, Frost, and Novstrup and Senators Hundstad and Sutton (Duane)

A LEGISLATIVE COMMEMORATION, Honoring the life and career of Earl Sande, a professional jockey during the 1920s.

WHEREAS, Earl Sande was born November 13, 1898, at Groton, South Dakota, to John and Tillie Sande. He learned to ride horses on H.W. Cassel's farm; and

WHEREAS, Earl Sande went on to become one of the top jockeys of all time, with five Belmont Stakes wins; three Kentucky Derby wins; one Preakness win; one Triple Crown win riding Gallant Fox, making him one of only eleven jockeys to win a triple crown; five Jockey Club Gold Cups; four Withers Stakes; three Lawrence Realizations; three Suburban Handicaps; three Dwyer Stakes; third on the Lifetime Winning Percentage List; and more than sixty percent of all mounts finishing in the money; and

WHEREAS, Earl Sande's life and career are described by Richard J. Maturi in his book *Triple Crown Winner: the Earl Sande Saga* with invaluable help from Stacy and Steve Swenson, publishers and owners of the *Groton Independent* and the back files of the *Independent* which were able to establish the residency and livelihood of the Sande family in Groton:

NOW, THEREFORE, BE IT COMMEMORATED, by the Eightieth Legislature of the State of South Dakota, that Earl Sande, a native South Dakotan, who gained national prominence as a jockey in the 1920s, the Golden Age of Sports, is arguably the best all-time jockey America has yet produced.

Dennis Daugaard
President of the Senate

Matthew Michels
Speaker of the House

Patricia Adam
Secretary of the Senate

Karen Gerdes
Chief Clerk of the House

South Dakota Legislature Commemoration of Earl Sande. Authors' collection.

ed us with numerous family photos and a rare personally autographed photo by Earl to her uncle, Burr Scott. We enjoyed our visits with Josephine over several years and are in debt to her graciousness and tremendous spirit. Doc Hinshaw, a friend of Doc Pardee, provided great insight into Doc Pardee and initiated the 2007 Doc Pardee/Earl Sande Purse and Earl Sande-Triple Crown Winner Purse at Yavapai Downs in Prescott Valley, Arizona. Doc writes, "The expanded edition of the Earl Sande saga is a great idea and will be greatly welcomed. We are keeping the Doc Pardee/Earl Sande connection and memories alive here at Yavapai Downs with races sponsored by the Arizona Thoroughbred Breeders Association, which Doc Pardee founded and served as its first president."

Mary Maturi, Stacy Swenson, Rick Maturi and Steve Swenson at South Dakota Legislature. Courtesy Stacy Swenson.

At Hollywood Park we met talented equine artist, Joyce Canaday. Joyce writes, "My painting honors Earl Sande, one of the great jockeys in history, and his Triple Crown winning rides on Gallant Fox. Earl Sande was expertly portrayed in Richard J. Maturi's book, *Triple Crown Winner: The Earl Sande Saga*. Through this book I was taken along on an adventure and inspired to paint the new edition's cover. I learned that Earl Sande had nerves of steel, calm and communicative hands and a warm smile. He was a race rider who brought in winners and prompted poets to write verse. In 1930, prominent trainer 'Sunny' Jim Fitzsimmons needed a top rider for Belair Stud's three-year-old colt, Gallant Fox—the chestnut with the 'wild eye' and independent nature. Sande and the Fox won nine major stakes races in 1930 and roared down the stretch to win the Preakness, Kentucky Derby, and the Belmont Stakes; the second Triple Crown in history! They were beaten only one time, by Jim Dandy in the Travers."

During our travels we met some of horse racing's greats. What a pleasure to talk with Triple Crown Winner Steve Cauthen, who stopped by our book signing booth at the Saratoga Springs Race Course. While he had graciously provided a jacket quote for the hard cover edition, we had never met before in person. Also at Saratoga Springs, we sat with the Manny Ycaza family at the Hall of Fame luncheon. Hall of Fame jockey Manny took the time and consideration to send a nice letter on the Sande book, part of which is quoted here, "Rick, I like the way you prepared the race,

Mary Maturi, Debbie Crompton and Mary Tomlinson at Idaho Legislature. Authors' collection.

Rick Maturi, Brett Crompton and Sande Tomlinson at Idaho Legislature. Authors' collection.

how you broke out of the gate, positioned yourself, and how you finished. You did a fine job of paying tribute to a great talent. You portrayed Sande with dignity, professionalism and honesty. I enjoyed the book very much. Congratulations."

]]]]   LEGISLATURE OF THE STATE OF IDAHO   ]]]]
Fifty-eighth Legislature   First Regular Session - 2005

IN THE HOUSE OF REPRESENTATIVES

HOUSE PROCLAMATION NO. 3

BY STATE AFFAIRS COMMITTEE

1   A PROCLAMATION
2   COMMENDING THE LATE EARL SANDE FOR HIS CONTRIBUTION TO
    THOROUGHBRED RACING.

3   We, the members of the House of Representatives of the State of Idaho
4   assembled in the First Regular Session of the Fifty-eighth Idaho Legislature,
5   recognize and commend the late Earl Sande, of American Falls, Idaho, for his
6   contribution to thoroughbred racing.

7   WHEREAS, the family of Earl Sande moved to American Falls in 1908, where
8   John and Tillie Sande homesteaded a farm in the Fairfield section; and
9   WHEREAS, young Earl Sande raced his first competitive race in the 1914
10 American Falls Fourth of July festivities and the late Burr Scott of American
11 Falls gave Sande his first break riding and took him on the "Leaky-Roof Cir-
12 cuit" to begin Sande's racing career; and
13   WHEREAS, Earl Sande compiled a 26.4% lifetime winning percentage, which is
14 the third highest of all time, and a 60.9% lifetime percentage of in-the-money
15 mounts; and
16   WHEREAS, Earl Sande became known as the "Idaho Hot Potato" and his life
17 and career are described in a new book, for which the back files of the Ameri-
18 can Falls Press were used as a research source.
19   NOW, THEREFORE, BE IT PROCLAIMED by the members of the House of
20 Representatives assembled in the First Regular Session of the Fifty-eighth Idaho Leg-
21 islature, that we recognize and commend a native Idahoan who gained national
22 prominence as a jockey in the 1920s during the Golden Age of thoroughbred
23 racing, who won the 1930 Triple Crown on Gallant Fox, who was elected into the
24 Racing Hall of Fame with the first inductee class, and who ranks as the top
25 jockey of all time and Idaho's contribution to thoroughbred racing, and we
26 celebrate the late Earl Sande in 2005 as this year marks the 75th anniversary
27 of his winning the 1930 Triple Crown as well as his third Kentucky Derby and
28 fifth Belmont Stakes.
29
30 Speaker of the House of Representatives Bruce Newcomb
31 Representative Scott Bedke

Idaho Legislature Proclamation. Authors' collection.

Inaugural Doc Pardee/Earl Sande Purse, Doc Hinshaw far right, middle photo. Courtesy Coady Photography, Phoenix.

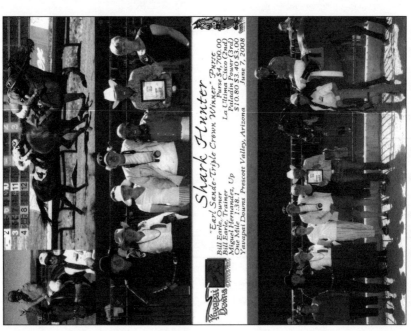

2008 Earl Sande-Triple Crown Winner Purse. Rt to lf middle photo: Rick Maturi, Mary Maturi, Mary Tomlinson, Sande Tomlinson, Miguel Hernandez, Doc Hinshaw and Sue Grundy. Courtesy Coady Photography, Phoenix.

A book signing at Wyoming Downs in Evanston, Wyoming resulted in a wonderful surprise as we accepted an invitation to meet the guest steward. We climbed the many stairs to the top of the stands and entered a room overlooking the track, where Hall of Fame jockey and five-time Kentucky Derby win-

Rick Maturi with Hall of Fame Jockey and five-time Kentucky Derby Winner, William Hartack. Authors' collection.

ner Bill Hartack greeted us.

During a visit to Pimlico for the Preakness, I used my press pass to meet turf writers from across the country to inform them of Sande's achievements and the new book on Sande. Mary recalls her day, "We all remember the heart-stopping near fall of the courageous 2005 Preakness winner Afleet Alex and the tremendous cry of horror from the record crowd. Earlier in the day, I visited with the mother of another Philadelphia Alex. As I spoke with Liz Scott, my eyes moistened when she told me of her young daughter's valiant efforts raising money to fight the childhood cancer which took her life. We were so touched by Alex's story, we donated all of our proceeds from our book signing at Canada's

Richard Maturi/Earl Sande Saga press pass for 130th Preakness. Authors' collection.

Woodbine poster for book signing donated to Alex's Lemonade Stand Foundation. Authors' collection.

Woodbine Racetrack to the Alex's Lemonade Stand Foundation."

We wish to thank Arlington Park in Chicago, Calder Race Course in Miami and other racetracks across the country for their hospitality and efforts in promoting the Earl Sande story by hosting book signings, track interviews, and program announcements. We literally went from A to Z (Arapahoe Park to Zia Park) and coast-to-coast (Los Alamitos to Delaware Park). We also wish to thank Pam Williams, Manager Historic Properties and Museums and Jason Illari, Curator for the City of Bowie, Maryland for vintage

Rick Maturi presenting winning trophy at Arlington Park. Courtesy Four Footed Fotos, Issaquah, WA.

Rick and Mary Maturi presenting book to jockey M. Cruz at Calder Race Course. Courtesy Jim Lisa Photos, Calder Race Course.

Earl Sande aboard Gallant Fox at 1930 Preakness. Courtesy City of Bowie Museums.

William Woodward leading Sande and Gallant Fox at 1930 Belmont Stakes. Courtesy City of Bowie Museums.

photos which further enrich the Sande legacy. For more information on the Belair Stable Museum and other City of Bowie Museums check out their website at www.cityofbowie.org/museum.

Three years after Sande won the "Race of the Century" by piloting Zev to victory in the 1923 International Match Race over Steve Donoghue aboard Papyrus, Sande competed in an out-of-the country competition, the Cofforth Handicap and other races at Aqua Caliente in Tijuana, Mexico. In its heyday, Aqua Caliente, not bothered by alcohol prohibition and Sunday Blue Laws, thrived as Hollywood stars and other California wealthy patrons spent their money lavishly at Tijuana card tables and horse races.

More than eighty years later, we have become good friends with Jose Naveja. Jose will tell you the rest of the story. "I work in a place where I meet a lot of people. I had known Mr. and Mrs. Maturi for several years before I found out they are writers. I say, 'It is a great honor to know a writer.' Several days later, someone left a package for me. Inside, I find a note that says, 'Enjoy the ride, Jose,' attached to a book about Triple Crown Winner, Earl Sande. My thoughts went immediately to the greatest horseman I have ever known, my father, Eladio Naveja, who broke horses and worked at Aqua Caliente for 29 years. I started to cry because the book brought back memories of my father.

Ever since I could remember, on the first Saturday of May, he would say, 'Today is the Kentucky Derby.' I didn't know what he was talking about but I could see it made him feel alive. He always told me stories of the great horses and jockeys that raced at Aqua Caliente such as Seabiscuit and Phar Lap and George Woolf, Eddie Arcaro and Bill Shoemaker. I

Eladio Naveja. Courtesy Jose Naveja.

always wanted to do something about this 'great man,' my hero, who I call, Father. He passed away several years ago but I always dreamed that I would be able to have my father's name connected to something he loved, horses and horse racing.

The next time I saw Mr. and Mrs. Maturi I asked them if they knew my love for horse racing. They said no, they just wanted me to have one of their books. I believe my father connected us and every time I see them, I think of my father and feel a very special relationship with them."

It's possible that Earl Sande and Eladio Naveja met in Tijuana, or at least, we're sure that Mr. Naveja knew of Earl's accomplishments. We're certain Earl would have approved of Mr. Naveja's talents with horses and his horsemanship.

Finally, we are indebted to Earl Sande's nephew, Sande Tomlinson, for his insight into Earl's talents. Not only was Earl the consummate jockey, he excelled at every thing he tried off the race track. He mastered golf, swimming and even singing, with his debut at the famed New York Stork

Eladio Naveja holding the halter of horse at Aqua Caliente, Tijuana, Mexico. Courtesy Jose Naveja.

Club. We value the friendship that has grown between Sande, his wife, Mary, and us.

Even when we weren't in search of Earl, he seemed to follow us. While on vacation in Sydney, Nova Scotia, we ventured into the library and googled Commander Ross, the Canadian owner of the first Triple Crown Winner, Sir Barton, and for whom Sande rode from 1918 into the early 1920s. Lo and behold, we found out that Commander Ross's picture hangs in the Sydney Yacht Club and his stately home is now part of the Meridian Hotel. That evening we dined in the hotel's restaurant (once Commander Ross's dining room), embellished with bevelled glass and rich oak trim and bookcases. After a delicious meal and images of Commander Ross and Earl Sande seated in this very room talking strategy in the off-season, I followed a noise downstairs to discover a basement OTB (Off-Track-Betting) establishment. I think Commander Ross and Earl Sande would have enjoyed the appropriateness of the location.